Astrology and the

Evolution of Consciousness

Lee Linsley
many Bless *Maukie*

Volume One

Nu Orleans
2012

Astrology Fundamentals, the Moon, the Sun,

and the Evolutionary Levels of Consciousness

Maurice Fernandez

Editor: *LeAnn Plank*
Additional editors: *Jinny Rodrigo and Julia Fay Hornick*
Cover and inside artwork: *Jeff Lohrius*

©Copyright 2009 Maurice Fernandez

Printed in the United States
ISBN 978-0-615-29654-8

Published by Evolutionary Astrology, Inc.
Land O' Lakes, Florida.
Order Contact: majorsky@earthlink.net

For more information about

Astrology and the Evolution of Consciousness

The Author

Study Programs

Presentation Schedule and Location

Catalog of Recorded Material

Visit the website:

www.mauricefernandez.com

Available from the same author

NEPTUNE
THE 12TH HOUSE AND PISCES

ISBN 1-4120-4028-0
978-1-4120-4028-0

 Acknowledgments

Writing a book is a significant task that requires a tremendous amount of resources whether in the form of time, knowledge, linguistic skills, high-tech equipment, money, inspiration, character, or a support system. The author receives the credit for the work with his or her name printed on the cover, but this book is the product of multiple feeding sources. Some of these sources are obvious, while others are less so. I wish to acknowledge those whom I can identify as having made working on the book a possible and better flowing experience. The value of their contribution cannot be adequately expressed.

My gratitude to my parents Sara and David who have always provided unconditional love and support in every form, something that allows me every day to stay sane and functioning in a challenging world.

For LeAnn Plank, a being made of angel dust, who made it her priority to transform my notes into a presentable book, spending countless hours to get everything right. I can only feel love and gratitude.

To Albert Alhadeff whose patience and service I can never repay.

To Jeffrey Green who has elevated astrology to completely new levels.

From my heart straight to all of you who have been there to keep me and the work going particularly Jeff Lohrius, Julia Fay Hornik, Jinny Rodrigo, Tom Lescher, Philip Sedgwick, Robert Blaschke, Michael Lutin, Kim Marie, Leroy Wiemer, Steven Forrest, Laura Nalbandian, Maggie Nalbandian, Vanya Innendorfer, Moses Siregar III, Adam Gainsburg, Kristin Fontana, Rita Rishe, Michelle Davidson, Naomi Landau, Lisa Busch, Yogi Bhajan, John of God, and Rabbi Elazar of Adderet.

Table of Contents

Foreword

By Robert Blaschke

With his new book, *Astrology and the Evolution of Consciousness—Volume One*, Maurice Fernandez has crafted a well-written treatise, designed to teach beginning students of astrology its first principles through a spiritual lens focusing on how to perceive the ultimate alignment of the soul with Truth.

Maurice has distinguished himself as an author before the age of 40 by aligning his writing with spiritual principles that bring great depth and human understanding to his readers. He is following a tradition and a lineage of spiritual astrologers that preceded him, including both Jeffrey Green and Dane Rudhyar.

As a teaching astrologer for over twenty years, I have observed that the first two years of astrological study are crucial. How the beginning student learns the language of astrology from his teacher will shape his perceptions and open his insight. What makes this new book by Maurice Fernandez, the first in a series, so important is that it presents the fundamentals of astrology in a way that also enhances the student's spiritual understanding.

His lucid writing about the evolutionary levels of consciousness and the percentages of the human population that fall into these three broad categories of *consensus*, *individuated* and *spiritual* levels of being, with each level then further subdivided into three evolving states of awareness, provides the beginning student of astrology an invaluable spiritual context within which to learn.

Writing about this sacred knowledge, originally passed down to us from Swami Sri Yukteswar in his book, *The Holy Science*, and from his direct disciple, Paramahansa Yogananda, in his book, *Autobiography of a Yogi*, helps to preserve the important spiritual dimensions of astrology during an era when many within the younger generation of astrology students are taught as much about the history of astrology as they are about its core spiritual truths. The value of this teaching approach cannot be overstated.

Readers are presented the spiritual meaning of the four elements, the three modalities, the hemispheres and quadrants of the chart, and the twelve signs of the Zodiac as fundamental archetypes.

The Luminaries are then delineated by sign, house and aspect as archetypal combinations. Thus, a Pisces Moon, a Moon in the 12th house, or a Moon aspecting Neptune are shown to have a common evolutionary need and intent.

I can already hear the reviewer's critique about Mr Fernandez's conflation of signs with houses, but it is far better for a beginning student to learn astrology through this archetypal lens than to have his mind scattered to the four directions by an overly complex introduction to this divine science which focuses on the minutiae of the house meanings. These can be learned later on.

Chapter Seven on the Moon and the Sun in synthesis is especially beneficial as it provides readers with an orientation and outcome delineation for the 144 Sun-Moon combinations. A famous or historical figure is referenced for each in order to illustrate the evolutionary principles for the interaction of the two Luminaries.

An interesting parallel to Maurice's new book exists within the world of astrology itself; where fully 70% of those who find this divine science intriguing never go beyond Sun-sign horoscopes. Another 25% of astrology enthusiasts will eventually have their nativity calculated and interpreted, either by a professional astrologer or through a computerized report purchased on-line. The rare 5% of astrology students who immerse themselves into this cosmic science as a spiritual discipline and go on to practice, teach and lecture publicly will find their lives transformed for the better, and the lives of their clients and students equally enriched.

May this book carry the torch of evolutionary astrology forward into a new generation of students and spiritual seekers.

Robert P. Blaschke
6 May 2009
Santa Monica, California

Introduction

I was inspired to write this book to expose beginners right from the beginning to astrology's deeper spiritual content. Commonly at first, beginners in the field are introduced to new terms, generalized definitions, and the methodology, and only much later have access to more meaningful spiritual material. In other circumstances, beginners jump ahead directly to advanced knowledge because they are drawn to the spiritual essence but then end up feeling overwhelmed upon realizing they lack a solid foundation. The purpose of this book is to bridge these gaps by providing practical guidance without compromising the depth of content.

Diluting the content in order to simplify access would have defeated the very reason it was written. While the book delves into the complex spiritual layers of the soul's evolution and life meanings, I tried my best to write it in a way that makes astrology accessible to everyone regardless of their level of expertise.

Today, astrology is ever richer from the years of consistent research that has been conducted by numerous bright minds in the field. The content that is revealed gets ever deeper and wider when all streams merge together. Yet, astrology needs to be taken more seriously so that its incomparable quality can serve humanity the way it was destined to. Too many people interested in astrology believe that a one-dimensional "cookbook" will provide everything there is to know about it. Many are shocked or overwhelmed when they realize how rich and vast the content actually is. Through astrology we learn about life on a personal and a collective level; it cannot be simplistically approached. Those who are not intimidated by astrology's profundity are in for a fundamental life lifting experience.

The book is designed to be used as a manual; it is best to first read the entire book cover to cover and then refer back to specific chapters for reference. I believe many intermediary and advanced astrology practitioners will also find this volume tremendously insightful as it revisits fundamental concepts in a new and perhaps richer light.

This is the first volume in a series depicting the body of knowledge that I have developed inspired by what was passed on to me by my teachers and then by my personal research over the years. Time will tell how many volumes this series will contain, but I consider this first one to be the most important; it is a book I would have liked to have had access to when I first began my astrology studies.

All in all, the main message pervading the chapters of the book is that astrology is not separate from life; it is a tool to objectify our existence so that we can gain perspective and make better choices given what is available to us. Understanding the natural cycles of life through the study of astrology facilitates our ability to harmonize and align with the forces of existence. The more aligned we are with life principles, the more meaningful and beneficial our lives become. If this book inspires a person to realize astrology in its true light—as a map of life designed by the divine—then, the years of work behind it are well worth it!

I dedicate this book to all of those who are making their first steps into the realm of astrology—an amazing journey paved with epiphanies and awakening awaits! May those who will keep the torch burning be blessed with guidance and meaningful experiences.

With love and blessings,

Maurice Fernandez
Boulder, Colorado
April 2009

Chapter One

Explaining Astrology of the Evolution of Consciousness

Our understanding and use of astrology is evolving. This discipline, which correlates celestial constellations with life on Earth, has been used for different purposes and with varying levels of depth throughout the centuries including prediction, health diagnosis, and character definition. In our times, we are at the vital juncture where astrology can also be used as a tool to identify a person's evolutionary path of consciousness.

This astrological perspective is rooted in the conceptual understanding that life does not manifest randomly; there are reasons promoting evolution that influence all events. From this viewpoint, one of the main reasons for existence is to evolve to a higher level of consciousness. As one's consciousness expands more of the Truth of life is realized; accordingly, realizing more of the Truth helps one more effectively navigate life's challenges and participate with greater meaning and success.

We are born into circumstances that serve as a platform for our evolutionary journey. For this purpose conditioning factors such as the early life environment, family dynamics, and resources available during childhood are in place to direct the flow of evolution. These factors are not coincidental; they are synchronized with our evolutionary needs. In the course of our lives challenges arise that prompt us to ask questions about existence, forcing us out of complacency and ignorance so that we gain more awareness—setting evolution in motion as the vessel of consciousness expands through these learning experiences.

Learning about and gaining more awareness of life is a work in progress as it usually occurs through continuing education or trial and error. Since human beings did not create life, they do not fully grasp its mechanism; no one is born with an instruction manual. At first naïve and ignorant, people make mistakes and consequently experience limitation or pain. Resulting discomfort prompts a person to try and do better and further decode life's mechanism. With learning comes a greater chance of success; the more pieces that are added to the puzzle of Truth the better life is understood and the more one's consciousness expands.

The evolutionary journey is a lengthy one because the learning process must be emotionally assimilated through recurring experiences. Intellectualizing an experience is not enough; learning must be emotionally digested so that it can be fully integrated into our consciousness. For example, a person may intellectually understand the solution to a problem and yet keep repeating the same mistake again and again. This happens because the solution has not yet been emotionally integrated; consequently, it remains theory rather than practice. Repeated exposure and experience facilitate emotional assimilation, hence the necessity for time when learning about life.

The extended path of evolution commences before birth and comprises both past and future lives as one lifetime is too brief a sojourn to completely master the experience of life on Earth. *Individual consciousness is carried from one life to another through the soul*—that which defines us beyond our physical self. Newborn babies are not devoid of consciousness; they already have a conditioned awareness based on their past life experiences and come into this life charged with character, desires, needs, and fears. Some may claim that a baby's defined inclinations are inherited through its genes, but an astrologer adopting this approach will ask why one baby ends up with particular genes while a sibling receives others. From an evolutionary perspective it is not a coincidence but rather the soul's evolutionary state and needs; in order to pursue its learning path, the soul continually reincarnates through time, space, and forms that respond to its evolutionary requirements.

Astrology that focuses on the evolution of consciousness provides some of the most sophisticated knowledge identifying the soul's evolutionary purpose in the current life and beyond. When analyzing an astrological birth chart, we can use this modality to describe the nature of past life themes that have shaped the soul's awareness prior to the current incarnation; the chart not only reveals qualities acquired through past life experiences, but most importantly describes the person's current life lessons and orientation, and given that how to make the best of existence *in the present* relative to that background. Thus an astrological chart simultaneously represents the past, the present, and the potential future.

This astrological approach not only identifies particular personality traits and future trends but also attempts to decode why things happen the way they do on both a personal and a collective level. What are the lessons behind events given that we are here to learn about life and make the best of it? Upon gaining such a perspective, valuable advice and guidance can be offered directing the individual toward the fundamental purposes of his or her life.

Importantly, the evolutionary perspective considers *free will* a crucial factor when interpreting a birth chart. The positions of the planets describe the qualities and themes of the person's nature and evolutionary path; however, each person has a choice in determining how far and how deep he or she will go on this path. It is not possible to know in advance how much of the chart's potential will be realized.

For example, two people born exactly at the same time and place will share the same chart; yet despite the similarities each one has free will in realizing the chart's qualities according to his or her individual level of awareness. It is important to remember that astrology is a language of symbols representing many possible layers of application and experience. The use of free will and the level of the individual's awareness determines which layer will be accessed. This is something that cannot be fully predicted according to the chart alone.

For example, if the chart describes a tendency for intense power struggles, two people sharing the same chart will likely address this issue differently: one consistently expressing defiance and anger, the other learning techniques to address the problem and possibly even becoming a mediator to help others with power struggle issues. The chart energy is the same but the choice of action is different and thus the results are too. The birth chart does not condemn the person to a sealed fate; rather it describes trends and themes that one can address in various ways according to one's level of consciousness.

The Course of the Evolution of Consciousness

Time and space break life experiences into fragments so that our system can process existence step-by-step rather than being overwhelmed with instant exposure to the Truth; such an experience would be similar to a light bulb that shatters when exposed to a current intensity it cannot handle. Instead, we only experience a fragment of life through a particular time and space, allowing for a more gradual integration of each experience. For example, a person born in Baghdad at the dawn of the twenty-first century will have a specific life experience relative to that setting. The person's gender will further narrow the nature of the experience. Depending on what is accomplished under the given circumstances in that life, new conditions will be set in place for the following incarnation; thus the evolutionary process is broken into numerous segments in the form of life chapters or incarnations, each one defined by a different time and space. Gradually experiencing the sum of all segments allows us to better integrate the whole life experience.

While all beings may be equal when evolution commences and aim for the same final goal of realizing the Truth, different paces and evolutionary orientations set people apart. Gaps of consciousness are created as each person goes through a different sequence of events in the course of his or her evolutionary journey. Time and space are the cause of this division and necessarily so.

In my book, *Neptune, the 12th House and Pisces*, I explain that the evolution of consciousness starts from a place of *absolute innocence*. In this phase consciousness is very dim; therefore, the person remains passive and assumes that everything in life is trustworthy. There is no understanding of choice, change, ambition, or discrimination; instead, the person drifts on the currents of life directed by external circumstances or unconscious survival impulses such as hunger. This state can be described as "being in the womb of the universe" where one surrenders to the forces of existence just as a baby surrenders to its mother not knowing anything different. In a state of innocence, nothing is questioned: air, water, earth, and energy are provided from above and allow one to survive seemingly without effort.

With innocence there is a degree of ignorance as well as purity. Because everything is taken for granted, the impulse to learn is minimal, leaving one initially ignorant. Similarly passive acceptance makes one unaware of negativity and keeps one's state of mind pure. However, inexperience in managing natural resources eventually leads to discomfort and pain as excesses or deficiencies are bound to cause diverse crises; for example, in a state of innocence a crisis may be as simple as getting a sunburn when unaware of the danger of overexposure to the Sun.

Following discomfort the person starts to think and strategize to avoid repeating the unpleasant experience. Through recurrent trial and error the realization emerges that nothing is really free as it first appeared when one was innocent, but rather it takes *effort* to properly use resources and maintain one's sense of well-being. Discomfort, pain, illness, and eventually the threat of death force the person out of complacency. Gradually it becomes clear that one needs to learn how to manage life instead of blindly going through the motions—the effort needed is not solely physical but also *an effort of consciousness.*

Upon facing existential challenges the person is birthed out of "the womb of innocence," and this is the turning point that causes him or her to realize that *happiness is not a given.* The prospect of pain creates pressure that forces the development of intelligence through expanding consciousness. As one learns to discriminate what works from what doesn't, more of the Truth of life is understood. *As innocence decreases consciousness increases* and so does the contrast between the *Truth and illusion.* When the veil of ignorance is lifted the Truth emerges, and living in the Truth provides happiness and answers the initial desire for well-being.

As consciousness expands *the ego* develops. The ego is the separate sense of self; it serves to process personal experiences and is like the "digestive system" of the soul. Through the ego the person feels, relates, assesses, identifies, likes, dislikes, judges, and discriminates: it is the medium through which one *personalizes* life and chooses. As personal consciousness expands the ego matures. Through the ego the person becomes emotionally attached to people, experiences, or concepts, and those attachments generate a personal connection. Only when such a connection is made can related experiences be processed.

For example, when the person makes a personal connection to a lover, the ego forms an attachment to that chosen person. At that point, every experience related to the lover can be processed and assimilated into the person's system. When the experience is complete, the attachment is released, eventually spurring new attachments.

As evolution unfolds, more knowledge is acquired and life is better managed; pain and limitations are handled more effectively and feelings of happiness are experienced more consistently. It is not always a linear process, but generally the more one's consciousness evolves, the more fulfilling life becomes.

As consciousness expands, independence and control over existential circumstances increases. For example, stronger houses are built and cures for diseases are found. Usually, control increases a sense of security and improves the odds of attaining better life conditions.

Coming from a place of passivity and innocence in the initial stages of evolution, the person increasingly becomes more proactive. As learning and effort is applied, self-reliance increases while disruptive external circumstances decrease. Gaining control also boosts *creative competence*, allowing the ego to play a more meaningful role in life's unfolding. Through creativity, one manifests destiny and participates in making life happen instead of accepting circumstances as fated.

Ultimately in the higher states of evolution, spiritual ripeness and maturity are attained. After experiencing the privileges of control and creative freedom, the ego recognizes that happiness is found in the sole attachment to the Truth instead of ephemeral gratifications or through blind attachment to security. While egocentric control enhances security, it does not provide lasting happiness and freedom from pain; consequently, there is still a need to further refine one's approach to existence. Instead of solely acting on personal projections, wishes, and assumptions, one realizes that the Truth is what really matters—the Truth reflecting universal laws that created and govern existence. Accepting that it does not have all the answers and that it cannot own the Truth, the ego surrenders its need for absolute control; accepting that learning is never-ending keeps the ego humble and alert.

In a place of maturity, the ego realizes that it is part of a larger mechanism and becomes inspired by it. Accordingly, aligning one's ego with the Truth and directing creative capacities toward that end fosters greater harmony with existence. In doing so the person gets in touch with the source of Creation—the intelligence behind life. The evolution of consciousness is a direct result of realizing the Truth; it is an ongoing process. The more precisely one aligns to the Truth, the deeper the sense of harmony with life and the more one is open to divine inspiration.

Glossary of Spiritual Terms

- *Consciousness:* One's current level of understanding of the Truth.

- *Truth:* The sum of all principles and laws governing life within and beyond the realm of human understanding: what works. Divine intelligence and order.

- *Soul:* One's consciousness incarnated and evolving throughout lifetimes.

- *Ego:* The operating arm of the soul in the current life through which one forms attachments necessary for the evolutionary process. These attachments come to define one's separate sense of self and identity; through the ego, all of life's experiences are emotionally processed.

- *Evolution of consciousness:* Increasing the understanding of the Truth.

- *Karma:* The subordination of personal action to divine order. Corrective measures and possibly negative consequences that occur when a person's actions are misaligned to divine order. Conversely, positive circumstances that result from aligned actions. The law of cause and effect that is in force through one's incarnations.

- *Dharma:* The fulfillment of one's destiny by living in the Truth that results in one's contribution to existence; as a result, Dharma enhances the essence of love.

- *Spirituality:* The study and practice of aligning the ego with the soul and the soul with the Truth.

Chapter Two

The Language of Astrology

Astrology is a symbolic language; understanding it is like reading a map of life. The celestial configurations are perfectly synchronized with occurrences in our reality. The art of astrology involves reading a chart effectively; for despite the wealth of information, it takes a vast awareness to interpret a chart well. Since astrology is a symbolic language, there are many levels of interpretation; the challenge is to penetrate through the surface to access the deeper layers.

Each astrological sign is ruled by a planet and associated with a house. Together *the sign, the ruling planet, and the house form are a unit—they form an archetype*. For example, the Aries archetype comprises the sign of Aries, its ruling planet Mars, and the first house in the birth chart wheel. In astrology, there are twelve primary archetypes at play that relate to the twelve astrological signs; each archetype represents a particular aspect of life, and when all twelve archetypes are unified, they describe the totality of life (see table 1).

Table 1: The twelve archetypes and the associated glyphs

Sign	Glyph	Planet or Luminary	Glyph	House
ARIES	♈	MARS	♂	1st
TAURUS	♉	VENUS	♀	2nd
GEMINI	♊	MERCURY	☿	3rd
CANCER	♋	MOON	☽	4th
LEO	♌	SUN	☉	5th
VIRGO	♍	MERCURY	☿	6th
LIBRA	♎	VENUS	♀	7th
SCORPIO	♏	PLUTO	♆ or ♇	8th
SAGITTARIUS	♐	JUPITER	♃	9th
CAPRICORN	♑ or ♑	SATURN	♄	10th
AQUARIUS	♒	URANUS	♅	11th
PISCES	♓	NEPTUNE	♆	12th

Aries is considered to be the first sign because it symbolizes the birth of one's separate sense of being. Astronomically speaking, each sign is a constellation of stars. Together, the twelve astrological signs represent the constellations that the Sun passes through in the course of one year—the path of the Sun is called the *ecliptic*. The twelve signs form a 360 degree astrology ring around the Earth; each of the twelve signs has 30 degrees.

Each sign (or constellation) is in fact a location in the sky. A planet or luminary (the Sun and the Moon are luminaries, not planets) rules one or two signs, but physically the planet or the luminary can be in any sign as it moves from one constellation to the next. For example, Saturn rules the sign of Capricorn, but as Saturn travels around the Sun, it can be found in any sign (location) at the time of a person's birth; it is like an ambassador promoting the affairs of his or her nation in another "country" (see figure 1).

Figure 1: Saturn traveling through the signs

In most house systems, houses are delineated according to the points of intersection between the Earth and the ecliptic (the path of the

Sun). For example, when the eastern horizon line meets the ecliptic (the path of the Sun), this point of intersection represents the beginning of the first house, also called *the Ascendant.* When the western horizon line meets the ecliptic, this point of intersection represents the beginning of the seventh house, also called *the Descendant.* As seen from the Earth, the highest point on the ecliptic is the *MC—the Medium Coeli,* Latin for "middle of the sky"—and it marks the tenth house. The lowest point under Earth, the *IC—the Imum Coeli,* Latin for "bottom of the sky"—marks the fourth house.

Figure 2: The Ascendant, the IC, the Descendant, and the MC mark the angular houses (houses 1, 4, 7, 10)

Figure 2 shows the intersecting points between the Earth and the ecliptic that mark the beginning of the angular houses: the Ascendant marks the first house, the IC marks the fourth house, the Descendant marks the seventh house, and the MC marks the tenth house. A more thorough definition of each sign, planet, and house can be found in Chapter Four.

A planet's position is defined by both its sign and house placement. For example, Mars can be in the sign of Aquarius and in the fifth house. The particular position of each planet, by sign and house in the birth chart, describes very specific features about one's character and evolutionary path. For the readers who are new to astrology, these terms and combinations might seem overwhelming at first, but over time it becomes much easier—it is like learning a new language.

The Astrology Chart

An astrology chart is a frozen moment in time that shows the positions of the planets and the signs as they appear from the Earth's perspective—it is like a photograph of the sky. A chart can be erected for any new beginning, be it the birth of a baby or the start of a new business. The chart describes everything about the nature of what it is erected for and relies on the concept that the starting moment leaves an indelible signature that symbolically carries all meaning for the person or event. *An entity beginning its independent existence on Earth will completely relate to its birth chart throughout its entire life, at all moments, until its last breath.*

A birth chart describes the qualities of the person in question including what he or she is about, personal life themes and possible circumstances, the lessons he or she needs to learn, potential challenges ahead, and also what he or she brings from past lives: talents, unconscious memories, and or emotional scars. The chart describes where the person left off and based on that what the course of evolution for the current incarnation is—however, it does not foretell how far one may go with the current course of evolution.

The chart describes the themes and energy available for the person to work with. These themes can be approached either constructively or destructively; the way the person uses the available energy depends on free will or on how conscious his or her soul is. For example, Mahatma Gandhi's chart describes a great deal of anger that could have been expressed in a destructive way. Nevertheless, because Gandhi's soul was in a highly evolved state of consciousness, he used that anger as a vehicle for change and destruction for the sake of renewal. A lesser evolved person with the same chart might have used the intense energy negatively, becoming a sex offender or a tyrant. Our chart reflects the evolutionary themes we need to master—*we are not free to choose our chart and its themes, but we are free to make the best or the worst of it.* As counselors, our purpose is to inspire the client to move toward a higher level of expression of the chart, taking the person one step further—the key being "one step further" given that rushing a person too fast forward can be damaging.

The chart reflects the kind of evolutionary themes the person is facing, where the soul left off in the past incarnation, and the direction the soul is taking in the present incarnation. It describes all life issues including family dynamics, relationship needs and interactions, vocational orientations, health conditions and risks, and spiritual potential. Through the chart, we can identify the themes of the past and the prospects for the future including one's Karma (past actions and consequences) and Dharma (one's sense of destiny and contribution).

The Elements: Fire, Earth, Air, Water

The four primary elements of nature—*Fire, Earth, Air,* and *Water*—each include three astrological archetypes (signs). The elements are fundamental forces that in varying amounts constitute everything in life from matter to spirit.

Fire

Signs: *Aries, Leo, Sagittarius*
Planets: *Mars, Sun, Jupiter*
Houses: *1, 5, 9*

Figure 3: The fire triad

Fire represents energy—it is the life force. This force sustains itself by consuming and producing; it generates the fundamental feeling of being alive. Through fire, we are given a personal consciousness and start to feel, relate, express, and proceed *independently*; it is the spark that awakens our individual sense of being. Fire is not expressed intellectually, but purely instinctually and emotionally. Symbolizing the individual active force in the evolutionary equation, fire represents the urge to separate from the womb, the need to become a separate entity, the urge to take charge of our own life, and the desire to engage in life, perform, and develop our personal capacity; it symbolizes the individual active force. Consequently, fire embodies the soul's effort to be, express, create, and overcome obstacles and challenges. This element represents the soul's urge and imperative to independently *participate* in life; it is the egocentric spirit and engine from which personal desires emerge and are creatively acted upon.

Representing individuality, separate consciousness, and egocentric productivity, fire is naturally subjective and personal. Therefore, it portrays uniqueness and personality, as well as the weight and impact of one's presence in life. The emotional quality is extroverted, unrefined, and unreserved; consequently, fire is dramatic—the person feels the essence of each experience and moment. Under this influence, there are no initial filters, making one's expression natural, transparent, authentic, pure, simple, and upfront.

Positively, this natural form of expression promotes vitality, a healthy circulation of emotion, as well as an effective metabolism that diminishes repression and stagnation. When mismanaged, this dynamic results in a lack of boundaries that generates emotional excess, inappropriateness, and unhealthy indulgence—there is an inclination to get carried away in expression, action, and expectation, resulting in possible disappointment or damage.

With fire, the person acknowledges the possibility of having an impact on life. There is an urge to take charge of one's destiny and make things happen, rather than wait for God or someone else to act on one's behalf. Hence fire represents the need to separate for the sake of independently pursuing what one believes in—it is the effort we make to be. This individuation process demands a great deal of energy; however, one can feel empowered by discovering the internal capacity to perform or to be a catalyst for action.

Through fire, the person learns he or she has power. Action generates motion, interference, and change; it creates an impact. Creating an impact requires one to confront potential resistance and defiance because when taking action, personal forces converge with universal forces always at play. Just as the birthing process is an effort, the person must invest resources and conquer resistance to execute any action; the very act of standing can be seen as a defiance of gravity. The success of one's effort proves one's strength and exposes options for further accomplishments. Through fire, the person acknowledges the capacity to direct and influence life instead of feeling anonymously at the mercy of external events. Successful action promotes a sense of exaltation through which a feeling of significance and confidence is gained; as a result, one believes in opportunity and change—*through fire one defies fate and creates destiny.*

Beyond generating motion through action, through fire the person is able to create: the essence of one's being can expand and manifest through many different forms of creativity whether art, initiating projects, or having children. The creative process is orgasmic and ecstatic by nature as it brings one in touch with divine energy and power; it allows one to be godlike, or more accurately an active force that contributes to the greater scheme of things. Creativity is the main factor of participation, fostering personal involvement in the continual development of life. Personal investment and generosity are the foundations of creativity. Through fire, one becomes "a freelance executive" of universal forces and proceeds on the basis of what personally feels best at any given moment. There is a great deal of independence in this role; although, it is important to note that with freedom of action and power also comes responsibility.

Fire keywords

Being, instinct, vitality, individualism, action, autonomy, strength, creativity, inspiration, defensiveness, reactive behavior, emotionality, impulsiveness, expressiveness, authenticity.

Fire signs

- *Aries'* influence represents the impulse and effort to initially separate from the universal womb in order to be. Consequently, there is pressure to develop a defense mechanism so that one can independently stand up to challenging forces and carry out actions deemed necessary to promote universal right over wrong.

- *Leo's* influence represents the individual creative process that is fundamental to the continuation and development of life. Through Leo, destiny unfolds as the ego gets fully in touch with its capacities and role—it allows one to leave a legacy and guarantees that life goes on.

- *Sagittarius's* influence addresses the gradual alignment between the individual's personal sense of destiny and higher life meaning. Therefore, it promotes the expansion of one's personal potential and creative capacity as more of the Truth is realized. The search for the Truth is processed through intuition, speculation, and belief.

Earth

Signs: *Taurus, Virgo, Capricorn*
Planets: *Venus, Mercury, Saturn*
Houses: *2, 6, 10*

Figure 4: The earth triad

Earth represents the integration of spirit into matter; consequently, it relates to the phenomenon of gravity which naturally increases the density of molecules that manifests in form creation. The purpose of matter is crystallization, which brings tangibility both literally and figuratively; through earth, life's processes can be measured and evaluated.

Matter, form, and tangibility can only be sustained when they are in harmony with the laws of life; otherwise, they disintegrate. Only something that works can be materialized and hold over time. Earth exposes us to objective conditions and laws existing beyond us that we must consider in order to manage things successfully; these conditions and laws are the crystallization of the Truth—that which works. Although the whole Truth and the laws of life are not immediately revealed, earth's influence provides a point of reference when navigating through life. Boundaries are emphasized through this dynamic, revealing the value of accuracy upon proceeding.

As evolution unfolds and change occurs, earth represents the building or maturation process through which one form is built on the foundation of the previous one. If one stage or form intrinsic to the maturation process is not dependable, everything built on its reference will crumble. Thus through earth, reliability and credibility are imperative and measured according to what stands the test of time. Challenges keep testing the consistency of established notions. Accordingly, when earth is involved, continuity and durability are proof of worth as they reflect the harmonious adaptation to life's complexity. When something remains reliable and promotes well-being over years or even centuries, it means that it embodies truthful qualities and thus has great worth. The person gains security when he or she is able to rely on a concept or a product that has been proven to work and that has stood the test of time, compared to something that did not work and failed to hold. Over time, structures are established reflecting what is considered valuable and reliable.

Through earth, creative impulses are regulated and constructively channeled in order to adapt to and fit established references. Thus earth describes the maturity of self-control, patience, consistency, and the ability to adapt to environmental requirements. It also inspires responsibility and the use of discrimination and judgment to diminish the odds of error and failure.

When earth's influence is mismanaged, a fear of failure may cause an excessive attachment to established structures and notions. Failing to recognize that everything that has been established must, at some point, be upgraded, the person tends to become overly attached to what was once proven reliable and unable to accept that structures and notions become obsolete over time. Resisting progress and change results from a suspicion that new and untested concepts might fail and leave one without solid and reliable references. One may believe that current established references are absolute and do not need further development, resulting in the potential for rigidity and stagnation.

Since earth represents constructive development, it naturally describes maturation processes. One can foresee how the maturation process may unfold and therefore decide what result to aim for. There is a defined course of action one can plan and prepare for, knowing what challenges to expect and what the harvest will be. For example, a high-school student might aim to become a doctor and foresee what steps to take in order to materialize the goal. Time is an important factor here because time engenders progressive maturation—one cannot skip steps if one wants to achieve results that have lasting value.

As solid as structures and plans must be under earth's influence, they must also be flexible enough to adapt and develop with personal and collective evolution. When well managed, the person aiming for defined goals and achievements is also ready to face unexpected challenges and deviations. As fully prepared as one might try to be, there are always surprises along the way. Thus new skills and capacities must be developed to overcome the unexpected when it arises. Inner strength and maturity are measured according to having a plan of action, where objectives are defined and challenges anticipated, and being able to adapt when the unexpected happens.

Earth keywords

Tangibility, credibility, value, solidity, endurance, function, longevity, maintenance, rightful, efficient, plan, measure, harmony, boundaries, restraint, maturity, strength, responsibility, development, improvement.

Earth signs

- *Taurus's* influence represents the acknowledgement and establishment of form. When the spirit integrates into matter and the body, the senses awake. Through the senses, the person can relate to and evaluate life's components and resources, and assess what is worth keeping. What is kept will be protected to assure that it grows stronger and can withstand challenges through time.

- *Virgo's* influence represents the need to acknowledge that available resources are limited. This realization heightens one's awareness about using and properly maintaining them in order to avoid waste. Particularly concerned about the limitation of time as a resource, Virgo's influence pressures the person to become more efficient and improve and refine modes of operation in order to increase quality and productivity. In this process, skills and control abilities are perfected, continually increasing the worth and reliability of matter.

- *Capricorn's* influence represents the need to preserve knowledge acquired from experience in order to ensure that development continues on top of established foundations. Consequently, the person's concern is focused on education and the right way of handling life through matter to guarantee that present and future generations will benefit from the sum of efforts so far.

Air

Signs: *Gemini, Libra, Aquarius*
Planets: *Mercury, Venus, Uranus*
Houses: *3, 7, 11*

Figure 5: The air triad

The air element represents the understanding that each separate component or being is limited in its capacity to fully encompass the vastness of existence. Consequently, effort is oriented toward bridging between separate factors or people to create new units that result from the combination of separate items. Air's purpose is to build a network of cooperation that allows for greater achievement through unity, strengthening resistance to potential danger. In nature, air is conductive and motioned by changing pressure—flying creatures are considered messengers that connect separate entities such as the pollinating bee or the homing pigeon. Moving from one person or location to the next, we are exposed to different dimensions of life, time, and space, and consequently gain a wider perspective on life.

Since the air element provides perspective, it naturally stimulates an awareness of existing limitations and encourages one to open up to new alternatives. The focus is external since the answer to limitation is seen in cooperation and union with others. Consequently, air stimulates the person to step out of him or herself in order to explore the realities of others which promotes learning; in this process, a more objective outlook is developed about life while new knowledge is gained. Learning from the fruit of other people's experiences accelerates the evolutionary process as it saves one the time of repeating it all. In this context, air emphasizes a theoretical and intellectual approach when learning about and addressing life.

It becomes clear through the air element that life operates on the foundations of logic and synchronicity. Since experiences can be shared between separate beings, it means that life has a common thread for all and that everything is interconnected. Without logic, learning would not be possible; there would not be any consistency or sense, but only random occurrences. The perception of logic provides clues that a higher intelligence operates behind the mechanism of life; one's learning process adheres to the task of decoding the logic of that higher intelligence and objectifying one's existence in a larger context.

Enhancing the qualities of the mind, air's influence promotes observation, awareness, and education. With higher awareness, impulsive drives are better directed; air's influence promotes the upgrading of primitive expression and the refinement of personal creativity to higher levels of sophistication. Innovation ensues, prompting the development of civilization—modern times are constantly in the making, leaving the obsolete in the past. None of the air signs are symbolized by animals, reflecting the potential access to objective perspective and emotional neutrality.

As mentioned previously, the air element accelerates the pace of life's processes because there is constant learning and upgrading. Operations that used to take a certain amount of time can be accomplished at a faster rate because of the increasing knowledge that the present brings; ironically, the present is already obsolete when compared to what the future will bring. With increasing speed, the person approaches ever more sophisticated and complex knowledge, accessing more dimensions in less time.

When mismanaged, air may heighten nervousness and tension. Speed may overwhelm the emotional body to the point of creating internal fragmentation that manifests in scattering, disassociation, and impatience; the mind may consequently override the emotions, spurring snobbery and disdain toward what is considered dense or obsolete. Additionally, air's influence can induce a disproportionate focus on the external world and cause an unhealthy idealization of other people, leading to a potential loss of self in others.

Positively, the air element facilitates exchange and emancipation. As a result, it fosters social dynamics and generates motion. The person is on the move physically or mentally in order to learn, experience, and gather new elements from diverse sources. These diverse elements are then combined together to offer a more expansive viewpoint and new opportunities, depicting the reality that even though there is only one Truth in life, this Truth takes many shapes and forms. Only when the variety of forms comes together can the greater Truth be realized.

Through air, greater tolerance emerges stemming from a higher understanding that life is not one sided. One comes to understand that everything is relative—relativity engenders diversity. Yet eventually, all diverse forms must unify to make things work because ultimately they all aim for the same thing—the absolute Truth.

Air keywords

Internal lack, external stimulation, openness, learning, adaptation, motion, exchange, social, mental, objective, perspective, relativity, awareness, speed, progressive, modern, sophisticated, civilized, cooperative.

Air signs

- *Gemini's* influence represents the need to learn about the immediate and larger environment in order to better integrate into it and successfully navigate through life. Survival pressures stimulate the person to understand the different components of existence and decode the logic of life. This learning process stimulates physical and mental motion.

- *Libra's* influence represents the experience of duality where two opposites create a center of gravity: the middle way. Feeling a sense of inner lack, the person branches out to learn about other people's realities and is consequently exposed to polarities and different perspectives. Satisfaction is gained when managing to harmonize and balance opposites. Through Libra, there is a greater interest in what each person represents and has to share; thus it encourages relationship dynamics.

- *Aquarius's* influence represents the urge to find new solutions for existential problems. Using the mind as a creative instrument, there is pressure to foster progress. Combining seemingly nonaffiliated components, the person challenges linear development in order to research new alternatives that are outside of currently existing paradigms. When succeeding, progress, refinement, and sophistication are attained and new solutions are implemented. Aquarius's influence yearns to bring capable minds together in order to gain greater understanding; it encourages think-tank dynamics, community, and social exchange.

Water

Signs: *Cancer, Scorpio, Pisces*
Planets: *Moon, Pluto, Neptune*
Houses: *4, 8, 12*

Figure 6: The water triad

The water element represents the assimilation process of life experiences into our system in order for growth to occur. Assimilation occurs primarily through the emotional body as our soul digests life experiences through the emotions. During our life, the sum of all interactions must eventually be processed, filtered, and absorbed into our consciousness the same way that food must be ingested and eventually absorbed into the bloodstream. Accordingly, consciousness grows and matures. Water represents the mutation of consciousness intrinsic to evolution.

Assimilating life experiences requires isolation because the person must tune into his or her own personal rhythm while undisturbed; the external rhythm of life must be neutralized so that one's internal rhythm can take its course. In this process, water serves as an insulating factor that is necessary for creating intimacy. Intimacy requires supportive conditions and protection from potentially disturbing factors so that our emotions can be processed in a healthy way and a sense of safety and security can be established. For example, it is during the surrendering time of sleep that a child processes life and grows in size just as a fetus matures in the protective watery womb.

The assimilation process can also happen through interacting with other people. When wishing to take in what someone else has to offer, intimacy is created between two people so that an exchange can take place; such a fusion can manifest on all levels whether physically, emotionally, intellectually, or spiritually. The need to create intimacy can be observed in many random activities: the doors of the classrooms are shut when learning proceeds, lovers isolate from the world when making love, and families gather in their protected homes when nurturing and educating each other—in all these different scenarios a womb effect is created that is essential for emotional processing and exchange. In the trusting space of intimacy, defense mechanisms can be surrendered and the person can be in a receptive mode.

However, the risk of getting hurt or traumatized increases accordingly during intimacy when circumstances are subsequently revealed to be hostile. Emotionally exposed in an intimate atmosphere, a person may be violated, stressed, and shocked; for example, a lover might turn out to be abusive or a family might fall apart because of a divorce. Consequently, as water represents emotional intimacy, it also reflects potential emotional wounds and trauma that result from being exposed.

Nevertheless, despite the potential for pain, the risk is necessary because the benefits of intimacy are essential for the evolutionary process. One can filter negative experiences by proceeding with caution before forming an intimate relationship, but there never are any absolute guarantees.

Through intimacy, one can also identify vulnerabilities that must be worked on. Experiencing emotional pain, one realizes that something is not right and needs processing. For example, one may recognize the fear of abandonment when feeling jealous at the sight of one's partner interacting with other people; the experience makes one feel vulnerable, but as uncomfortable as it may be, it is an opportunity to heal this fear, possibly through a therapy process. Paradoxically, in order to establish intimacy and process life, the water element not only aspires for security and trust, but also for risk and change in order to outgrow weakness and enhance growth.

When the person processes and digests something into his or her system, something new is internalized and an inner change occurs. A new self eventually emerges once the new content has been emotionally assimilated.

Water inspires a mutational process so that consciousness can expand and reach new dimensions. However, because there is an element of danger in emotional exposure, water's influence can generate mood fluctuations. The balance can swing between trust and caution, openness and unavailability, or conservativeness and the need for change.

When mismanaged, water's influence can result in exaggerated processing and a reluctance to leave the intimate space, sometimes in excessive distrust of the outside world. Consequently, the person may fail to perform and rebuff external pressure, preferring to stay away from anything unfamiliar. Emotional pain may remain untreated to a point of creating displaced emotions that result in a debilitating sense of insecurity, potentially leading to obsessive or manipulative behavior.

Overall, water manifests in a sensitive, protective, and nurturing nature. Recognizing weaknesses renders one more humble and human, preventing one from being too proud to ask for assistance and being able to depend on others when necessary. Values of forgiveness and empathy may be present, and patience for processes to take their course fosters a more natural developmental course.

Water keywords
Processing, assimilation, intimacy, internal rhythm, immunity, fusion, vulnerability, trust, security, nurturing, growth, mutation of form, evolution.

Water signs
- *Cancer's* influence relates to the need to emotionally process life experiences so that one can develop in a healthy way. When something is processed, it becomes personal and even part of one's being. Personal connections are created with family, people, one's country, or particular ideas and tastes; these elements shape the person's identity. What becomes personal is also intimate, promoting a nurturing and protective approach.

- *Scorpio's* influence represents the recognition of personal limitations and the desire to outgrow them. The need for growth prompts one to include external elements or people who are considered worthy into one's intimate space. Consequently, what was initially foreign becomes close and intimate, allowing an exchange to occur. From this delicate and intense intimacy, empowerment and evolution can result; however, possible disappointment and wounding can occur after forming an intimacy with something or someone who is later revealed to be detrimental or hostile. Trust depends on mutual well-being and gain.

- *Pisces'* influence confronts the person with his or her mortality and permanent imperfection. Consequently, it inspires one to fuse with the collective and transcend one's sense of separation and individuality. When merging with the collective, a timeless experience of oneness is created; consequently, the person emotionally processes circumstances that occur on a more public, collective, and spiritual level.

Element Combinations

In most cases, more than one element is prominent in an astrology chart. When that is the case, the basic psychological inclinations can be described as follows.

Fire-Earth: Creation

With an emphasis of fire and earth elements in a chart, autonomy, strength, and creativity is accentuated. When facing challenges, this type of individual is highly competent and soundly resists attack. Strong, predominantly self-reliant, self-regulated, and vital, the person is focused on facts and inspired to take action. The pronounced resourcefulness of this combination promotes constructiveness, reliability, physical endurance, and usually outstanding artistic talent.

However, the potent and distinct sense of personality comes at the expense of compromise and flexibility. Requiring freedom of action, one is usually not keen on giving in or giving up principles or habits. Compliance and dependence are last resorts as fire and earth emphasize self-made qualities.

Fire-Air: Motion

With an emphasis of fire and air elements in a chart, exposure, mobility, and stimulation through social and creative interactions are highlighted. Strong communicative needs, backed with initiative and vision bring about a colorful personality with pronounced coordinating skills. The fusion between impulse and perspective promotes imagination, inventiveness, and originality.

With a tendency to proceed relatively quickly, boredom and impatience may surface quite regularly. In further extremes, one may end up scattered and restless, leaving loose ends while operating on many levels at once. The accelerated mode of operation may upset processing needs and leave one ungrounded. In order to stay composed, the person may need constant learning and interaction.

Fire-Water: Involvement

With an emphasis of fire and water elements in a chart, emotions dominate the consciousness. The individual personalizes every aspect of his or her existence and feels strongly involved with whatever choices are made. Fluctuating between reactive or defensive behavior and accentuated generosity, there is a tendency to be completely absorbed by whatever one has chosen or whomever one is with, and to expect equal intensity in return. A healthy expression of this combination manifests in a person who is authentic, natural, attentive, and compassionate.

The lack of boundaries intrinsic to this emotional emphasis often generates a tendency to get carried away in either optimism or distrust. Drama makes one feel alive, yet it fuels excess. Consequently, the person may lack perspective when immersed in emotions such as passion or anger and become hypersensitive. Whether through crisis or excitement, the predominant inclination is the need to feel alive.

Earth-Air: Reference

With an emphasis of earth and air elements in a chart, neutrality and maturity are the adopted mode of operation. Cerebral qualities are emphasized and offer a broad and more accurate understanding of dynamics. Knowledge, awareness, and sensibility engender greater efficiency, refinement, culture, delicacy, precision, technical skills, and taste. This combination promotes objectivity, sophistication, and professionalism.

However, the need for perspective and correctness may result in excessive control and a lack of spontaneity. Consequently, unpredictable deviations may trigger nervous tension or even panic as they threaten the regulated and proficient mechanism of things. Alternatively, the person can become sarcastic or show disdain toward dramatic and untamed behavior often considered primitive. With earth and air, the need for sense and reason is essential.

Earth–Water: Maturation

With an emphasis of earth and water elements in a chart, protective and nurturing qualities are in the forefront. Inclined to introversion, the person is highly aware of needs and the care that is necessary to secure the proper function and development of things. Patience, attention, and sensitivity reduce the pace of action as earth and water are oriented toward gradual development. Preferring the depth of the inner world and the cultivation of internal gifts, the person is usually more discreet and reclusive, shying away from excessive outward stimulation.

Sometimes, this combination results in a lack of vitality and communication problems. High sensitivity can also generate a strong attachment to security needs, inducing stagnation and anxiety. Because of the tendency toward attachment, the need to process life may be exaggerated; to counterbalance potential stagnation, one may be confronted by shocking changes in order for evolution to proceed. With this combination, finding the right pace and timing is very important—haste or delay requires adjustments.

Air-Water: Growth

With an emphasis of air and water elements in a chart, a strong need for exchange and bonding is stimulated. Mind and emotions easily interrelate, prompting one to gain psychological insight. Consequently, there is a stronger focus on relationship involvement and emotional exchange. Counseling skills, a broad awareness, openness, liberalism, and caring qualities foster unification and mutuality. Conscious of the need to share resources in order to enhance development, the person is flexible and compromises when necessary. The need for growth is constant and conducive to emotional depth.

However, a permanent sense of lack may generate a tendency to become dependent on others. Positively, lack stimulates a search for ways to grow; yet when ungrounded it causes emotional instability and spinelessness. Individuals may lose themselves in others and end up weakened instead of empowered by relationships. With air and water, relating and gaining psychological perspective are natural inclinations, but this must first start with the self-acceptance.

Low Presence of an Element

All elements manifest in every chart to a certain degree. There is no absolute deficiency since a chart comprises all the signs, even if the signs are not populated by planets. However in a given chart, an element, or even two, may be strikingly low or even absent.

When an element is lacking, it does not necessarily imply that the person is impaired or ignorant in that area. In one way, it can simply mean that there is less conscious focus in that direction from an evolutionary point of view. However, since balance is ultimately necessary for healthy function, the person eventually yearns to complement or compensate for that, at least to some degree. Often the person finds balance by attracting another person whose chart is abundantly populated by the lacking element—this may be through a partner, or even one's own child.

Alternatively, the person will use existing resources in his or her chart to attain a desired sense of balance and will be cautious about maintaining it. Sometimes, one will go through phases of overcompensation, ardently clinging to a symbol representing that element. For example a person lacking fire, yet having the fiery planet Mars in a prominent position in the birth chart, may go through phases of extreme rebellion or confrontational behavior in an attempt to affirm the individuality intrinsic to the fire element. When balance is secured, compensation through excess is reduced.

Low Presence of Fire

A low dosage of fire can encourage a more cooperative and mild-mannered approach to life. Because there is less focus on individualism, the person's behavior is not as reactive and there is more room for reason and adaptation. Drama and creative self-expression are likely to be relatively cooled and the tendency to get carried away better tamed. This may manifest in a more placid and or detached personality.

When the lack is not compensated for in some way, vitality may be low, sometimes to the point of blocking the circulation of energy and possibly causing health disturbances. The individual may end up dispassionate, ineffectual, or shy when having to protect personal interests or promote personal causes. Possible outcomes include the feeling of not owning one's life and living according to external obligations or dancing to other people's tunes. A low presence of fire may narrow release outlets and either neutralize passion and emotions or repress them. The person may fear causing a disturbance and end up blocking his or her natural self-expression.

To establish balance, the work of consciousness requires the person to eventually develop expressive communication skills and define personal goals. There is also a need to defend one's personal sense of justice rather than sink into helplessness or comply when facing adversity and challenges. When healthily compensating for the lack, we may find a person pointedly attached to personal goals and causes but able to promote them with diplomacy

Low Presence of Earth

A low dosage of earth can induce a lifestyle that is more fluid and open to sudden changes. There is less focus on regularity and a reluctance to completely commit to structure; consequently, the person may be considered somewhat different for following a less predicable life path that might, at times, happen to be more cumbersome, less practical, and yet, more exciting and fulfilling than the norm. Meaning may become more important than efficiency and security.

When a lack of earth is not compensated for, energy may be easily scattered and wasted, inducing general inefficiency and even poor health. When facing discomfort, a lack of grounding may cause inconsistency and childlike expectations for immediate relief. The person may also poorly manage personal energy and resources and end up investing much more effort than was necessary. At worst, this may lead to repeated failures without any concrete results.

To establish balance, the work of consciousness requires the person to remain focused on a path, however uneven that path may be. Patience must be cultivated and boundaries respected for proper development to unfold. When healthily compensating for the lack, we may find the person to be eccentric and yet inwardly self-disciplined, sometimes even to the point of austerity.

Low Presence of Air

A low dosage of air can decrease the focus and interest in external stimulation and renewed variety. The person will likely be more grounded and centered within him or herself and less troubled by the erratic pace of trends or social interactions. This dynamic may also manifest as a relative disinterest in foreign and impersonal matters, the person preferring the here and now.

When not compensated for, the lack of air can result in a certain narrowness of spirit, possibly inducing prejudice. In a different way, this lack of perspective may cause too much focus on particular things and spur various forms of compulsions. In the same vein, the person may sink into emotional patterns or unhealthy situations without the capacity to rationalize and detach from them. As a result, one may get stuck and fail to move on with life when necessary.

To establish balance, the work of consciousness requires the person to keep an open spirit and realize the relativity of life; nothing is one-sided as air reflects the phenomenon of duality and balance. Similarly, healthy self-doubt and a reflective approach allow one to periodically upgrade personal standards by staying tuned to new trends and life dynamics. When healthily compensating for the lack, the person will be grounded, consistent, and yet, widely aware and educated about life and its diversity.

Low Presence of Water

A low dosage of water can decrease the time spent on processing needs and instead emphasize action, external stimulation, and or achievement. The person is likely to exhibit more clarity and direction, preferring to avoid innuendos and expressions of vulnerability. There is a stronger aspiration to perform with assured productivity and a high level of mastery.

Failing to compensate for the lack, the person may proceed in ways that are too abrupt and fail to emotionally digest encountered experiences; this attitude can manifest in attempting to always have everything perfectly regulated. Pain and chaos are not properly dealt with and often denied. The expectation for a high level of productivity can be projected onto others by assuming they can rapidly get over their vulnerabilities. Fearing weakness and moving forward too rapidly in life, one is likely to eventually experience emotional shocks. Sometimes this predisposition can describe a situation where a support system is lacking, rendering one distrustful and thus inaccessible in the deeper levels of intimacy.

To establish balance, the work of consciousness requires the person to become aware that it is not always possible to be on top of every situation and have the answers for all quandaries; vulnerabilities are part of the learning process. Weaknesses must be exposed in order to be healed and overcome; thus more patience and forgiveness must be developed toward imperfection. Despite the possibility of pain, one must take rational risks and learn to trust in order to be able to surrender and receive. When managing to compensate for a lack of water, the individual becomes aware of his or her own hunger and can assert surfacing needs for closeness. More consciousness will be oriented toward taking the time to process experiences and dwell in them while remaining highly functional and effective.

The Modes: Cardinal, Fixed, Mutable

Another classification of the astrology signs is called the modes which refer to "mode of action." There are three different modes—*cardinal, fixed,* and *mutable*—and each one consists of a sign in each element. Similar to the elements, the modes describe fundamental themes that are intrinsic to natural development.

Cardinal

Signs: *Aries, Cancer, Libra, Capricorn*
Planets: *Mars, Moon, Venus, Saturn*
Houses: *1, 4, 7, 10*

Figure 7: The cardinal cross

The meaning of the word cardinal is synonymous with important and essential, and indeed the signs of the cardinal mode serve as foundations and launching points that set new processes in motion. The central concern intrinsic to this mode is to establish security and reliability as new cycles are launched. On the one hand, the emotional orientation is active because there is a need to create new foundations, yet at the same time it is defensive because there is a need to protect those foundations. Through this mode, there is a sense of engagement, urgency, responsibility, and concern, making one aware, alert, and task oriented.

The cardinal mode represents new cycles of evolution. There is a constant feeling of transition between what needs to be left behind and what now needs to be established. Under these influences, the person cyclically experiences new beginnings, new births. The sense of transition generates a need to define the new direction and recognize what was, what is, and what is now going to be.

Accordingly, the cardinal quality heightens a person's sensitivity to timing and phases in life. The emphasis on new processes stimulates an awareness that there is a need to cut ties with a previous phase, now considered obsolete, so that something fresh can be promoted. The person becomes sensitive to the right timing for each phase of life; it is about sensing when a new chapter must begin while making sure the previous chapter is properly "sealed." Sometimes, the sense of transition can linger for years and the person swings back and forth between the past and the future—between where one came from and where one aspires to go to. The past is only released when it is properly sealed. The cardinal mode reflects the continual process of becoming via these developmental shifts.

The "back and forth" motion is also caused by an internal paradox within the cardinal signs: the need to launch new cycles and the need to solidify foundations. These urges create simultaneous needs— moving forward and staying put—and they often manifest in going two steps forward and then one step back. Action toward the new is often followed by hesitation. Ultimately, a more cautious development ensues.

The new cycles launched through the cardinal mode are motivated by personal causes, values, and identity questions. New beginnings also mean establishing a new identity and experiencing a continual sense of becoming. Consequently, the person is more emotionally charged when choosing a new direction; it is important for the person to define what he or she stands for.

Cardinal keywords

Ending and beginning of cycles, transitions, cyclic renewal, birth, continual state of becoming, launching, initiating, protectiveness, defined direction, foundations, maturation process, development.

Cardinal signs

- *Aries'* influence reflects the launch of a new individual developmental and evolutionary process. The Aries archetype represents a desire to actively initiate a separation from previous commitments or patterns of behavior so that new ones can be created and better conditions established that support personal and collective development. What came before is considered either complete or deficient, urging one to break away in hope of creating something better. With Aries, beginning new chapters and reinventing oneself occurs cyclically, and as a result, creativity and passion abound. While actions are taken to create new conditions, the transition is not always immediate, and the person may dwell in the "in between" for a while. When associating with a new sense and definition of self, the person tends to react defensively toward any external factor that threatens to hinder or slow down his or her action and expression.

- *Cancer's* influence reflects the beginning of a new maturation and growth phase. Through Cancer, the person gets in touch with the inner child who is in the continual process of becoming, regardless of one's age. Maturation can apply on different dimensions; it can be purely biological, or otherwise emotional, intellectual, or spiritual. As one starts a new phase of becoming, an entire emotional process is launched for the sake of assimilating new conditions. For example, if the person moves to a new location, he or she feels like a child in that new environment and requires time to process the move; part of the emotional adjustment includes asking for assistance to orient oneself and learn about the different dynamics of the new place. Emotional processes allow one to digest new experiences and grow into new conditions; therefore, the sense of becoming is continual.

- *Libra's* influence represents the necessity to experience polarities so that balance can be eventually attained—it is about finding the middle way. Hence the cardinal quality intrinsic to Libra stimulates a transfer from one extreme or polarity to the other. The shift occurs as a reaction to the feeling of limitation and lack when experiencing one side of things, triggering the desire for completion through the opposite polarity. Just like a person who has the urge to bond with someone in order to overcome personal limitation, Libra breaks away from one side to realize the other. For example, after having been employed by a company for many years, one may seek to experience the polarity of that experience by becoming self-employed. Or, after having been single, one may shift to engage in a relationship. Shifting from one experience to its opposite, naturally generates a continual sense of becoming.

- *Capricorn's* influence represents the need to establish references and structures that reflect the person's current level of maturation. The structure is the crystallization of all the experiences or concepts that have been processed up to the present moment. For example, a family structure may embody all the values and knowledge that the family authority has acquired and processed up to that time. As new emotional processes and changes are launched through the preceding cardinal signs, new references are established and structures must incorporate these developments and adapt to them. Hence Capricorn reflects the shift within structures that is necessary to integrate recent developmental efforts. The change of references is also stimulated by an urge to mature and move to a higher level of performance thus cyclically pushing the person up the ladder. As one matures, there is a calling for new challenges. However, the need to adapt to newly established references also brings resistance for fear that the new is not truly reliable. Hence heavy consideration precedes action and the launch of new cycles.

Capricorn also emphasizes the importance of defining the right amount of time for each phase in life so that under or overextension is avoided. Capricorn regulates the biological clock and one's life span. It rules time, and thus it indicates when the moment arrives to move on to new levels of being. Under this influence, it is assessed whether one is ripe enough for the next step in life.

Fixed

Signs: *Taurus, Leo, Scorpio, Aquarius*
Planets: *Venus, Sun, Pluto, Uranus*
Houses: *2, 5, 8, 11*

The fixed mode refers to creativity through the right use of resources. This mode highlights the need to invest material and or psychological resources in order to materialize and execute chosen goals. Through the fixed mode a greater concentration of energy is created, generating greater intensity and focus. Fixed signs boost personality presence and strength of character; the person gets fully in touch with the source of his or her creativity and is inspired to uniquely contribute to the process of life.

Figure 8: The fixed cross

Accordingly, the fixed mode signs represent one's personal sense of power; these signs are strongly associated with what one has, and therefore define self-esteem, value, and worth. They represent the availability and use of resources thereby defining the person's creative capacity and potential—therein lies the sense of power. The power to choose, to have an impact, and to change is recognized under these influences, allowing one to lead one's way rather than being swept by circumstances. The person grows into his or her personal power, presence, and capacity for influence through the fixed signs.

The term 'fixed' is often misinterpreted as a tendency toward stubbornness and stagnation. This is a misconception as the influence of this mode points to a constant need for depth. The first two signs,

Taurus and Leo (and their respective planets and houses) are geared toward establishing one's identity, resources, and purposes while the remaining two, Scorpio and Aquarius (and their respective planets and houses) are oriented toward constantly redefining one's sense of self to promote growth and progress.

Fixed keywords

Concentration, focus, determination, intensity, strength, resources, individuality, personal power, creativity, uniqueness, presence, implementation, having an impact, change, growth.

Fixed signs

- *Taurus's* influence points to the need to establish existence in the material dimension. The focus is on integrating into the body, defining one's territory, and recognizing one's worth measured in personal qualities, innate talents, or material possessions—these resources serve as currency of exchange. The stronger one's currency, the stronger one's appeal. Relying on personal resources, the person learns to stand firm and gradually build a foundation to survive life challenges. A greater focus on the physical world engenders the awakening of the senses such as taste, smell, and touch. With a rich inner world, self-sufficiency becomes a natural way of life. Immersed in one's private universe, strength and immense creativity keep one potent.

- *Leo's* influence symbolizes the impulse to make use of personal assets and qualities in order to creatively actualize what one represents or stands for. Inspiration abounds from serving as an engine of creativity and having, as a result, a meaningful impact on the environment. The need to participate in life stems from the confidence that one can create destiny and overcome fate by generating better existential conditions. This proactive approach increases one's power over life's development. Through creativity the flame of life continues to burn, possibly even outliving one's own death when leaving a legacy.

- *Scorpio's* influence represents the constant impulse to outgrow limitations and expand one's sense of power. The sense of power is measured according to the strength of one's currency when exchanging resources with others; it relies on how attractive and appealing one can become whether the exchange occurs on a material, emotional, intellectual, or spiritual level. Confronted by potential rejection or a lack of satisfaction with one's life, the need for introspection emerges to identify what needs to change inwardly and or outwardly. The tendency for soul searching generates intensity and penetrating insights into the hidden side of things.

- *Aquarius's* influence symbolizes the need to upgrade conditions of being and operating. The focus is on generating progress when the conditions of the present appear to have been fully exploited to the point where further creativity and development is not supported. Upon failing to resolve a problem, new research is launched with the aim of gaining greater insight or discovering new ways of addressing existing quandaries. When solutions are investigated, the mind is the main instrument of creativity. Creativity is also stimulated through community activities and bringing like-minded people together.

Mutable

Signs: *Gemini, Virgo, Sagittarius, Pisces*
Planets: *Mercury, Jupiter, Neptune*
Houses: *3, 6, 9, 12*

Figure 9: The mutable cross

The mutable mode represents the natural law of holism. It describes the need to assimilate separate components of life into the greater scheme of things. It relies on the idea that despite the differences between one another, we are all interdependent and affect each other whether we are conscious of it or not. Through these influences, a person realizes that it is not possible to remain completely separate from the rest of existence, regardless of how isolated or independent one may be. Every living being breathes the same air and depends on the same Sun. Consequently, this mode incites one to become aware of collective dynamics and adapt to the collective rhythm—this includes learning about all encompassing spiritual meanings and the laws of life. There is a requirement to step outside of oneself, observe, and understand life's mechanism. The pressure to assimilate is stronger, inducing the need to cooperate and interrelate with others in a spirit of oneness.

The search for larger meanings spurs the development of culture as human beings attempt to interpret existence from the viewpoint of their experience in a particular geographical location. Accordingly, the desire to travel and explore different cultures emerges as an attempt to understand and unify different perspectives; however, cultural clashes commonly occur when such attempts fail.

Similarly, the mutable signs represent the necessity of releasing the fruits of personal creativity to the larger public. Everything that was individually processed and created through the previous modes must now be integrated into the greater scheme of things. The person loses his or her sense of individuality and territoriality, surrendering to the collective flow. Failing to integrate into the larger whole, the person may feel awkward, misunderstood, or become overwhelmed by larger circumstances. When integration is successful, networking and larger scale development occurs by connecting with larger frameworks.

Mutable keywords

Adapting, releasing, decoding the larger framework of existence, holism, the search for meaning, spiritual attunement, greater sense of duty, cultural trends, ideas and concepts, opinions and beliefs, constant motion and flow, travel, internationalism, larger scale production.

Mutable signs

- *Gemini's* influence represents the survival pressure to integrate into life's rhythm. Through this influence, knowledge of the way life works is gathered in order to be able to orient oneself and adapt to the vastness of existence. The learning process reveals there is logic behind life's function which the individual strives to gradually decode through theory and practice.

The learning process begins with exposure to the immediate environment and expands to encompass further geographic locations, fostering travel and multicultural experiences. Information is gathered from everyday life encounters and from academic references in order to establish a wealth of general knowledge. When assembling the knowledge gathered in different spaces and times, pieces of the big life puzzle fall into place. As new knowledge is integrated into the whole, new cultural trends emerge.

- *Virgo's* influence refers to the necessity of integrating one's creativity and services into a larger chain of services. This dynamic emphasizes the interdependence between one another as each person depends on the service of another in order to be able to perform and produce. For example, the baker depends on the service of the farmer to do his or her work, and so on. The pressure to excel increases because the quality of one's service affects the service of another. All of the details must be synchronized in order for the whole to function productively.

- *Sagittarius's* influence stimulates the impulse to realize a potential that is larger than what is currently known; it is a search for the greater Truth that governs existence. A feeling of limitation ignites the thought that there must be more to life than what is currently known, motivating a personal search for greater opportunity and meaning. Intuition, speculation, and faith inspire one to follow through on different assumptions and attempt to realize a greater potential. When successful,

Sagittarius stimulates expansion, growth, and spiritual development. Conversely, when missing a target, waste and excess can cause negative consequences. Since potential is initially abstract, realizing it is always a gamble. The search for and interpretation of the Truth engenders the creation of belief systems, rituals, and cultures.

- *Pisces'* influence refers to the need to completely unify individuality with the larger whole and totality of life. One realizes that despite existing differences, every being shares similar goals such as well-being, health, and love. The person becomes aware that a greater life mechanism governs the totality and life, and well-being depends on harmonizing with higher life principles; the individual is inspired to surrender control and flow with life. When surrendering to larger life forces, a more responsive and adaptive attitude replaces active initiation. In identifying with the larger whole, one may tap into the collective conscious and unconscious, and have an impact on the public.

Note: To measure how influential a particular element or mode is in a chart, first count the populated signs in that element or mode, then the populated houses, then finally the strength of the planets. For example, if there are no planets in a fire sign, compensation can occur if a fire house contains planets or if the fire planets are in prominent positions. However, the primary measure of an element or mode's prominence in a chart is having the appropriate signs populated by planets.

Summary of the Signs, the Elements, and the Modes

- **Aries:** *fire, cardinal*—breaking through to usher in a new cycle of becoming.

- **Taurus:** *earth, fixed*—establishing one's territory and self-worth.

- **Gemini:** *air, mutable*—learning about life in order to adapt to the environment and navigate existence.

- **Cancer:** *water, cardinal*—emotionally processing a new cycle of becoming.

- **Leo:** *fire, fixed*—creatively actualizing one's personal sense of meaning.

- **Virgo:** *earth, mutable*—effectively managing resources to optimize productivity and the quality of service.

- **Libra:** *air, cardinal*—shifting direction through the embrace of opposites.

- **Scorpio:** *water, fixed*—processing exchange through intimacy for the sake of growth.

- **Sagittarius:** *fire, mutable*—uncovering a greater potential for existence on a personal and a collective level.

- **Capricorn:** *earth, cardinal*—introducing reliable standards of ethics and performance.

- **Aquarius:** *air, fixed*—upgrading standards of living by fostering creativity through personal and combined efforts.

- **Pisces,** *water, mutable*—attuning personal powers to meanings higher than the self.

The Hemispheres and the Quadrants

An astrological chart describes the particular placement of the celestial constellations at a given moment in time. To refer to these celestial placements from our view on Earth, we use four points of intersection where the Earth meets the sky. As discussed earlier in this chapter, the first two meeting points are *the Ascendant*, where the eastern horizon line meets the ecliptic, and *the Descendant*, where the western horizon line meets the ecliptic. *(Note*: When you look at a chart, east is on the left side.) The other two points are the *Midheaven* (or *MC*) and its opposite the *Lower Midheaven* (or *IC*). These points are called *the angles* (see figure 2); they vary according to the geographical location and the time of year.

The four intersection points (angles) divide the chart into *four hemispheres and four quadrants.* When a majority of the planets populates a specific hemisphere or quadrant, the hemisphere or quadrant meaning is emphasized and provides general clues about the person's evolutionary orientation.

Although when referring to quadrants and hemispheres the primary focus is on house population (for example, the first quadrant includes the first house through the third house), the description of hemispheres and quadrants also applies to the respective signs (for example, the first quadrant description also applies to the signs of Aries, Taurus, and Gemini).

It is common to have more than one quadrant or hemisphere populated in a chart. The astrologer must synthesize the sum of these influences to understand how everything works together.

The Lower Hemisphere: Personal Reality

From the Ascendant to the Descendant passing through the IC.
From the first house through the sixth house.
From Aries to Virgo.

Figure 10: The lower hemisphere

The lower hemisphere refers to the formation of one's personal reality—the ego is being established and its orientation or purpose defined. This is where one personally connects with life. As the ego develops, it serves as a personal point of reference in existence. Consequently, this hemisphere represents the building process of one's personal life through which the person learns to survive independently, form an identity, and strengthen the foundation of his or her existence.

Emotional attachments are created with specific elements in life that allow one to feel a sense of association and direction.

Through the lower hemisphere personal meaning is defined and asserted, and the person gains the ability to better regulate his or her personal life. The lower hemisphere represents the survival and creative process through which security, a reliable foundation, and a personal purpose is established.

Lower hemisphere keywords
Personal, subjective, unique, guarded, intimate, nurturing, attentive, detail-oriented, emotional, attached, identified with, security-oriented, constructive, creative, expressive.

The Upper Hemisphere: Transpersonal Reality
From the Descendant to the Ascendant passing through the MC.
From the seventh house to the twelfth house.
From Libra to Pisces.

The upper hemisphere refers to egocentric expansion, growth, and transcendence. Once the ego is established through the lower hemisphere, it faces its limitations as a separate entity and learns to reach out in order to grow. Associations are made with external elements in order to gain greater perspective and exchange resources; thus adaptation and performing skills are strengthened. The sense of self is challenged, pressuring the person to mature and develop a higher perspective on existence.

Figure 11: The upper hemisphere

Through the upper hemisphere, the person steps outside of his or her comfort zone and security to explore larger realities through relationships, public involvement, and spiritual meanings. As one's personal reality is adjusted to respond to larger circumstances, a more objective perspective is developed. The need for growth stimulates change; consequently, the person learns to release emotional attachments accordingly.

Upper hemisphere keywords
Perspective, objectivity, reflection, self-doubt, cooperation, inner lack, receptivity, maturity, development, increase, growth.

The Eastern Hemisphere: Facing Life Circumstances

From the MC to the IC passing through the Ascendant.
From the tenth house to the third house.
From Capricorn to Gemini.

Figure 12: The eastern hemisphere

The eastern hemisphere refers to the person's response to the stronger forces of existence such as fate, natural forces, and or collective dynamics. Through this hemisphere, one is subject to larger life currents and compelled to forge his or her way through life—adapting, persevering, and surviving. Confronted with existential challenges, the person has less control over the unfolding of his or her existence as life is experienced in a less predictable fashion. Personal attunement to these larger dynamics requires inner strength and improvisation skills.

There is a common misunderstanding about the meaning of the eastern hemisphere. It is often said to represent personal initiatives and therefore personal control abilities; however, this hemisphere is more about the pressure to personally address larger circumstances rather than have a defined and consistent sense of direction, hence the confusion.

Eastern hemisphere keywords

The individual facing existence, adaptation, response to larger circumstances, necessity, attunement, surviving challenges, fortitude, fate.

The Western Hemisphere: Creating Life Circumstances

From the IC to the MC passing through the Descendant.
From the fourth house to the ninth house.
From Cancer to Sagittarius.

The western hemisphere refers to the impact the person has, or can have, on existence; it symbolizes free will and the power to make things happen or stimulate change. Through the western hemisphere, the person cultivates control abilities and the capacity to choose—establishing conditions that would support personal needs and purposes. Here one's sense of identity is better defined. The environment is better understood, more easily regulated, and it is used to facilitate personal causes. Talents, skills, and culture thrive and are enhanced, opening up opportunities for expression and development. The ego is in its empowerment phase, contributing to the whole and processing its own growth.

Figure 13: The western hemisphere

There is a common misunderstanding about the meaning of the western hemisphere; it is often thought to represent the need to surrender and respond to "others." However, this hemisphere reflects egocentric ripeness, and thus even if it includes interactions with others, these interactions are the fruit of a conscious choice based on one's conscious desire for growth. The need for personal expansion is what drives the person to form relationships; he or she chooses whom to be with. Therefore, the ego remains in relative control of the direction of events.

Western hemisphere keywords
Having an impact, control, choice of direction, involvement, management, talents, input, legacy, personal development, increase, change, growth.

The First Quadrant: Existing

From the Ascendant to the IC.
First house, second house, third house.
Aries, Taurus, Gemini.

Figure 14: The first quadrant

The lower eastern quadrant refers to developing skills to face life on one's own; strength and survival capacities increase as an independent sense of self emerges. Foundations are established to better address challenges, resist turbulence, and take charge of one's life.

These circumstances prompt a more defensive stance and promote self-sufficiency. Consequently, personal skills and talents are developed and an inner world is cultivated. Trust in others is reduced in this quadrant; whether isolated or networking with others, the person is mostly self-reliant.

First quadrant keywords
Separation, defensiveness, autonomy, independence, resourcefulness, talent, inner wealth, strength, resistance, survival.

First quadrant signs
- *Aries*: Individualizing, acknowledging one's power to take action, forging one's way, confronting challenges, defense.

- *Taurus*: Defining territory, grounding, using the senses, gathering and using personal resources, self-sufficiency.

- *Gemini*: Finding direction in the environment amidst survival pressure, figuring life out, intellectual perspective, navigation.

The Second Quadrant: Generating
From the IC to the Descendant.
Fourth house, fifth house, sixth house.
Cancer, Leo, Virgo.

The lower western quadrant represents egocentric expression and creativity. The sense of self is better defined and loyalty to personal values is established, allowing the person to have a better understanding of what he or she wants out of life, more attentively address details, and manifest private goals.

Greater control over one's environment and objectives is gained and the flow of one's life is more effectively directed. As personality and creativity blossom, expectations rise toward finding personal fulfillment; a strong need emerges to make one's life meaningful.

Figure 15: The second quadrant

Second quadrant keywords

Creativity, personal attention, detail-oriented, control of development, self-motivated, loyalty to one's personal vision, output, production.

Second quadrant signs

- *Cancer*: Remaining loyal to one's personal rhythm and needs, establishing a personal connection with life.

- *Leo*: Expressing creative qualities, finding a personal purpose, asserting one's role in life.

- *Virgo*: Controlling and refining the use of resources to guarantee productivity and success.

The Third Quadrant: Growing

From the Descendant to the MC.
Seventh house, eighth house, ninth house.
Libra, Scorpio, Sagittarius.

Figure 16: The third quadrant

The upper western hemisphere refers to egocentric development and expansion. Through this quadrant, the person experiences a deep sense of inner lack and is consequently stimulated to find ways to fulfill a higher potential and gain new ground in life.

There is tendency to reach out and identify what one is missing, making one more of a seeker and doubtful of the status quo. Bonding with others, gaining new perspectives, and challenging security and boundaries are the ways this growth process unfolds. Doubt naturally fosters a more confrontational approach toward both personal and external limitations so that change can occur. The need for "more" promotes development and invites risk taking.

Third quadrant keywords

The need for more, lack, hunger, doubt, stepping out of oneself, relationships, reaching out, increase, change, growth, expansion, constant redefinition.

Third quadrant signs

- *Libra*: Confronting lack and imbalance, reaching out to find a sense of completion.

- *Scorpio*: Aspiring to outgrow a sense of limitation through merging with symbols of power, continual redefinition, change, and growth.

- *Sagittarius*: Taking risks to search for greater potential and meaning, both for oneself and the collective.

The Fourth Quadrant: Aligning

From the MC to the Ascendant.
Tenth house, eleventh house, twelfth house.
Capricorn, Aquarius, Pisces.

The upper eastern hemisphere refers to the need for the ego to adapt to realities larger than itself. The person is exposed to meanings and paths in life that apply on a mass scale and accordingly directs personal effort to meet the larger collective orientation.

Figure 17: The fourth quadrant

This dynamic is first stimulated by the understanding that merging with the collective increases the odds of personal survival and well-being. When resources are shared, forces are combined to combat greater challenges. Personally associating with larger meanings stems from realizing one's mortality; the person feels small when compared to greater universal currents and is incited to adopt longer-lasting values that are rooted in collective heritage or spiritual truth. Circumstances incite the person to let go of personal attachments when necessary and better flow with what life requires. Identifying with greater collective needs and currents, the person can have an impact on public needs through this quadrant.

Fourth quadrant keywords

Collective, impersonal, transcendence, mature, adaptation, conformity, higher duty, sacrifice, community, public function, higher meaning.

Fourth quadrant signs

- *Capricorn*: Aligning the ego with moral values and reliable codes to live by as a collective.

- *Aquarius*: Developing civilization by fostering collective creativity and progress.

- *Pisces*: Dedicating oneself to a public role and or spiritual meaning, merging with the general flow of life.

Chapter Three

The Twelve Archetypes

The twelve astrology signs can also be thought of as archetypes. Each of the archetypes (or signs) represents a life theme, and when all twelve of them are united, the totality of life is at play. Studying the astrological archetypes is a way to understand the fundamental forces operating in our existence and universe. It is important to understand each archetype separately before analyzing how they interrelate with one another.

Each of the twelve astrology archetypes manifests through three primary forms in the chart: *the sign, the planet, and the house*. For example, the Aries archetype expresses itself through the sign of Aries, its ruling planet Mars, and its representative house—the first house. Consequently, the themes and meanings embodied in Aries operate through these three forms. Further clarification of the difference between each of the forms—the sign, the planet, and the house—is explored in the next chapter.

To understand the nature of an astrological archetype, it is important to observe the placement of the corresponding constellation in the heavens because there is a natural development from one placement to the next. For example, the fact that the constellation of Aries succeeds Pisces and precedes Taurus is significant because there is a logical development from one archetype to the next: the order is not random. Similarly, archetypes that oppose each other share important interactive themes. For example in the case of Aries, the opposing archetype is Libra (see figure 18).

Figure 18: The Aries-Libra polarity

Our cycles of development are reflected by the progression of a planet from one sign to the next. After a planet completes a full cycle through the twelve signs and returns to Pisces, it begins a new cycle right away when moving into Aries. When a new cycle begins, new dynamics that pertain to the passage of the planet through the houses and signs are experienced.

Below is a description of each of the twelve astrological archetypes. While reading these descriptions, it is important to remember that these associations reflect the general evolutionary themes pertaining to the sign—they are not specific to the placement of a specific planet in that sign.

The Aries ♈ Archetype
Including the sign of Aries, the planet Mars, and the 1ˢᵗ house
Fire—Cardinal—Extroverted

Aries is the first archetype; however, it does not represent the absolute beginning of life, but rather the commencement of individuation and the birth of one's separate consciousness. In the natural order of the signs, Aries follows Pisces. As Pisces represents a more passive and impersonal approach to life through the need to merge with collective currents, moving on to Aries reflects the evolutionary need to separate and develop one's own sense of being. Through the Aries influence, an effort is made to pierce through resistance and forge one's way in life, just like a baby pushes through the birth canal and separates from the womb. Pisces represents the womb of the universe where all is one; the urge to separate, ignited through Aries, stems from a need to participate and develop one's own unique way of being in life instead of remaining passive within the womb.

Through Aries, the person learns to make life happen rather than wait for it to happen: Aries reflects the principle of taking action and becoming a creative force. Under the preceding influence of Pisces, personal boundaries were blurred because one identified with larger causes and ideals generating circumstances where collective influences directed the flow of personal life occurrences. With Aries, one learns to think for oneself and aspires to proceed independently at one's own risk.

The motivation behind this surge of independence is the fear of losing oneself and being helpless when challenges or adversity emerge. As one gradually takes charge of one's life through Aries, a defense mechanism is developed, diminishing the odds of being controlled or even victimized by others. Through personal initiative and effort, the person grows into his or her own power and becomes capable of independently handling and promoting life.

Like a toddler experiencing a sense of elation upon making his or her first step, the person discovers capabilities that were never considered prior to having taken action. The process of self-discovery provides one with more confidence and a greater sense of security. With freedom and independence, personal desires are addressed and life is directed toward fulfilling personal aspirations.

In some cases, the urge to individualize and take independent action stems from being confronted with injustice. The person may experience abuse or neglect and feel the need to react in order to change the circumstances. Injustice can trigger anger that in turn makes one realize that when the need arises it is not always viable to wait for outside help, or even expect divine intervention; one must develop the capacity to independently face potential threats and create change.

Anger makes a person realize that something is wrong and that change is required. In a healthy way, anger leads to corrective action or even activism. Under the Aries influence, the person cannot sit and wait for problems to pass; there is an urgent need to act that makes one an agent of change on a personal level, sometimes even a collective level. The aspiration for change incites one to launch new life cycles with the aim of creating more just and meaningful dynamics.

For example, some women with a strong Aries signature in their chart tend to embrace feminism. With a memory of having been taken for granted or having lost their identity through submissiveness, they aspire to break patterns of injustice and take appropriate action to protect women's rights. Realizing that change will not occur unless they become personally involved and protest, they want to usher in a new cycle to prevent history from repeating itself. Not every person necessarily becomes an activist per se and takes political action under these influences, for such an orientation can simply manifest as instinctive defensiveness when personal rights are denied.

The need to launch a new cycle is not always motivated by a feeling of injustice or a crisis; it may also gradually emerge because of a need for personal development and growth. Having led a particular lifestyle, the person may cyclically feel that whatever he or she had been involved with has been fully exploited and that it is time for something new. This shift can manifest in changing careers, relocating, or breaking away from relationships—with new starts, one feels revitalized.

Emotions are strong and instinctive under the Aries influence. The person acts from primal urges and yearns to freely express whatever is felt whether excitement, passion, enthusiasm, or conversely, anger. Through these emotions, one feels alive and strongly involved in the immediacy of the moment. Unrestrained expression usually renders one emotionally transparent as everything is conveyed in an open and straightforward manner.

When confronted with injustice, the person may react defiantly either through a frontal response or by quitting the scene. For example, if feeling unfairly treated at work, it is not uncommon for the person to quit on the spur of a moment. Abuse, corruption, or restrictive control triggers a strong reaction, and the rush of adrenaline that ensues promises a charged response of some sort—temper is obviously on the warmer side.

While reactive and rebellious behavior is recurrent, strong attachments are formed when the person feels passionate about a cause or another person. Conquered by strong emotions, one is completely dedicated when finding something or someone to identify with. Such a commitment manifests in generosity, support, and protectiveness. Conversely, the moment negative feelings arise and trust is threatened, an equally strong reaction may be expressed in the opposite way resulting in a defensive and confrontational stance. Sometimes one gets caught in a "black and white" vision of people and the world that is split between those that are in "one's camp" and those that are not. When in agreement, everything of oneself is given, but when antagonized, one may only see enmity in the other. It is not uncommon to suddenly perceive people one was once affectionate with as adversaries and then address them rather mercilessly. The fear of victimization and injustice, blended with strong emotions, is the cause for this potentially radical approach and sharp change of position from friend to foe. If these inclinations are not well managed, the person may get carried away in creating a commotion.

The strong instinctual nature of the Aries archetype keeps the person very authentic and natural. Life's direction can be unpredictable as one is mostly driven by feelings, passion, and emerging challenges. There is a need to identify with every aspect of one's personal life instead of performing out of obligation or because of external requests. For example, one may fair better when self-employed or at least when given creative freedom if under another authority.

Naturalness and instinctive emotions also manifest in a strong sexual nature. Sexual desires are usually acted upon with the person usually taking the assertive role when courting a potential partner. Women with these chart influences tend to defy the stereotypical role of passivity and usually are more sexually liberated, challenging judgment or repression. They may yearn for a partner that is not intimidated by their more proactive approach.

Similarly, individuals with a strong Aries signature abound with creative talent. It may manifest in entrepreneurial inclinations or simply through artistic expression. Immersed in their inner world and free to express themselves, they are inspired and often find it most appropriate to "speak" through their canvases or other creative outlets.

The archetype opposing Aries is Libra. The opposing archetype serves as a point of balance, and here through Libra there is a need to develop a more neutral approach to life. Aries tends toward more extreme categorizations such as "good or bad," "love or anger," or "friend or foe." To counterbalance this rather radical approach, the Libra influence inspires understanding, consideration, and balance in one's approach to life and people. There is an evolutionary lesson to better direct personal power and create win/win situations when possible. When considering an adversary's motivation, the person learns the broader meaning of justice and sees that the other person may also have a valid point. When approaching others from a place of neutrality, one may feel more secure and therefore more likely to be able to compromise rather than react defensively out of a fear losing oneself. With greater perspective and understanding of "the other," relationships become more equal and mellow.

General associations
Being, expressing, taking action, beginning new cycles, reacting, defending, fighting, defying, asserting, activism, justice-fighters, sharp objects, war, weapons, impulse, sexuality, phallus, separation, ruptures, change, excitement, empowerment, courage, dedication, passion, creativity, the color red.

Health associations
The skull area, red blood cells, the adrenal glands and adrenaline, male hormones, sex organs, sex drive, vitality, inflammation, cuts, immunity response.

Professional associations
Entrepreneurship, self-employment, freelance, art, sales, activism, combat, the defense industry, rescue, acupuncture.

Relationship inclinations
Passionate, reactive, complete self-investment, personally attentive, romantic, sexual, defiant, confrontational, competitive, hot to cold mood swings, enthusiastic.

The Taurus ♉ Archetype
Including the sign of Taurus, the planet Venus, and the 2nd house
Earth—Fixed—Introverted

Under the Taurus archetype, there is an evolutionary need to integrate spirit into matter and to solidify form. Following the charged emotion that stimulated a new cycle of being through Aries, one realizes through Taurus that survival depends on giving form to one's life and harmonizing it with the flow of existence. The person aspires to maximize the life span in the realm of matter and consequently seeks stability, consistency, and strength.

Under this influence, aesthetic attributes are revered because beauty is associated with quality of form: there is balance and harmony in beauty, something that promises longer-lasting value. But it is not only in external appearances that one recognizes quality—strength, authenticity, and inner wealth are equally valued. In a different and more abstract way, a strong attraction to the harmony of music reflects the yearning for beauty.

The initial impulse to break away and individuate that preceded through Aries is now internalized through Taurus, and the person shifts his or her approach from extroverted self-assertion to a more territorial and self-sufficient approach. Establishing and defining a private territory upon which a solid foundation can be established allows one to build life progressively.

The person aspires for autonomy and self-sufficiency because dependence is perceived as a potential threat to one's stability and survival: giving other people influence over one's well-being is not welcome. Therefore, one gets in touch with private resources in the form of talents and assets to take care of survival needs and productivity. Commonly an individual with a strong Taurus influence is highly resourceful and blessed with inborn capacities that secure self-sufficiency. Helping to generate a source of income, these talents may be manual, musical, artistic, or in the form of self-taught knowledge.

Often people under this influence isolate themselves from the external world with its excessive stimulation and prefer to spend time in their own private world, cultivating personal capabilities and taking care of themselves. Spending hours gardening, listening to music, or regrouping in their own space is a form of therapy. Partners may, at times, feel threatened by such autonomy, but they must understand it is an essential need. Sometimes this orientation manifests in choosing a more rural lifestyle, away from urban stress.

Through developing an inner world, one's personal sense of worth is evaluated. Value is based on what stands the test of time and outlives eventual tribulation: the more solid and consistent a quality is the greater its worth. Through the Taurus archetype, value associations are defined starting from self-esteem to identifying what is worth keeping or losing. When exchanging resources with others, the individual aspires to have a strong currency; hence self-worth and the value of assets are constantly worked on so they can be improved and more likely appreciated by others.

However, the focus on one's inner world may create a tendency to be overly attached to personal values and possessions in an uncompromising way. The desire for continuity generates a dislike of endings or change. The person may hold on tight to his or her private vision of harmony and potentially become too resistant when compromise and cooperation are necessary.

Moreover, a fear of death and endings may prevent one from letting go when it is time to move on. This orientation not only manifests in being attached to physical things such as land, a house, or a piece of art, but also to one's ways and principles in spite of external pressure; the individual strives to maintain his or her inner world intact as the rest of the world goes through changing tides and trends. There are advantages to such a fixed stance, until it becomes excessive.

The evolutionary impulse to integrate spirit into matter makes the person highly aware of the physical and material dimension of life. To be able to proceed on its course, the soul needs a body and a concrete form. Such an orientation can manifest in various ways, possibly even emerging as an attraction to the physicality of the natural world, especially the vegetal realm. In this context botany, or any other earth-related interest or activity, is often considered very soothing as the richness of soil reflects one's own inner wealth. Similarly through Taurus, the person strongly connects to the physical body considering it a temple of the soul; thus the senses and sensuality bloom, helping one appreciate earthly pleasures such as food, physical comfort, and sexuality. Consequently, one may indulge in the senses, demonstrating an appreciation of the richness of life.

Sexuality is highly emphasized under the Taurus influence as it reflects the need to get in touch with the body; in this context orgasms serve to bring spirit into flesh. Because of the autonomous orientation, masturbation is a common way to bond with one's body. Similarly, sexual activity with another partner may be motivated by this conscious or unconscious appreciation of sensuality instead of only having sex for procreative purposes. Once again, sexuality is validated as a way to stimulate the senses and integrate into the material dimension. However when imbalanced, this orientation may manifest in perceiving others as sexual objects or becoming oneself only an object of pleasure because values are wrongly defined.

Aware of the physical dimension and the value of things, the person may direct effort toward developing financial resources and acquiring tangible assets. Personal assets may also be quantified as inborn talents that serve as a source of income. Overall, material security and abundance rise in importance under this influence because survival within the realm of matter is a strong focus. When excessive, money may be substituted for love, or self-worth measured according to material possessions. Despite the fact that financial development is an integral part of survival, materialism must serve as a means rather than an end. When better managed, the ability to generate abundance allows one to share resources and help others prosper as well.

The archetype opposing Taurus is Scorpio. The opposing archetype serves as a point of balance, and here through Scorpio there is a need to embrace the reality of impermanence. From a Scorpio point of view, nothing lasts forever in manifested Creation. Since we are constantly evolving, everything is bound to be redefined. Scorpio exposes what doesn't work anymore and thus it inspires change and growth. In this context, the Scorpio influence confronts the potential for excessive attachment to matter through Taurus. Physical form has to adapt to the changes the soul goes through; otherwise, it confines it. Scorpio's influence reminds us that soul development is the higher goal and that excessive attachment to the status quo or matter is bound to hinder one's growth. Ultimately, if change is resisted when necessary, survival suffers. As Taurus yearns for stability and Scorpio for growth, a balance can be found between cycles of stability and cycles of doubt and redefinition.

From another perspective, the Scorpio influence also emphasizes the fact that at some point the self-sufficiency and isolation preferred by Taurus can render one vulnerable in the long run. The need to merge and exchange resources with others serves a survival need as it revitalizes one's inner world. We need others and dependence cannot be completely avoided.

General associations
Form, matter, tangibility, density, rooting, solidity, earth, vegetation, smells, sensuality, sexuality, beauty, harmony, pastel colors, food, acceptance, appreciation, worth, talents, music, sculpture, construction, assets, possessions, finances, comfort, durability, self-sufficiency.

Health associations
The throat, vocal cords, weight management, sugar processing mechanisms, female hormones, the senses, physical soundness.

Professional associations
Agriculture, botany, farming, finances, asset management, gastronomy, art, music, design and aesthetics, construction, carpentry.

Relationship inclinations
Accepting, harmony and calm seeking, non-confrontational, independent, territorial, practical, sensual, sexual, simple.

The Gemini ♊ Archetype

Including the sign of Gemini, the planet Mercury, and the 3rd house
Air—Mutable—Extroverted

Under the Gemini archetype, there is an evolutionary need to learn about life by interrelating and integrating into the external environmental rhythm. After the isolation that fostered self-sufficiency through the Taurus phase, one realizes through Gemini that withdrawing from external dynamics can be detrimental to one's survival because we are all part of a larger chain of events; understanding the various environmental components helps us better navigate life. For example, the simplest things, such as the air that we all breathe or the flow of a river, serve as a conduit from what is external to what is private—thus there is a need to be informed about what happens in the outside world. The person is confronted with the reality that many currents simultaneously intercross in life and that failing to synchronize with them may lead to disorientation, the mismanagement of resources, and exposure to danger. Consequently, being informed of what goes on in one's environment and the world at large is a survival necessity.

The Gemini influence makes one aware of the changing nature of time and space, and the need to keep up with it. Getting acquainted with the local space and current time improves navigation through life; as a result, learning and "figuring life out" is an ongoing effort. There is pressure to come out of the shell and explore one's surroundings, gather information, gain understanding, and communicate with various factors in the environment. Survival depends on education as it becomes clear that ignorance and innocence weaken one's ability to make it and develop—being informed helps one avoid quandaries and seize existing opportunities.

Born into a universe that existed before our birth, everything appears magically self-regulating; through Gemini the person strives to decode the mechanism of things and demystify life's function through knowledge. As knowledge increases, the odds of chaos decrease and life is better managed. The learning process starts by observing and correlating life events in the current space and time, and from there it expands to exploring neighboring environments and different time periods. Learning may occur through formal education within the structure of school, or by spontaneously observing life. Whether immersed in books or "street smart," the person is mentally alert; every bit of information is a new piece that is added to the big puzzle of life.

The Gemini archetype reflects the birth of language—the word results from understanding. When the mind comprehends a life phenomenon, it can name it and relate to it. An elaborate and rich language mirrors the depth and intelligence of a culture. Beyond the action of labeling life's phenomena, through Gemini the person realizes the interrelationship between each particle of life; life appears in fragments but the fragments communicate, influence, and depend on each other. For example, what happens in the city impacts what happens in the country. The carnivore depends on the herbivore, which depends on vegetation, which depends on rain—learning about one leads to all the others. As learning unfolds, it becomes clear that there is sense in all life occurrences: nothing is random but instead all is connected by a thread of logic. While most of the logic of life remains veiled and is left to be uncovered, one realizes that there must be higher intelligence at play. Figuring out the intelligence of life fosters one's own intelligence. Learning through the Gemini influence spurs the development of language, communication, culture, science, and literature.

Learning about life is strongly conditioned by the environment the person lives in: someone living in a desert has a different life experience than someone living in a rainforest. Knowledge spurs a whole way of life that in turn sets in motion activity and a rhythm— since the search for understanding is never ending, the need for more knowledge incites the person to venture beyond the immediate space to explore new environments. The move to a new environment is not always by choice; life circumstances may expose one to different cultures without one's conscious control.

Multicultural experiences and lifestyles are common under this influence the purpose of which is to progressively synthesize the diversity that is encountered and see how each culture interprets life phenomena in a unique fashion. Moving from location to location—either virtually through literature or literally through travel—one learns about different perspectives and expands the learning process. A bridge is built between all the seemingly separate fragments.

Gemini's influence is strongly associated with modernity and current trends because modernity represents the implementation of newly acquired information. Since new knowledge is constantly uncovered, the need to update one's reality accordingly keeps one continually alert and on the move. In this context, the past may be perceived as obsolete because in most cases it contains less knowledge than the present where everything happens and new learning occurs. In this light, the person maintains a youthful spirit and an open mind, always yearning for mental stimulation. There is a strong appeal for science, culture, fashion, new ideas, foreign exchange, and diversity; consequently, the person is inclined to disassociate from conservative values and single-minded perspectives.

Because of integration pressures, learning must occur promptly because the threat of disorientation and chaos is always looming. Similar to visiting a foreign country, where one has to quickly compute new dynamics, the person is pressured to synthesize new impressions and data in everyday life. This dynamic significantly stimulates the nervous system, often leading to restlessness and impatience. Constantly maintaining a faster pace, one may also get easily bored if the environment does not offer learning opportunities.

Moreover, the need to be informed is also a result of the tendency to feel self-conscious; one may be concerned about being publicly inappropriate, shamed, or considered intellectually inferior. On these bases, there is an inclination to develop a social image that portrays self-control and "coolness"—weaknesses and insecurities tend to be camouflaged beneath a confident external appearance.

A strong Gemini influence in one's chart often manifests as an easy-going personality that is equipped with a relatively good understanding of the way the world works. Quick to assimilate and catch on to things, the person lives at a faster pace and seeks learning experiences. Exposure to the media, involvement with people, studies, and travel keep the mental acrobatics going and fight off the threat of boredom and disorientation. Respect is often lost for people who resist change and hold on to what is perceived as obsolete. Overall, despite a social nature, a very independent and self-motivated spirit is behind the wheel.

The archetype opposing Gemini is Sagittarius. The opposing archetype serves as a point of balance, and here through Sagittarius there is a need to maintain a level of authenticity to avoid losing oneself in the complexity of external life dynamics. Concerned about learning and adapting, the Gemini influence may pull the person in many directions without a solid center; the Sagittarius influence points to the need to remain natural and in touch with one's internal truth.

When embracing the Sagittarius polarity, the person frees his or her spirit and is able to decrease nervous tension. This dynamic also encourages the person to speak up and voice his or her personal perspective, even if it is not to other people's liking—the student can get in touch with the inner orator or teacher through this polarity. Moreover, the Sagittarius polarity inspires one to look at the bigger picture when engaged in the learning process. Logic is complemented by abstract thought and intuition—this implies identifying the larger and more general themes that are common to all diverse life expressions.

General associations
External life rhythm, adaptation, rhythm, integration, the intellect, learning, schools, books, language, observation, culture, trends, modernity, urbanism, media, information, communication, mobility, all means of transport, travel, the environment, internationalism, cross-cultural experiences, anthropology, siblings, neighbors, extended family, diversity.

Health associations
Lungs and the respiratory system, the nervous system, the left-brain hemisphere and right side of the body, motor skills, limbs and hands.

Professional associations
Communication, media, transport, teaching, literature, multicultural orientation, culture, fashion, internationalism, travel, language, math.

Relationship inclinations
Seeking stimulation and growth, intellectual, verbal, communicative, reflective, open-minded, witty, social, entertaining, pleasurable, exciting.

The Cancer ♋ Archetype
Including the sign of Cancer, the Moon, and the 4ᵗʰ house
Water—Cardinal—Introverted

Under the Cancer archetype, there is an evolutionary need to personalize existence through creating emotional attachments. Following the pressure to assimilate the myriad of facts and elements that were studied and experienced through Gemini, one realizes through Cancer that to develop in a healthy way there is a need to be able to choose what to personally associate with. Personal attachments allow the person to be connected within the vastness of existence and have a life; without emotional attachment, one's approach to life would become utterly impersonal and even robotic. This personal approach is a function of the ego which is established through Cancer. The ego is the personal lens through which one perceives and processes life—it serves as the vehicle of the soul.

Emotional attachments generate associations with people, things, or ideas. For example in becoming attached, the person can form a family, feel a sense of belonging, or adopt a philosophy. An identity is formed through the personalizing process. For example, a citizen of India is more emotionally involved and therefore closer to affairs occurring in India than other countries. While knowing about other countries, the person in this case personalizes India, and India becomes part of his or her egocentric identity; consequently, this is the country through which the person has stronger life experiences and learns soul lessons.

Following the Gemini phase where one was pressured to integrate into the external crosscurrents of life, the focus through Cancer is to attune to one's personal internal rhythm and choices in life. These choices are not always fully conscious—life circumstances influence what one naturally gravitates toward based on the soul's evolutionary requirements. For example, the person does not consciously choose what country he or she is born into but rather associates with it because it is chosen on a soul level.

As one emotionally bonds and becomes attached to particular elements, more attention and care is given to them. Under the Cancer influence, intimate relationships and familiarity with people, things, or ideas is developed. Through intimacy the person is able to let go of his or her defenses and become inclusive, emotionally processing life experiences in a healthy way. For example, after managing stressful situations all day at work, coming back home to a familiar and safe environment allows one to process what went on through the day and absorb it into one's system. This dynamic can be compared to shopping for food, cooking it, and then digesting it into the blood stream. Emotional processing and digestion is more effective in a stress-free and supportive environment; hence through Cancer there is an urge to find and establish safety, insulation, warmth, and support.

This process is similar to a baby needing to be sheltered in the womb in order to develop. The Cancer influence symbolizes the parental nurturing and care that support a child's processing and maturation needs. However, this does not only apply in the literal sense. We all are children who are growing and developing on some level, no matter what biological age we may be. Through Cancer, we can get in touch with the inner child who is always in need of guidance and support. Consequently, one alternates between the role of the parent and the child through providing a support system for others and then requiring support in return.

Family dynamics and the relationship with one's parents, especially the mother, are described through this influence. Ideally one's family represents something personal through which one can deal with the world in a more securing way. Cancer represents one's support system and in times of need the privilege to help and be helped by those with whom we are emotionally attached to. The person realizes it is not always possible to be strong and face life's challenges alone; vulnerabilities incite one to establish a support system without which one's mental health and the ability to perform adequately might be compromised when facing life on one's own.

Since emotions are predominantly activated through Cancer, the person is naturally very sensitive. Emotions are the core of our being and our human nature—they serve as a point of reference. Everything is registered through them; they are what make us who we are. If a person likes cheese, is afraid of airplanes, or believes in Allah, emotions are behind it. Since life experiences are processed through emotions and we register everything through them, maturation and evolution are an outcome of our emotional processes. This is the reason why evolution occurs through the emotional body; failing that, it is not really integrated.

In the same vein, the person gets in touch with weakness and imperfection under the Cancer influence—if one needs to continually mature and grow, it means that one is in a permanent state of imperfection. This imperfection is what renders us human—we are in fact all children who are growing up. Thus the Cancer archetype represents the recognition of personal imperfection and the ability to accept it in oneself and others.

As the individual is emotionally exposed when opening up in an intimate setting, the danger of being wounded and traumatized increases accordingly. For example, one's family may be dysfunctional and because of the emotional attachment the painful experiences may have a deeper impact—the environment that is supposed to be safe and supportive can be hostile on some occasions. When emotional trauma is severe, it can stunt emotional processing and consequently arrest the maturation process. The person may grow in size and age but remain emotionally immature. Symptoms such as chronic insecurity, the avoidance of responsibility, or an insatiable emotional hunger reflect the damage. Emotional therapy is then required to heal the trauma and reactivate emotional maturation.

A person with a strong Cancer influence in the chart aims to avoid unnecessary stress and tends to be rather protective of what he or she associates with. Being more attuned to personal rhythms, there is a tendency to avoid potentially disruptive pressure from the outside. For example, one may prefer to work from home rather than follow the regulated schedule of an office or respond to demanding authority figures. There is a tendency to be more casual and simple, and not deprive oneself of personal needs and wants. This dynamic induces generosity and warmth when one is hosting others in his or her private space.

Similarly under this influence, the person is usually less interested in proving his or her personal worth and capacity to the external world. While one may have strong needs and an uncompromising nature, it is not oriented toward ambition and achievement. Determination is more focused on creating a lifestyle and conditions that completely resonate with one's authentic nature and aspirations.

The archetype opposing Cancer is Capricorn. The opposing archetype serves as a point of balance, and here through Capricorn there is a requirement to understand appropriate timing and boundaries. Through this polarity, an individual learns that emotional processing is important but that it cannot last forever; at some point, one must account for what one is processing. The Capricorn influence requires one to act maturely and perform accordingly when the time comes. For example, one cannot remain a student forever, never feeling ready to work. At specific junctures, duty calls. Capricorn represents a test of ripeness when credibility and capacity are assessed, and reflects the pressure to be taken seriously when assuming responsibility.

The Capricorn influence reminds one of a sense of duty, encouraging the person to take action and lead when needed. As a baby learns to walk, it assumes responsibility for its movement and ceases to rely on aid for that purpose. Serving as a counterbalance to the emotional fragility of Cancer, Capricorn renders the person more resistant and capable of handling stress.

General associations
Personal rhythm, emotional processing, emotional attachments, the ego, identity, personal associations, support system, nurturing, parenting, the inner child, needs, vulnerability, intimacy, acceptance of one's condition as a human being with imperfections, maturation and development, home, family, the mother, womb, roots, belonging, nationalism, real estate, food, lenience, patience.

Health associations
The stomach, digestion, breasts and female organs, general hormonal function.

Professional associations
The hospitality industry, gastronomy, social care, real estate, freelance work, stay-at-home parent.

Relationship inclinations
Intimate, nurturing, needy, emotional, supportive, moody with possible inconsistencies, warm, attentive, familial.

The Leo ♌ Archetype
Including the sign of Leo, the Sun, and the 5th house
Fire—Fixed—Extroverted

Under the Leo archetype, there is an evolutionary need for the ego to be involved and participate in the development of life. Following the processing phase that supported emotional growth and maturation through Cancer, one feels ready through Leo to express one's creativity and make an individual contribution to life. One is inspired to self-actualize and in that process leave a legacy that might benefit others as well. Consequently through this influence, the person is significantly empowered through finding a role and gaining meaning in his or her personal life.

Creativity brings the person closer to the divine for it makes one an infinite source of life—death is defied through creativity. On both biological and functional levels, the Leo influence fosters fertility through launching projects, creating art, or having children. The person is constantly producing, making him or her naturally generous and giving, and in return respect and support are expected. Without individual creative effort, life could become extinct. In order to enhance and keep the flame of life burning, each person must contribute—creativity is a responsibility.

The evolutionary need to participate in life often manifests as an inborn sense of destiny. One may come into this world with a feeling of having something special to accomplish and a path to follow. This dynamic generates an aura around the person and magnetizes expectations to be successful or even heroic; not much value is attributed to being average. Parents may project their hopes on their child and consciously or unconsciously impose personal ambitions. Sometimes, when one child appears more promising than another, this approach induces favoritism, commonly breeding jealousy and competition. The person with an emphasized Leo influence may be on either end of this equation: the parent, the favored child, or the discriminated child.

Following the Cancer phase, through Leo the approach to life remains emotional because the outlook on life is still highly personal and subjective. Emotional attachment makes one engaged, caring, and inspired to invest. However, attachment may also lead to possessiveness and emotional control. For example, the Leo influence can generate benevolent dictators who on the one hand are very generous and supportive, but on the other hand very demanding in return expecting absolute commitment and surrender to their personal causes. For example, parents may pay for their child's higher education and living expenses provided the child studies what the parents decide. When excessive and rigid, this attitude is bound to backfire through revolt and crisis.

A person must realize that his or her creations have a life of their own and cannot be considered mere extensions of oneself. Biologically, this is why a child is a product of two parents; he or she is never identical to either one of them. When mismanaged, this influence can manifest in emotional abuse and the control of others, similar to a slave and patron dynamic. Positively, the person remains generous and frees the creation to pursue its independent course; using another analogy, the artist must at some point separate from his or her painting and let it have a life of its own.

Generally speaking, the emotional approach makes existence more dramatic. Because the focus is on enhancing life through creativity, there is a tendency to give meaning to every fragment. Details are considered important because they are perceived as essential to the greater scheme of things; the person understands that everyone deserves their share of respect. For example, one may remember people's birthdays and look forward to celebrating them; it is a form of acknowledgment and a way to give attention to life. However when excessive, too much focus may be directed toward trivial things. Everything can end up being taken too seriously because so many emotions are involved. Sometimes the tendency for drama derives from the need for attention through creating a crisis and in such a way compensates for a lack of achievement in life. In other cases, the person may sink into depression because he or she dramatizes negative emotions such as the fear of failure.

Generally speaking, praise and attention must be a result, not an end, and when centered in right values, one's accomplishments speak for themselves. In a positive way, the person under the Leo influence is passionate about life, feels inspired, and naturally radiates a loving spirit. Eventually, he or she may become a source of inspiration for others and naturally generate interest, support, and praise.

There is a need to make the best out of life, both through achievement and pleasure. Enjoying festive times and playfulness, the shift from a serious to more casual approach is common. Inspired, invested, and goal-oriented, the person often possesses leadership qualities and will look up to people who possess a strong spirit.

The archetype opposing Leo is Aquarius. The opposing archetype serves as a point of balance, and here through Aquarius there is a need to approach life more cerebrally to balance emotions with perspective when it is lacking. The Aquarius influence highlights the need to objectify dynamics through being more emotionally removed from things: the "bird's eye view" provides a wider outlook on life. Through Aquarius, one adopts a more neutral approach, reducing the inclination of getting emotionally carried away and overdramatizing situations. The lesson of perspective may, at times, be experienced unexpectedly when, for example, attracting criticism or indifference instead of praise. The deflation may be hard to take, but it allows one to mature and learn from criticism.

The Aquarian polarity also balances the more individualistic and leader-oriented approach common to Leo, with a more community-oriented approach. The person learns to work through groups of like-minded people and be on equal footing with them instead of always "going solo" with creative projects.

General associations
Creativity, keeping the flame of life burning, emotional involvement, potency, passion, drama, artistic qualities, performance, self-actualization, sense of purpose, egocentric expression and contribution, leadership, the stage, respect, dynasties, parents, children, the father, legacies, expectations, recognition, achievement, importance, the heart, love, gold, the Sun.

Health associations
The heart, blood pressure, cholesterol sensitivities, vitality, upper back, vision.

Professional associations
Entrepreneurship, leadership, performance, art, children-related, school teacher, pet industry, medicine.

Relationship inclinations
Intimate, warm, outgoing, generous, romantic, seeking mutual admiration, seeking excitement, competitive, sexual, pleasure-seeking, independent.

The Virgo ♍ Archetype
Including the sign of Virgo, the planet Mercury, and the 6th house
Earth—Mutable—Introverted

Under the Virgo archetype, there is an evolutionary need to refine one's creative output and maximize efficiency while integrating one's services and products into the environment. Following the need for meaning that encouraged a focus on personal creativity through Leo, one realizes through Virgo that individual contributions must interrelate with other contributions to form a chain of creativity and service. For example, the baker relies on the services of the electrician to bake the bread, who in turn relies on the engineer, and so on. In this context, if one performs inadequately, the whole chain of service is affected hence the pressure to be highly competent when operating. This pressure often makes one more self-conscious as the dread of failure or dysfunction generates a more attentive and conscientious approach. In order to prevent negative results or problems, one learns to pay attention to details and tries to gain more control.

Under the Virgo influence, the person battles the odds of chaos and strives to attain perfect function: negligence, inattention to detail, or a carefree attitude must be avoided to prevent a crisis. Through fighting chaos, one strives to overpower potential parasites or unexpected disturbances that can sabotage the quality of work. An analytical approach is adopted: one plans ahead and prepares for potential problems, and skills are developed to fix them. Gaining more control over function and development provides a sense of security.

Following Leo, creative expression is further refined and taken to a higher use. In this process, personal skills are naturally enhanced because of the pressure to meet increasing standards of performance. The person may excel in a wide variety of functions and abound with outstanding talents ranging from manual and technical skills, to artistic expression, design, or management capabilities.

In a different way, the pressure for improvement and refinement is also stimulated by the realization that available resources are limited: time, money, natural resources, energy, and potency are all exhaustible. Abundance is not everlasting, and consequently, beyond the stress of performing adequately, avoiding waste is also a major concern. One realizes that resources are not easily replaceable, if at all, and therefore must be used wisely.

The efficient use of resources includes the approach to one's own body—the person is bound to become progressively more health conscious, typically learning to better maintain the body through exercising, participating in sports, and eating a healthy diet. The person realizes that fighting chaos and parasites through preventive measures diminishes the odds of illness.

With a more analytical approach, the nervous system is naturally more stimulated because one tends to take a lot on oneself in the process of correcting all perceived wrongs. Positively, effort improves quality and accelerates the speed of performance—"faster and better" is a common goal of efficiency. The person constantly thinks about how to better use what is available and increase the value and quality of the products or services that he or she offers. For example, the results may include building stronger houses, reducing pollution, or ensuring wise financial investments. Conscious of limited resources, the value of maintenance and manufacturing quality is emphasized to reduce decline and erosion. Positively, the person is able to provide high quality services and products, and promote management efficiency in systems, sometimes restoring health to what was dysfunctional.

Beyond the focus on high productivity, values of refinement are also reflected on an aesthetic level. Sharp attention to detail makes one highly responsive to beauty and sophistication. The senses are further polished under the Virgo archetype, fostering one's taste and appreciation for elegance and quality. When confronted with something considered coarse, ugly, or plain, it often results in disdain, impatience, or even sarcasm. In the worst case, verbal abuse may be directed toward whatever is considered uncivilized and vulgar.

The Virgo archetype represents the necessity for people to have more control over nature in order to make better use of it. Without personal intervention, natural resources remain crude and difficult to access or use. Control and intervention can manifest in promoting better hygiene, fighting parasites and illnesses, developing agriculture, and domesticating animals. Simple actions such as washing and cutting hair and nails reflect the daily aspect of such a dynamic.

Life and Creation require proper maintenance and refinement. Thus interfering with nature is legitimate under this influence in order to properly use and care for it; the motivation must be sourced in benefiting the development of life rather than serving selfish needs. Acquired knowledge is implemented with the intent of improving life conditions. This archetype emphasizes the value of work, not only from a professional point of view, but also when applied to any effort—no gain is ever truly free of labor.

Having more control over nature's development, wildness is monitored and tamed. However, when managing nature comes from impure intentions, the danger of upsetting nature's delicate balance can cause dysfunction and chaos instead of improvement. If the underlying motive for development comes from a carefree attitude or greed, the person, or society at large, can pay a high price. While nature is a resource that can be further refined, it must be considered sacred and approached with reverence. Like any other resource it cannot be replaced once it has been mismanaged and wasted.

When excessive, the pressure to be in control can take its toll. The person can end up living a sterile existence where all is in its "right" place and the unexpected is perceived as a threat to order. Fearing chaos, the person may adopt an overly conservative approach to life that neutralizes risk and adventure. True, parasites must be deactivated, but aiming to stay completely safe may end up equally detrimental to development. The need for control can lead to obsessive behavior, fears, and problems trusting the larger life mechanism—one cannot be everywhere and do everything to guarantee safe function.

Moreover, striving for perfection may leave the person feeling chronically dissatisfied. If too much focus is directed toward what needs improvement, the person can become overly critical and negative. The ego must accept that it cannot control everything simply because it does not know everything—there is no way to foresee and avoid every possible predicament.

The archetype opposing Virgo is Pisces. The opposing archetype serves as a point of balance, and here through Pisces it inspires one to accept the unknown. The Pisces influence symbolizes the fact that life existed before mankind and continues hereafter, highlighting the reality that greater forces are behind life's operation and to better understand and manage existence one must learn about these spiritual forces. This does not undermine the need to extend personal effort in order to develop resources and gain more control, but it does inspire a more flexible, adaptable, and flowing approach. Trust enables one to let go of control and perfectionism—through Pisces, one learns that chaos is part of order.

General associations

Labor, work function, control and maintenance of resources, domestication, refinement, improvement, analysis, criticism, discrimination, perfection, beauty, sophistication, dexterity, talents, skill, order, hygiene, function, productivity, industry, repair, prevention, health, medicine, cures, diet, sports, fitness.

Health associations

The intestines, digestion, immune response, allergy sensitivities, motor skills, nervous system, body flexibility, diet regulation, general health management, response to stress, disease prevention, healing potential.

Professional associations

Medicine, technical orientation, engineering, infrastructure, hygiene, farming, agriculture, secretarial, administrative function, sports, fitness, yoga, design, aesthetics.

Relationship inclinations

Devoted, dutiful, beauty-seeking, practical, analytical, witty, seeking refinement, fixing, improving.

The Libra ♎ Archetype

Including the sign of Libra, the planet Venus, and the 7th house
Air—Cardinal—Extroverted

Under the Libra archetype, there is an evolutionary need to establish balance in one's life and find the middle way between extremes. Following the need to improve management that required one to perfect personal skills and develop control abilities through Virgo, one realizes through Libra that it is not possible to feel whole when doing everything alone. Under this influence, the person feels a sense of inner lack and as a result tries to find completion through connecting with others. The need to share duties or exchange resources and ideas compels one to reach out for partnership and learn from what others have to offer—union makes everyone stronger.

The need for balance unconsciously generates an attraction to people or concepts that are foreign or opposite to one's own. Forming relationships and exposing oneself to different perspectives allows one to grow. Whether the relationships are intimate, professional, or social, through them one unites pieces of life that were initially separate. For example, one may lead a fast-paced lifestyle revolving around professional achievement and then at some point feel that something is lacking. Attracting a friend or a partner who opens one up to other ways helps one understand life's polarities and eventually adopt a more wholesome perspective.

Before establishing balance the person tends to live in duality, tasting from one extreme then another. In this process, he or she cyclically shifts from being attracted to one thing and then its opposite. Such a dynamic applies to any aspect of life whether relationships, vocations, or philosophical orientations. For example, the person may live a conservative lifestyle and then attract a liberal partner. The lesson is to integrate both polarities and become more neutral without having a single-minded preference for one side over the other, finding balance between both. In this example, the person may end up appreciating the value of both a conservative and a liberal approach. In reality, this means being sensitive to the time when each approach is relevant.

Usually the need to find balance manifests in an attraction to what one does not have. For example, a person living in a capitalist country may find great interest in a socialist regime. There is an aversion to seeing only one side of the coin—the more one is pulled in one direction, the stronger the attraction to the opposite direction. Thus under this influence the person is often attracted to different cultures, systems of thought, or lifestyles, and through exposure to diversity learns about opposites.

At first there is a tendency to glamorize the polarity; for example if living in America, one may hold romantic notions about living in Europe or yet another continent. What one has and knows seems obsolete and complete; therefore, one may change lifestyles, religions, or professions, or at least think about it. When the new and idealized idea is finally integrated, greater satisfaction is experienced because these new encounters provide a sense of growth.

Nonetheless, the road does not end when new experiences have been assimilated. Because balance is the ultimate goal, the person often needs to return to his or her origins once having tasted from different perspectives—only then can a sense of wholeness be realized. It is important to understand, however, that coming back to one's origins does not mean returning to square one because tremendous experience and wisdom has been acquired along the way. Learning about different perspectives and the value each offers brings a sense of inner harmony. Once finding inner balance, one may become more grounded and less likely to get carried away by the perception that the grass is greener elsewhere.

Aspiring to balance extremes, the person may become highly argumentative because of the instinct to naturally gravitate toward the opposite point of view. For example when among "left-wingers," one may take the "right-wing" side even if only for the sake of creating balance in the way things are presented. The person wants to stand by the unrepresented side, whatever it might be. Such an approach may sometimes become excessive when systematically disagreeing with anything that is said and bringing up an opposing view even if frail and out of context.

In a different way, an interest in people may manifest in wanting to help and counsel them. Equipped with a broad perspective of life, a natural capacity to listen, and innate wisdom, the person easily sees through other people's difficulties and is predisposed to offer insight. Such an inclination is very valuable; however, the person must be careful not to become everyone's private psychologist as compensatory behavior—the sense of inner lack may engender a need to be needed.

Under this influence the person is usually socially conscious and appropriate. The capacity to put oneself in other people's shoes naturally makes one compassionate and a good listener. Being motivated by balance, there is a natural sensitivity to fairness and justice, and an aspiration to help people from all walks of life find a place in this world.

The archetype opposing Libra is Aries. The opposing archetype serves as a point of balance, and here through Aries there is a need to understand that without a core connection to oneself, relationships of any kind are prone to crisis. The Aries influence inspires one to remain ' to one's nature while opening up and learning from others.

Failing that, relationship problems are bound to accumulate on the basis that others are excessively idealized.

Moreover, the Aries influence accentuates the need to learn how to be more proactive and make a choice instead of dwelling in indecision when wanting to remain neutral. Choice is not just about deciding if one thing is better than another but rather about sensing what the present time requires and acting upon it. To avoid indecision, the person must focus on what the current circumstances inspire instead of only aspiring for ideals of perfect harmony and neutrality. The Aries influence calls for action in response to what life brings in the current moment, decreasing the tendency for excessive reflection about perfectly balanced solutions.

General associations
Relationships, union, polarities, extremes, duality, diplomacy, exchange, trade, harmony, peace, neutrality, balance, consideration of others, fairness, wisdom, justice, ideals, social skills, psychological skills, inner lack, growth, dependence.

Health associations
The kidneys, auditory system, equilibrium.

Professional associations
Mediation, counseling, law, diplomacy, social projects.

Relationship inclinations
Adaptive, communicative, dependent, conscious, open-minded, generous, social, fair, idealistic, seeking perspective and neutrality.

The Scorpio ♏ Archetype

Including the sign of Scorpio, the planet Pluto, and the 8ᵗʰ house
Water—Fixed—Introverted

Under the Scorpio archetype, there is an evolutionary need to evolve our consciousness and grow in order to attain greater dimensions of being. Following the feeling of lack that stimulated relationships through Libra, one realizes through Scorpio that the process of growth is stimulated by recognizing personal limitations and the subsequent desire to outgrow them. Limitations can manifest as any feeling of weakness such as the experience of failure, rejection, or meaninglessness; these are conditions that generate a feeling of powerlessness. Exposed to vulnerabilities and crises, emotional pain is experienced to varying degrees. The descent into the dark inner cave generates introspection; subsequently, the inspiration for change emerges and prompts a renewed ascension to power where a greater sense of well-being is integrated. The metamorphosis is then complete.

The sign of Scorpio is symbolized by three animals: the scorpion, the snake, and the eagle. The scorpion represents initiation into sacred mysteries. The snake embodies the regenerative power of transformation through the shedding of it skin. It also symbolizes the ascent of kundalini energy and spiritual transformation. The eagle is associated with the phoenix, a legendary creature that builds its own funeral pyre and throws itself into the flames to die only to rise again from the ashes—reborn for five hundred more years.

Under Scorpio influence, the need to find a solution for pain generates introspection and an attempt to uncover the behavioral or strategic reasons that led to crises. Through this process, one is inspired to change and outgrow weakness in order to heal pain and avoid repeating dysfunctional patterns. The need to regain a sense of well-being is what induces the metamorphosis—values, behavior, and choices are then radically redefined. There is a death of the old self and a rebirth into a new state of being.

It is not uncommon for individuals with a strong Scorpio influence in their chart to begin their lives with insecurities and compromised self-esteem. These limitations cause frustration prompting them to change and find ways to gain power through growth. Innocence is often lost early during childhood when the person is confronted with problems that need solutions. Circumstances, such as familial dysfunction, a fear of rejection, or meager means, keep one reflective and more conscious of ongoing dynamics. Psychological skills are developed in order to identify the blockages that prevent more positive circumstances from unfolding. Feeling limitation or pain prevents one from living in denial because only an honest and straightforward approach can bring genuine solutions; as a result, the person is more consciously awake.

Upon facing a crisis, the person is confronted with a truth that may be inconvenient; yet it forces him or her to deal with the issue and master it. One encounters the shadows and what lies underneath appearances, playing detective to uncover hidden motivations or schemes. Commonly as one becomes accustomed to change and the need for growth, this approach is also projected on to the environment. In hoping for change, there is a tendency to become confrontational and also expose other people's limitations and emotional dysfunctions. Naturally, the person develops penetrating psychological skills to identify dysfunction or corruption from afar. Under this influence, naiveté does not subsist for too long.

Following the Libra archetype, Scorpio continues the desire to merge with others in order to gain greater strength. The aspiration for growth renders the person hungry for more in life—more choices, more influence, more resources, more love, more happiness, and more power in general. This hunger for growth keeps one constantly seeking, questioning, and testing boundaries.

To gain strength, one may seek to exchange resources with others. The exchange may take various forms from emotional support, to reading an insightful book, to merging ideas for launching new projects. There is a natural attraction to people with strong personalities and intensity who have substantial content to share and who serve as a source of inspiration. Likewise, one aspires to meaningfully affect people in the same way. Relationship partners are carefully chosen to answer precise needs; if these conditions are not met, there is a preference to remain alone.

Once finding something or someone with meaningful content to learn from, the fusion is total. There is a desire to merge with who the person is—or what he or she represents—in order to absorb the energy. This dynamic may take the form of falling in love and wanting to spend all of one's time with that person, or finding a spiritual teacher or a business partner who embodies what one needs in order to grow. The source of attraction can be intellectual, spiritual, emotional, or sexual, but it always affects one emotionally because it is through emotions that one grows.

Sexuality plays an important role under this influence because it serves as a means to merge and absorb what another has to offer. The need to penetrate the other is primarily emotional, and sexuality is a means to induce the merging process. Nevertheless, intimacy can occur without sexuality. For example, a discussion with a therapist who exposes vulnerabilities so they can be healed can be very intimate and help one resolve internal conflicts.

However, when creating intimacy with someone, the potential for pain and deceit is substantial because one is emotionally bare. For example, becoming attached to a lover is an emotional risk because at some point the lover may leave. Hence there is a reluctance to commit to people too quickly. A person plays detective and assesses if the other person is trustworthy and has what it takes to form a relationship. Reliability, potency, and content are evaluated to reduce the risk of disappointment. However, life offers no absolute guarantees for security prompting the person to take these emotional risks, albeit more cautiously so.

When feeling the need to expand and transcend limitations, one must face the fact that personal desires also depend on other people's cooperation. If a person is drawn to another and wants to be with him or her, the success of that choice obviously depends on the agreement of the other. Similarly if one wants to buy a house, having the money is not always enough because the house has to be for sale. Consequently, the sense of power intrinsic to Scorpio does not solely rely on making the right choice but also on being chosen in return. In the course of life, attraction is not always mutual and simultaneous; therefore, the fear of rejection and abandonment is recurrent. When failing to be chosen, one's self-esteem can drop and raise questions as to how to ascend and regain a sense of potency. For example, if a person is not hired for a job, he or she may become introspective in order to evaluate how to improve the odds of being hired.

Whether professionally or emotionally, the person works on increasing his or her appeal; it is like having a powerful magnet—the stronger the magnet, the fewer the rejections and the higher the odds of fulfilling one's choices. Increasing one's appeal may include getting a better education, earning more money, mastering a new skill, becoming sexier, or acquiring more wisdom: each person finds a different way to increase the value of his or her currency.

When mismanaged, the pain intrinsic to rejection may compel the person to use force or manipulation in order to get what is wanted at any cost. Trying to compensate for the fear of rejection, intimidation may be used to maintain a relationship. Even though this attitude provides a false sense of power, it only temporarily keeps one from facing the loss. Typically this approach generates a form of vampirism through which one takes from others without giving anything in return. Under the Scorpio influence, one may experience either side of this dynamic: either being the manipulator or attracting one. Ultimately these circumstances only generate more limitations.

Positively, the growth process manifests in having a stronger immune system, better coping abilities, more resources, increased magnetism, more meaningful relationships, and overall, a deeper and better flowing connection with life. A strong and penetrating personality emerges from the metamorphosis that is capable of having a strong impact and inspiring others. Tremendous courage and resilience are acquired when going through the highs and lows, rendering one able to face shadows or difficult circumstances with might.

The archetype opposing Scorpio is Taurus. The opposing archetype serves as a point of balance, and here through Taurus there is a need to realize that growth must be rooted in solid ground. Before seeking answers and rescue through external sources, lessons of self-reliance and self-worth must be learned. If the person approaches others with low self-esteem and few resources, relationships are prone to be crisis oriented and pain more accentuated. Learning to appreciate oneself and what one has to offer calms the hunger for more and strengthens one's inner core. Once feeling more centered in inner values, the potential to form healthier relationships increases.

Similarly, the Taurus polarity inspires calm and consistency. While Scorpio is oriented toward growth and change, one needs to learn that acceptance and stability is also necessary. Before changing and destroying something considered limited, one must assess if the decision is rushed because sometimes patience alone can resolve problems. The Taurus influence describes the need to stay centered and composed when facing challenges because such an attitude helps one better manage the situation.

General associations

Evolution, change, empowerment, power, resources, money, value, self-esteem, attraction, magnetism, emotions, fusion, love, sexuality, intimacy, attachment, trust, intensity, emotional crises, abandonment, powerlessness, shadows, anger, limitations, introspection, psychology, impermanence, death, ruptures, destruction, renewal, growth.

Health associations

Sexual organs and glands, intestinal biochemistry, enzymes, elimination mechanisms, cancer (the disease).

Professional associations

Psychology and therapy, defense, criminology, banking.

Relationship inclinations

Symbiotic, seeking intensity, emotionally attached, strong attraction-rejection modes, growth seeking, introspective, sexual, private, straightforward, confrontational, nurturing.

The Sagittarius ♐ Archetype

Including the sign of Sagittarius, the planet Jupiter, and the 9th house
Fire—Mutable—Extroverted

Under the Sagittarius archetype, there is an evolutionary need to uncover the highest possible potential of personal creativity, expansion, and life meaning under the current conditions. Following the powerful emotional experiences that lead to upheaval through Scorpio, one is inspired through Sagittarius to find greater meaning so that personal experiences can be given a greater context and perspective—understanding there is more to life than the immediate reality helps one better cope with eventual difficulties.

There is a drive to explore how far one can go and, how vast life is, and what the meaning of everything is. Attempting to clarify these concepts, the person is incited to go beyond what is currently established to a place of possibilities, spiritual meanings, and abstract thought.

What is currently known no longer satisfies the person—the Truth must be greater than what meets the eye. Yet searching for greater meaning is a journey with an unknown destination that requires an adventurous spirit willing to gamble and take risks. When facing open roads, intuition is an important guiding factor—through intuition, one develops belief and faith.

Through Scorpio, the person realizes that there is limitation and pain, and strives to conquer them through transformation. Through Sagittarius, limitation is confronted through conceptualizing a higher meaning that engenders optimism and positive thinking—having faith increases the chance of growth and a positive outcome.

There is an inner knowing that life is greater than what is established and what most people dare to think—with faith, one ventures into new territory. These ventures may take place on different levels whether they are philosophically or practically oriented. Since greater intuited potential is not initially uncovered, at first it remains abstract and the fruit of speculation. One has to risk security and push boundaries in order to assess what the hidden potential really is. It is a gamble, and through trial and error, facts are established.

At first, the search to fulfill a greater potential is completely theoretical and therefore without a guarantee of success. There is no clear design for this journey thus no clear indication of where and when to stop after engaging. For example, if one believes a business can increase its profits, there is no precise understanding of the actual amount but rather only a general idea. Therefore, when transcending a boundary considered obsolete, a new boundary must eventually replace it—one that better matches the current circumstances. To find the new boundary the person must trespass it in order to recognize it. There is a need to go overboard, at least a little bit, and then step back when having passed the new boundary. The Sagittarius influence invites excess as part of the search for a greater potential—indulgence is necessary for the expansion process.

However, the amount of excess may present a concern. Will the person recognize the new boundary and know when to stop the expansion effort, or instead go way overboard and possibly waste resources and cause damage until finally readjusting? This dynamic is illustrated in the simplest way when children test their parents' boundaries. Pushing the limits more and more to see how far they can go, they can become overconfident and end up completely out of line, finally having to face the consequences of their actions. The initiative to dare pushing is healthy because it promotes new discoveries, yet wisdom also means knowing when to stop because going too far causes damage.

What often prevents one from stopping at a reasonable point is the tendency to get overly attached to one's beliefs, faith, or speculations.

Wanting to make one's vision and faith happen at all costs and ardently holding on to convictions, the person loses touch with facts and bulldozes his or her way onward. Instead of being truthful, the person is attached to "being right" and thus becomes dogmatic. Typically such a person is highly argumentative, dominates conversations, and is charged with a fair dose of self-righteousness. Having a grandiose plan or a strong opinion, there is a tendency to get carried away with subjective interpretations of the Truth.

Personal beliefs must eventually be tested in reality. Intuiting a larger potential is healthy for chances are it is true and must be realized. Still, because the potential for expansion is initially abstract, at some point a theory has to show positive results to truly be of use. For example, if the person believes in the nearing end of the world, time will tell if he or she is right or wrong. If the person believes in the success of a business, numbers must eventually prove that.

It may take a long time for a belief to be validated, but sooner or later, faith must refer to reality. For example, existing religions offer different interpretations of the meanings of life, and these concepts live on without anyone really knowing how truthful they are. For this reason, they become the basis of arguments and wars. A tangible way to assess the validity of any belief is to see if following it promotes health, emancipation, and consistent well-being or, conversely, if it induces dysfunction and conflict.

Since Sagittarius reflects a search for the Truth, it stimulates cultural development, similar to Gemini. Groups of people living in particular environments experience life from a particular angle and naturally develop specific beliefs, customs, and ideologies; over time, the sum of these accepted notions becomes the foundation of a whole culture. Positively, each culture highlights something important about life and inspires people in their own individual search. Negatively, cultures may clash, leading to bigotry and religious wars. Such an orientation commonly engenders "convince and convert" agendas and the desire to forcefully spread one's personal truth.

Solutions to ideological or cultural conflicts are found in accepting that no one owns the absolute Truth. We can only capture fragments of it; therefore, learning is a never ending process. If someone is indeed wrong, there is no need to forcefully prove it to him or her. One's own life circumstances will make one aware of possible mistakes. Accepting this leads to a more relaxed approach when faced with different points of views or lifestyles. The Truth cannot be imposed; it is something one must naturally gravitate toward.

On another level, the Sagittarius archetype reflects a yearning for transparency and straightforwardness. Stripped of artifices, the need for the Truth connects one to a more natural approach to life; the person's appearance may be more plain and causal. Similarly, a love of open spaces and wildlife reflects one's own free spirit. With an adventurous and more daring attitude, life often turns into a colorful journey rich with associations, experiences, and play. Through this influence one may generate abundance, live authentically, and find deeper meaning. Holding on to faith and optimism makes it easier to create positive opportunities and experiences.

The polarity of Sagittarius is the Gemini archetype. The opposing archetype serves as a point of balance, and here through Gemini there is an evolutionary need to understand that development and learning is first attained through better communication. Instead of potentially voicing personal beliefs in an opposing way, or defending them argumentatively, Gemini inspires one to listen and gain a greater perspective. Relying on the values of logic and common sense, Gemini serves as a critic and observer of Sagittarius's inspired intuition and faith. It may trigger a corrective reaction if the optimism of Sagittarius becomes compulsive or blind. Through this polarity, the person learns to consider diversity and understand that life has many crosscurrents.

Moreover, the Gemini polarity reflects the need to adapt to existing circumstances and environmental conditions as the Sagittarius influence may manifest in coming on too strong or acting inappropriately or awkwardly. When the polarity is integrated, authenticity and naturalness are well balanced with sensitivity to environmental conditions, and the person remains loyal to his or her truth yet humble enough to remain flexible and adaptable.

General associations
Expansion, truth seeking, spirituality, faith, beliefs, ideologies, religion, knowledge, right-brain hemisphere, wisdom, teaching, intuition, speculation, gambling, excess, exaggeration, vulgarity, inappropriateness, confidence, courage, optimism, vision, risk, new horizons, travel, culture, ethnicity, nature, open spaces, wildness, wildlife, honesty, authenticity.

Health associations
The liver, hips, lower back, cholesterol sensitivity, weight management, right-brain hemisphere and the left side of the body, the thyroid and pituitary glands, the sugar-processing mechanism.

Professional associations
Teaching, religion and philosophy, nature, wildlife, publishing, distribution, travel, sales, entrepreneurship.

Relationship inclinations
Excited, passionate, straightforward, natural, casual, extroverted, independent, philosophical.

The Capricorn ♑ Archetype
Including the sign of Capricorn, the planet Saturn, and the 10th house
Earth—Cardinal—Introverted

Under the Capricorn archetype, there is an evolutionary need to practically implement in everyday life what is perceived as truthful and right. Following the search for a higher potential and the Truth through Sagittarius, one realizes through Capricorn that there is a need to establish a structure that embodies the captured meanings of life: theory must be put into practice. Through the Capricorn influence, the person recognizes the value of boundaries, right conduct, and the laws of life. One realizes that life is not about what one wants—but about what works. Having faced failure and crisis because of excess or mismanagement, one comes to recognize that not everything in life is possible and that every whim cannot be naively followed—there are consequences to choices and actions. Thus to lead a life that works, one learns to realign personal values and behavior according to the notions of correctness and the Truth.

Being a Cardinal archetype that opens the last quarter of the astrology signs, Capricorn represents a new orientation to life. Entering this phase, the person is pressured to consider larger life circumstances and adapt to them, as opposed to perceiving him or herself as the one in control of one's destiny. Gaining more maturity, one considers the benefit of general function over personal immediate gratification. This may manifest as simply as stopping at a red traffic light to let other vehicles pass, even if it takes more time.

Even though responding to laws seems to limit an immediate sense of freedom, ultimately the gain shows in the long run when well-being and success ensue. For example, eating ice cream all the time may be more fun, but the natural laws of life do not support such a habit and negative health consequences are bound to result. Capricorn inspires the person to humbly align with what works and relinquish whimsical desires that have little truthful value. Upon aligning with these larger principles, one's approach becomes increasingly more transpersonal—the ego releases its attachments when they do not match a greater sense of rightness.

There are two dimensions of law—societal and universal—and societal laws are inspired by universal laws. The product of divine creation, universal laws govern existence with or without human understanding. Established by human beings, societal laws derive from what humans manage to capture from universal laws; societal laws govern civilization and promote a collective code of rightness. For example, the societal law that forbids theft is inspired by universal principles of rightness. As human beings gain greater awareness, societal laws upgrade to better match universal laws. For example, laws that forbade women to vote were eventually seen as obsolete because over time they did not match universal principles.

However, when upgrading human societal laws, there may be a concern that new ideas that are appealing at first may later be revealed to be inconsistent. Therefore, to change structures and incorporate new concepts, these novelties must be tested over and over again to guarantee that they do not cause damage. Consequently, there is with Capricorn a necessary resistance to modifying tradition and structure; one cannot afford to be easily swept away by innovative or fanciful theories. New realizations must be tested for their reliability because once implemented the whole society responds to them. The downside of this dynamic is that societal laws and customs that are obsolete may take longer to be adjusted; thus wrong judgment, prejudice, and even unjust prosecution may linger.

When the society one belongs to consists of laws that one considers obsolete or misaligned, the person may instead find a source of guidance and reference in alternative systems and authority figures. In this case, one may conform to societal laws out of respect for a general sense of order, but privately refer to different ethical models when personally judging right from wrong. There may be a gap between society's view of ethics and the code of conduct the person adheres to, but in most cases it is a manageable gap that still allows the person to function relatively safely in society. If the gap between one's personal interpretation of rightness is significantly at odds with society's laws, then deep alienation and even persecution or anarchy may occur.

When living in an environment where laws are outdated, unnatural guilt may occur; the person is made to feel guilty for something that is not truly wrong. Life is full of such examples, and the most common ones include discriminating against the human rights of minority groups within society. Racial segregation laws or gender-based discrimination may lead to unjust sentences. Easily biased by their own conditioning, people holding positions of authority are the keepers of the law. In this situation, there is the potential that some will manipulate the legislation of laws according to their private agendas. While the aim is to objectify rightful behavior and live by it, corruption does occur through the abuse of authority and the implementation of laws for private gain.

Natural guilt, however, results from genuine wrongdoing and the need for correction and realignment. The person may be judged by his or her environment and required to realign his or her behavior—or in more extreme scenarios actually face prosecution in a court of law. If the person does wrong and is not exposed by the system, he or she will be judged according to universal laws: this is when negative karma is created whereby every action has a consequence. The need to align to what is right and what is truthful is a concept that lies beyond the realm of societal legislation—it is between the individual and the forces of Creation. For example, the person may live in a society where beating children for "correctional purposes" is lawful and accepted; yet from a universal standpoint violence against vulnerable beings is wrong. Such a conduct engenders negative karma and consequences— when hurting a child natural guilt may ensue.

Being inspired to do what is right and follow guiding principles, the person becomes attentive to what is credible versus what is unreliable in life. Judgment is used to assess what can be trusted and is valuable as opposed to what is implausible and fanciful. There is a yearning for true wisdom that leads to tangible results. Accordingly, one may fear not being taken seriously and having personal views and opinion dismissed. The person may feel tremendous pressure to prove his or her expertise and trustworthiness in order to pass tests of credibility. Approval is gained when achievements and results speak for themselves. In this light, one may become an authority figure in one's field and use successful experience as a basis for asserted views.

Born with a strong Capricorn influence in one's birth chart, the person is inclined to act more maturely beginning from a younger age. Sometimes family circumstances pressure the child to step up and assume more responsibility. For example, taking care of younger siblings may incite one to act more seriously and learn about responsible behavior. Sometimes when too serious, one may become self-righteous and too attached to personal views of right and wrong. Similarly one may advocate righteous values but not meet those standards personally—these double standards induce hypocrisy.

Following effort, hard work, and rightful action, the person reaps the benefits and enjoys the fruit of achievement in life. Naturally, success provides one with more authority as other people seek one's cooperation and guidance. The Capricorn influence can boost ambition and the aspiration to gradually ascend to higher positions of influence. Climbing up the system's hierarchy reflects one's gained credibility. With the fulfillment of more important roles comes more responsibility and self investment as the level of performance increases.

Moreover, when properly managed, the Capricorn influence can manifest in tremendous wisdom and dedication. The person can serve as a mentor and a reliable guide for those seeking guidance in life. One can naturally assume a parental role and use the position of authority to lead and inspire in most constructive ways.

The polarity of Capricorn is the Cancer archetype. The opposing archetype serves as a point of balance, and here through Cancer there is a need to remain emotionally connected and sensitive to personal needs. The Cancer influence inspires one to remain human and understanding instead of applying rules and rightful conduct in a rigid way. It is a reminder that laws must serve and support people instead of intimidating and threatening them. Moreover, Cancer's influence reminds one that it takes time to learn how to do things the right way: maturation is a process not an inborn condition. In order to genuinely offer proper guidance, structure must maintain an organic rhythm that breathes and adapts to change. Through this polarity, an individual remembers to have an inner child who is always learning, vulnerable to mistakes, and cannot be expected to be perfect and on top of everything at all times. When well balanced, rigor and firmness work in tandem with support and forgiveness.

General associations

Boundaries, laws, morals and ethics, authorities, parents, the government, the police, reward and punishment, guilt, structures, social norms and regulations, consensus agreement, politics, conditioning, security, order, sanity, reliability, credibility, ambition, achievement, status, aging, maturity, the elderly, experience, wisdom, leadership, education, training, responsibility, care.

Health associations

The bones, joints, teeth, skin, body structure, anal muscle, pituitary gland, general health.

Professional associations

Law, law enforcement, architecture, art and music, training and coaching, elderly care.

Relationship inclinations

Serious, practical, seeking security, sexual, attraction-rejection toward social taboos, private, controlled, attentive, mature, familial, leader-follower roles.

The Aquarius ♒ Archetype

Including the sign of Aquarius, the planet Uranus, and the 11ᵗʰ house
Air—Fixed—Extroverted

Under the Aquarius archetype, there is an evolutionary need to unite creative efforts in order to enhance civilization and foster progress on both a personal and a collective scale. Following the incentive to establish a structure that provides reliable codes of ethics and conduct through Capricorn, one realizes through Aquarius that society must not only serve as a securing backbone and guiding reference, but also provide a medium of creativity and growth. Existing standards must be consistently elevated on every level whether socially, technologically, ethically, functionally, emotionally, and or spiritually. Therefore through this archetype, the value of intelligence and refinement is strongly emphasized for the best of each person is sought in order to contribute to the development of society and industry—there is an aspiration to find solutions for problems and enhance the quality of life.

Aspiring to promote progress, research is conducted to decode the mysteries of nature and the universe so that better ways of handling challenges may be uncovered. Overall, the person aspires to transcend mediocrity and foster greatness. The person often possesses a vision for a better future; intellectual creativity leads to the development of science, technology, and culture, and through this process one becomes more aware, conscious, and awake. As life mysteries are unveiled and knowledge is gained, better control and development ensues.

Progress results from elevating minimum standards. For example, a society that defines the minimum standard for each child as having a computer may be considered advanced compared to a society where many children remain illiterate. However, progress is not only measured through cutting edge technology, but also through the respect of rights, civilized behavior, and emotional or spiritual awareness—a society where the rights of animals and minority cultures are protected reflects higher ethical standards.

Wishing to belong to a more advanced community, the person may feel pressured to meet the minimum standards of that community in order to be accepted and enjoy the privileges therein; this dynamic may, for example, require one to refine capacities, open one's mind to new ideas, and have meaningful things to exchange. Wanting to belong to what is considered more progressive can be stimulating; however, it also spurs a fear of inadequacy and rejection. For example, a teenager who seeks the approval of a trendier circle of friends may suffer emotional stress when failing.

The aspiration for progress, sophistication, and emancipation may create communities and organizations that become very exclusive and inaccessible to commoners. Elite groups are formed and members carefully selected. This dynamic applies to all sectors and dimensions of society whether socially, economically, technologically, or spiritually oriented; the few that are considered capable are included, and the others are dismissed with the usually unspoken thought that they will taint the quality. On the one hand, there is a valid concern that standards must be protected, and discrimination serves that purpose. On the other hand if the selective approach is pure snobbery, it engenders negative cycles where only a handful of chosen ones have access to opportunities and resources—gaps between people and classes easily widen this way.

Exclusivity may even escalate to a feeling of supremacy that breeds racism and subjugation. Ideologies are used to legitimize segregation by focusing on who possesses better genes and has more intelligence. In the name of progress and civilization, historical counts include numerous communities that associated with such ideologies and engaged in barbaric behavior.

The ultimate purpose of progress is to benefit the masses instead of only isolated pockets of society. Effort must be invested on both sides to attain such a goal. Those with resources must make them more accessible while those seeking to upgrade must invest effort to improve their performance. A society that maintains such a balance can thrive both through establishing a reliable and secure foundation and by encouraging creativity and excellence.

The need for progress and development always keeps one alert and reflective. For example, even when belonging to an interesting community or organization in which stimulation and exchange abound, the time eventually comes when inconsistencies and obsolete approaches are uncovered, inciting one to voice concerns about the need for modification. Yet since change is not instantaneous, a feeling that things are not moving fast enough is common and sometimes generates a feeling of alienation. When accentuated, the person is subject to losing passion, becoming indifferent, or sharpening his or her criticism. In extreme cases, one may feel general standards are too low and that there is nothing worth belonging to and consequently withdraw and become cynical or sarcastic.

Standards are rising with the Aquarius archetype, and it becomes hard to find true meaning in everyday circumstances. Having a vision for a more advanced civilization founded on idealistic visions and a taste for sophistication, there is a strong tendency to be more on the cutting edge. The person's hunger for newness may increase to the point of potentially losing touch with simplicity.

When perceiving people or even life as mediocre, compared to what could be, the person may become numb, lackluster, and lose respect for others. However, while contemplating the "petty" world from one's ivory tower, in reality one may fear personal inadequacy—a fear of failing one's own standards. As a result, the person may refrain from taking action and performing, instead preferring to remain a spectator of life and assessing what others do or don't do. The person may concisely voice what needs to change in the world but refrain from personally engaging to create such a change; a lack of participation may reflect deep insecurities, not just a loss of passion.

The Aquarius influence is naturally future oriented because from the perspective of progress the present is already obsolete. Still, innovative perspectives and inventions have to be tested and proven reliable. Solutions at first considered brilliant can end up discarded if they ultimately cause more damage than good. For example, in the reality of the early twenty-first century, controversial discoveries about cloning must be fully investigated before being approved.

The Aquarius archetype reflects the need to emphasize mind over emotion. To find new solutions for life's challenges, a more neutral and objective perspective must be developed; the person learns to detach from emotions in order to diminish personal biases. Being more removed allows one to gain a bird's eye view on things and avoid projecting personal associations on what is being studied. Consequently, one tends to be more mature and reflective and therefore more aware and conscious. Possessing a neutral mind allows one to have more clarity. Emotions are not necessarily repressed but more consciously directed; instead of getting carried away by mood swings, one learns to express feelings with more maturity and in a less reactive way.

Ultimately, Aquarius reflects the highest creative potential that can be attained on an individual or a collective level; it seeks to bring the genius out of humanity in order to foster progress. Through this influence, we see how human beings can become full participants in the development of life instead of just being passive elements. The use of intelligence makes each of us capable of intervention and provides the human race with the tools to independently face life challenges. Instead of being obliviously swept away by circumstances, the mind helps us navigate and improve life conditions—intelligence is not necessarily measured by good grades or in scientific prowess; each person is unique, and when well managed this influence can bring these unique gifts to light.

Through intelligence and creativity, the human race diminishes its dependence on the divine and learns to independently direct the flow of life. For example when facing a health crisis, medical treatment replaces prayer. Science, technology, and self-awareness provide the tools for humankind to independently face life challenges and elevate life's quality. This does not mean that the person invariably negates spirituality—optimally, instead of subjugation to higher forces, cooperation between mankind and the divine force is established. Using the above example, both prayer and medical treatment can be used to address a health crisis.

The archetype opposing Aquarius is Leo. The opposing archetype serves as a point of balance, and here through Leo there is need to unite the mind with the heart. Naturally emotional and dramatic, the Leo attributes balance the cerebral and detached qualities of Aquarius. Leo's influence calls for involvement, participation, and playfulness to complement the tendency for neutral observation and analysis.

There is also a lesson about performing and participating in life even at the risk of making a fool out of oneself. Eventually, one realizes that the purpose of progress is not only to create a sophisticated civilization but first and foremost to live a happier life. As Aquarius builds the future through developing values, ideas, and resources, Leo creates a new generation that keeps the flame alive—children.

General associations
Community, friends, groups, like-minded people, social rights, the elevation of standards, upgrading, progress, civilization, the mind, the brain, intelligence, genius, sophistication, speed, cutting edge, objectivity, inventions, reforms, revolutions, sterilization, elitism, superiority, sarcasm, quality, technology, all sciences, electricity, outer space, the future.

Health associations
Overall brain mechanism and function, synapses, the hypothalamus, the nervous system, the respiratory system, the ankles, blood circulation, dehydration.

Professional associations
High-tech, internet, aviation, astronomy, sciences, technology, networking, alternative modalities, film and photography, sound engineering, DJ, community work, culture, politics.

Relationship inclinations
Conscious, communicative, reflective, mild tempered, controlled, seeking intelligence and refinement, friendship with heart, open-minded, experimental, social, witty, civilized.

The Pisces ♓ Archetype
Including the sign of Pisces, the planet Neptune, and the 12th house
Water—Mutable—Introverted

The Pisces archetype symbolizes the whole spectrum of Creation: what came before us, life on Earth in its totality, and what extends into the infinite, beyond our understanding. Following the erudite, sophisticated, and masterful qualities that led to the development of civilization through Aquarius, one realizes through Pisces that human intelligence, however elaborate it may be, is very limited in contrast to the immensity of existence. Consequently, Pisces represents what is still a mystery to humankind and what cannot yet be controlled. The more we learn through science, the more we realize there is left to learn. Through Pisces, we learn to harmonize our personal existence with higher forces and higher meanings—it is the meeting between humans and the untamed vastness of existence.

Higher forces include the forces of nature, the weather, universal mechanisms, and divine principles. We are born into a world that existed before we were born and that will continue to be after we die. Everything around us operates whether we understand it or not. Cycles of nature, such as life and death, and the diverse phenomena constituting existence, all pursue their course and one is left to wonder when it all started and where it is going.

Humankind will forever be confronted by chaos—that which cannot be governed or predicted. As one life mystery is resolved, a new one emerges. One is reminded that ultimately life has the upper hand in the turn of events, and it is up to each person to adapt to circumstances instead of expecting to always maintain control. The Pisces influence represents the universal intelligence operating behind life: it embodies higher meaning, the absolute Truth, and the origin of all things. Pisces represents the relationship between living beings and life or living beings and the source of Creation—cultivating this relationship is the foundation of spiritual development.

Not having full control over larger life circumstances, one is left to surrender in trust that it is all for a good purpose. No one controls the fact that the Sun rises and sets; it is a phenomenon that people accept. Similarly, going to sleep at night requires tremendous trust and surrendering of control. Hence just like a baby surrenders to the care and wisdom of its parents, everyone surrenders to universal forces and benefits from what is provided: air, food, water, light, and resources.

Born into the setup of existence, one follows the motions and is incited to go with the flow of events. Unable to assemble all the pieces of the larger scheme of things, questions about life remain unanswered and one learns to accept what is. These circumstances induce a more passive, simple, and flowing approach.

Acceptance may be unconscious and instinctive, in some cases even naïve and blind. Sometimes, the person may deny negative or painful aspects of life because surrendering is easier when all is perceived as good and positive. Living in simplicity, one may follow the motions without critical thinking. Trying to change things may seem foreign—either because one is oblivious to the possibility of change or because one consciously fears that change would create more harm than good. With trust in goodness, the person initially flows with life without much discrimination. There is an unconscious sense of union with Creation and a seeming acceptance of its beauty; for example, one may easily interrelate with strangers or spontaneously join an adventure without questioning the circumstances. The person wants to remain a free spirit and naturally avoids an overly regulated lifestyle. Simplicity keeps one appreciative, faithful, and trusting.

However when naiveté is excessive, it cannot subsist in the natural world because parasites, predators, and challenges are part of Creation as well, and they pose a threat to one's survival. The person may neglect the need to properly take care of his or her life and end up unprepared when facing adversity or hostility, possibly becoming easy prey or victimized in some way. Initially lacking an understanding of danger, one does not recognize personal vulnerabilities.

Living life in full trust as if invulnerable, the person may literally live on the edge and practice extreme sports. In another way, the feeling of invincibility can translate into a savior's complex whereby one is under the illusive impression of being able to take everything on one's shoulders. In an attempt to save other people from pain, personal needs are sacrificed. The word "no" may literally not be part of one's vocabulary—a manifestation of this sense of omnipotence.

Inattention to danger and excessive exposure can keep one's immune system underdeveloped. The immune system is not only physical, but also emotional and spiritual. One must not only learn to fend off viruses but also hostile people or illusive ideologies. Lacking proper self-management and discrimination, one's immune system may become imbalanced—either over or underactive.

At some point, shock may occur through disappointment, failure, and or pain; not having been prepared for negative outcomes, victimization ensues. Everything may seem unfair because the person feels they didn't do any harm and do not deserve the inflicted pain. While seeing oneself as good and pure, the whole world may appear to be the villain: one does not yet realize that the reason for the pain is likely naiveté and an overly simplistic approach to life.

Eventually, a more grounded understanding of life's complex nature gradually surfaces. One learns that life is not only about being and flowing but also about properly managing emerging circumstances. Accepting everything about existence means also accepting the challenges, not only the "good parts." Yet before a balanced approach is integrated, it is common to feel deeply confused and bewildered by the experience of life once bitten—swinging from seeing everything as good to the other extreme of seeing danger or evil everywhere.

Not knowing proper boundaries to filter good from bad or useful from useless, life can be experienced as chronically overwhelming—the person is either completely open or completely closed. Under these circumstances, one becomes easily "flooded" when situations that were expected to be simple turn out in reality to be much more complex. Being overwhelmed can lead to mismanaging or abandoning duties. In extreme cases, one may even become suicidal and desire to escape existence. In most cases, however, a better perspective is eventually gained and management skills acquired. Beyond learning about boundaries, one may also adopt a spiritual practice that helps one to gain a greater understanding of life's complexity.

It is understandable that one gets confused when confronted with both the beauty and uncompromising harshness of nature. Not having a complete grasp of why things happen the way they do, there is no immediate reference to help the person feel more secure or guided toward the adequate response to challenges; it is all trial and error, and errors can be painful. There is no written life manual that prepares a person for life's unpredictable nature.

Since the destination is clearly unknown, it is better to focus on the journey of life; accepting this fact allows one to benefit from each moment even when setbacks erupt. When facing the jungle of existence, adapting to circumstances and learning how to improvise are essential skills—there is a need for a more adventurous spirit.

In a different way, since the Pisces influence reflects the need to acknowledge and connect to the larger forces operating in life and the source of Creation, it also inspires a feeling of unity based on the premise that we are all in "the same boat." Despite our differences, we all originate from the same source. On this basis, the person may connect with the collective and resonate with common needs and aspirations. Therefore, one may deal with collective issues in one's personal life. This may literally apply in having a job that deals with the public through service or by being a part of large institutions that address public needs such as hospitals, public spaces, or the army. In some cases, tapping into public needs brings fame and the ability to inspire the masses.

The archetype opposing Pisces is Virgo. The opposing archetype serves as a point of balance, and here through Virgo the balance between control and surrendering is in question. Virgo suggests that while resources are freely available in nature, they are not free of labor; effort is required to make proper use of them. For example, a diamond needs to be polished to be brought to value. Through this polarity, one learns the balance between the wild and the tamed—what needs to be properly managed and what needs to remain completely natural. The individual can remain a free spirit yet without neglecting management requirements.

Even one's body is a resource that needs proper care; the Virgo influence raises awareness about the benefits of leading a healthy lifestyle. While Pisces represents larger life cycles and spiritual forces, Virgo represents an awareness of the details and the multiple components that constitute the larger whole—properly managing details is conducive to the function of the whole. With better function, one avoids feeling overwhelmed or victimized.

General associations

Nature, the primal elements, oceans, wildness, the free spirit, raw and natural resources, flow, higher forces, spirituality, divine intervention, ideologies, prayer, surrendering, purity, idealization, positivism, passivity, sleep, dreams, the unconscious, the immune system, parasites, negligence, denial, illusion, escapism, dysfunction, addiction, victimization, disillusionment, fear, the collective, masses, impersonal, profession and public function, fame and notoriety.

Health associations

The immune system, bone marrow, white blood cells, the thymus gland, the lymphatic system, the pineal gland, the right-brain hemisphere and the left side of the body, the feet.

Professional associations

Public administration, medicine, social care, politics, the movie industry, show business, crude natural resources, geology, wildlife and nature, oceanography, fishing and sailing.

Relationship inclinations

Accepting, open boundaries, idealistic, naïve, adaptive, passive, mild-tempered, devotional, sacrificial, indiscriminating, harmony-seeking, simplicity-seeking.

Chapter Four

Signs, Planets, and Houses

We all have the twelve signs, houses, and all planets in our birth chart. The difference between one chart and another is the change of emphases and the arrangement of these factors. Even though every chart consists of the same components, no two charts are disposed exactly the same way; therefore, each chart describes a unique influence and life orientation.

As previously mentioned in the second chapter, an archetype of the zodiac consists of a sign, a planet, and a house. For example, the archetype of Capricorn comprises the sign of Capricorn, the planet Saturn, and the tenth house. These three components reflect the same themes, meanings, and energy; however, each one plays a different role in the chart dynamics.

The Signs

The twelve signs that are used in astrology represent the celestial constellations through which we see the Sun passing from our perspective on Earth. The signs are like geographical locations that follow one another and form a ring around the Earth. The thread of these signs represents the path of the Sun (the ecliptic), and as a unit they are called *the zodiac*. The zodiac is similar to the ecliptic except that it extends approximately nine degrees on each side of the ecliptic—it forms a ring of constellations around the Earth. Since all the Solar System planets orbit around the Sun, they also travel through the zodiac.

In astrology, our subjective perspective of the heavens is the point of reference; consequently, from this standpoint the Earth is perceived as the center around which the celestial bodies rotate. Thus as the Earth revolves around its axis in the course of one day, it appears as if it is the signs that have completed a whole rotation around the Earth in that time period.

The whole ring of the zodiacal signs equals 360 degrees; since there are twelve signs, each sign comprises 30 degrees—from 0 to 29 degrees. Hence as the planets travel through the signs, they begin their passage from 0 degrees, and each one at its own pace progresses to the 29th degree before proceeding on to the next sign. When looking at a chart, it is important to identify not only which sign each planet is in, but also what degree of the sign.

The Planets and the Luminaries

The main bodies studied in astrology are the Solar System planets and the luminaries. In terms of influence, the luminaries—the Sun and the Moon—are as important as the planets.

The Solar System planets range from Mercury, closest to the Sun, to Pluto, farthest from the Sun. While the scientific community has demoted Pluto's status from a planet to a "Dwarf planet," within the astrological community Pluto is still considered to function as a planet, unlike other non-planet bodies. Given that it rules the sign of Scorpio, its importance remains paramount.

Currently, other "Dwarf planets" include Eris, Ceres, Makemake, and Haumea; they were discovered beyond Pluto's orbit and named around 2006. At the time this book is being written research is being conducted to decode the nature of their influence.

Other bodies belonging to the Solar System—such as the asteroids, Centaurs, and Kuiper Belt objects (located beyond Neptune)—are also analyzed by many astrologers; the heavens are vast and each body has its relevance. However in this volume, only the Solar System planets— from Mercury to Pluto and the Sun and the Moon—are studied because they are the only bodies archetypically associated with signs and houses. The other bodies are important but not associated with specific signs or houses.

From our perspective on Earth, the Solar System planets and the luminaries rotate around the Earth through the path of the ecliptic. When we look at the sky, the planets are positioned against the backdrop of a particular sign. For example, Mercury may be currently positioned against the backdrop of the constellation of Libra; then over the next few days it will progress to the backdrop of the following sign, Scorpio, and so on. It is as if Mercury is visiting these signs, and when it does, its influence on us is characterized by the particular sign it visits. The moment it moves to the next sign, we experience new dynamics represented by that particular sign.

As each planet passes through a sign, new realities are created on Earth that directly relate to these positions. The movement of the planets and the luminaries through the signs is totally synchronized with life occurrences on Earth both on an individual and a collective level. The way to interpret these influences begins by individually analyzing each planet's position and then by synthesizing the sum of all the planetary influences operating as a cohesive unit. (*Note*: Hereafter for the sake of simplicity, the term "planet" assumes that the luminaries, the Sun and the Moon, and Pluto are included.)

Each planet moves from sign to sign at a different speed. The closer a planet is to the Sun, the faster it completes its revolution (a complete cycle through the signs). Thus Pluto, being the farthest from the Sun, is the slowest moving planet, sometimes staying more than thirty years in a sign; Mercury, the planet closest to the Sun, only stays about two weeks in a sign.

The fastest moving body is not Mercury, however, but the Moon. Since the Moon is the closest to the Earth, its revolution (complete cycle) through the signs is the fastest from our perspective.

Since the Earth is perceived as the point of reference instead of the Sun, the Sun takes the place of the Earth when referring to its speed. Thus the Sun's speed is third in line after Mercury and Venus (just as the Earth would be in the actual Solar System). Table 2 lists the planets and the length of time it takes each planet to move through a sign.

Table 2: The speed of each planet as it moves through a sign

Planet	**Approximate length of time in each sign**
MOON	Two and a half days
MERCURY	From two weeks to two months if retrograde
VENUS	From three weeks to four months if retrograde
SUN	One month
MARS	From two months to seven months if retrograde
JUPITER	Thirteen months
SATURN	Two years
URANUS	Seven years
NEPTUNE	Fourteen years
PLUTO	From twelve to thirty-two years—its elliptical orbit accounts for the variation in speed.

As previously mentioned, each planet is part of an archetype; for example, Pluto is part of the Scorpio archetype. Additionally, each planet *rules* a sign—the ruler is also called the *despositor* of a sign; thus Pluto is the natural ruler or despositor of Scorpio. This does not mean that Pluto only stays in the sign of Scorpio; it moves through all the signs. As Pluto embodies Scorpio energy, it carries that energy and "distributes" it to each of the signs it passes through. This is a very simplified way of explaining it—we will learn more about this dynamic in subsequent chapters.

The Luminaries—The Moon and the Sun
The Luminaries include *the Moon* and *the Sun*. They represent the personal filters through which all life experiences are processed. Thus they represent the person's unique sense of self and control center. Sometimes the luminaries are also included with *personal planets.*

Personal Planets—Mercury, Venus, and Mars
The planets from *Mercury to Mars* are called the *personal planets* because they reflect personal development and life management. These planets represent themes such as personal survival issues, personal needs, personal resources, and one's subjective orientation and function in the world.

Social Planets—Jupiter and Saturn
Jupiter and Saturn are called the *social planets* because they reflect egocentric development and influence within the larger framework of society. Through Saturn and Jupiter, we can assess how the person integrates into social structures and how he or she gains authority and fulfills a role in guiding others.

Transpersonal (Outer) Planets—Uranus, Neptune, and Pluto
Uranus, Neptune, and Pluto are called the *outer planets.* The outer planets are not visible to the naked eye and consequently were only discovered in the last centuries following the development of the telescope. The outer planets are also called *transpersonal planets* because they are about transcending personal attachment and adopting a more holistic

approach to existence, shifting one's view from a subjective to more objective perspective.

The transpersonal planets are the force behind evolution because they constantly stimulate the need to gain a greater awareness of life and the Truth, and continually promote a redefinition of the self—they are the main agents of change. Through the influence of the transpersonal planets one learns to align personal views with the universal Truth, instead of projecting personal views on existence.

Traditional Rulership—Before Discovering the Outer Planets

Outer planets, Uranus, Neptune, and Pluto, are not visible to the naked eye and were consequently only discovered beginning in the eighteenth century after more powerful telescopes were invented. Today, Uranus rules Aquarius, Neptune rules Pisces, and Pluto rules Scorpio. But before their discovery, Scorpio was ruled by Mars, Aquarius was ruled by Saturn, and Pisces was ruled by Jupiter. Today the traditional rulers, Mars, Saturn, and Jupiter, are considered secondary rulers to Scorpio, Aquarius, and Pisces, respectively, while the outer planets are the primary rulers.

The Houses

Houses are formed relative to intersecting points between the Earth and the ecliptic or zodiac. Therefore, houses are the medium through which the earth and the skies connect. There are twelve houses that relate to the twelve signs.

The Angles—The Ascendant, the Descendant, the MC, the IC

The Ascendant, the Descendant, the MC, and the IC are four points that intersect the ecliptic. In many house systems, these four points determine *the angles* and mark the *cusp* (the beginning) of the first, fourth, seventh, and tenth houses (see figure 19). Some house systems do not use these four points to determine the angles, but this is a subject for future study beyond the scope of this volume. *The angles are determined according to the time and place of birth*. With the exact time of birth, we can calculate what degree of what sign lies on each angle. When the time of birth is not available, it is common to use the position of Sun as the Ascendant and divide all the houses accordingly into twelve equal parts—this is called a *Solar chart*; it is a less precise house division, but a valid one.

When having the time and place of birth, we find the first intersection point, called *the Ascendant,* which marks the cusp of the first house in most house systems. The Ascendant is the point on the *eastern horizon* that meets the ecliptic; thus the Ascendant sign is actually the sign that lies on the eastern horizon at a particular time. Approximately every two hours, a new sign is on the Ascendant or eastern horizon. All twelve signs pass through the Ascendant in the course of twenty-four hours relative to the Earth's complete rotation around its axis in one day.

Figure 19: The Ascendant, the Descendant, the MC, and the IC determine the angles of a birth chart in most house systems

Just as the Ascendant is the sign on the eastern horizon, the exact opposite sign lies on the *western horizon,* namely *the Descendant,* and it marks the cusp of the seventh house in most house systems. The Ascendant-Descendant axis cuts the whole ring of constellations into two equal parts above and below the horizon creating the upper and lower hemispheres (see figure 19).

The other intersection points between the Earth and the ecliptic are *the MC, Medium Coeli* in Latin, and *the IC, Imum Coeli* in Latin. The MC is also called the *Midheaven* and the IC is also called the *Nadir.* Astronomically, the MC or Midheaven is the intersection of the local meridian with the ecliptic. The MC marks the tenth house cusp while the IC is its exact opposite and marks the fourth house cusp in most house systems. The MC-IC axis divides the ring of the zodiac into the eastern and western hemispheres (see figure 19).

The Inner Houses

The remaining houses—the 2nd, 3rd, 5th, 6th, 8th, 9th, 11th, and 12th houses—are called *inner houses;* their cusps do not represent meeting points with the ecliptic but rather are derived from the angles. In other words, the inner houses are calculated relative to the angles and do not stand on their own.

House Systems

There are several different house systems in astrology. The main reason for the multiplicity of house systems originates from the different ways of dividing the inner houses once the angles have been determined. For example, to calculate the inner houses, some systems simply divide the number of degrees between each angle into three equal parts. This form of division is called the *Porphyry* house system, named after its initiator. With house systems such as *Koch* or *Placidus,* the inner houses are calculated using more complex equations.

Systems such as the *Equal* house system only consider the Ascendant and Descendant axis and from that reference divide the whole zodiac into twelve equal parts. For example, if the Ascendant (the cusp that marks the first house) is at five degrees Libra, all the other houses are equally divided into thirty degree sections; thus the second house opens at five degrees Scorpio, the third house at five degrees Sagittarius, and so on. Other house systems exist, but these are the ones most commonly used.

House Sizes

In the charts of people born near the equator, the astrological houses are more or less naturally equal in size. The reason for this is that on the equator, the Ascendant and the MC are usually ninety degrees from each another forming a symmetrical cross between the four points (see figure 19). The further north or south in latitude one is born, the more the houses vary in size.

Figure 20: Unequal houses

For example, in the chart of a person born in Scandinavia, the MC may be only thirty-five degrees away from the Ascendant (instead of ninety), causing very irregular house patterns. Thus the house formation of a chart varies greatly depending upon the geographical location (see figure 20). A bigger house is not more significant than a smaller house; however, it stands a greater chance of having more planets in it.

A Brief Description of the Houses

Each house represents a different area or theme in a person's life. The sign and planets residing in a house describe how the particular area or theme represented by the house is used, processed, and developed. A house unpopulated by planets remains important.

1st House—Aries Archetype

This area describes the urge to become—"the rising wave." The first house represents the impulse to separate and individuate; it is comparable to the effort of birth when the baby moves out of the womb to become an individual entity. Through the first house, new seeds of consciousness are planted and gradually grow—it describes the new orientation for the soul in the current life. This house represents the active and reactive defense mechanism the person develops as he or she learns how to become more independent and face life challenges alone. It reflects the emergence of personal desires (including sexual impulses) and the mode of action. The signs and the planets in the first house describe how these matters are addressed.

1st house themes
Becoming, new wave of consciousness, new life orientation, independent way of action, impulses, creative expression, sexual expression, strength to face challenges, defense strategy.

2nd House—Taurus Archetype

This area describes all matters pertaining to available resources and their management. The second house represents the inner bases from which the person stabilizes and solidifies foundations in order to survive in the material dimension. This includes inborn talents as well as material assets. The second house reflects the basis of one's worth and sense of self-worth; it reflects what one has and its value. It describes the basis from which the person relies on him or herself and the way he or she manages personal resources in order to remain self-sufficient. The second house also describes sensual and sexual needs as one learns to adapt to the physical and material dimensions of life on Earth. The signs and the planets in the second house describe how these matters addressed.

2nd house themes

Available resources, talents, financial management, self-worth, sensuality.

3rd House—Gemini Archetype

This area describes the pressure to integrate into the environment and learn how to navigate through life. This house represents the need to figure things out, decode the logic of life, and find common sense; thus it refers to orientation, adaptation, motion, and learning. The third house describes how the person learns about life and its diverse nature, and adapts to the environment; thus it depicts observation, learning, and communication skills. Moreover, this house refers to traveling to different environments so that one is exposed to life's diversity and learns from changing perspectives. The third house also describes one's relationship with siblings, extended family, and neighbors. The signs and the planets in the third house describe how these matters are addressed.

3rd house themes

Orientation, learning, schooling, communication, transportation, cultural development and multi-cultural exchange, travel, the environment, siblings, neighbors.

4th House—Cancer Archetype

This area describes the need to have a safe and intimate environment in order to be able to emotionally process life experiences while sheltered from disturbances. It refers to family life and parental nurturing and protection—especially the mother's involvement in providing security and affection. The fourth house describes one's personal development and the needs one may have to secure that development. Through this house the person establishes his or her sense of identity; it relates to all that one personally identifies with and becomes emotionally attached to. This house describes childhood dynamics and the eternal inner-child who constantly processes life experiences. The signs and the planets in the fourth house describe how these matters are addressed.

4th house themes

Intimate world, emotional response and processes, nurturing needs, family dynamics, the relationship with one's mother, the support system, development and maturation.

5th House—Leo Archetype

This area describes self-actualization and the need to find a personal sense of purpose and meaning in life. The fifth house describes one's creative potential and the capacity to impact life's development through leaving a legacy. In this regard, it also points to issues associated with children, such as fertility issues, and the relationship with one's own children. Additionally, the fifth house describes the support and expectations from one's parents to make something important out of one's life, and more particularly it refers to the father's influence. The signs and the planets in the fifth house describe how these matters are addressed.

5th house themes

Creative self-actualization, sense of purpose, output, the relationship with one's father, fertility, the relationship with one's children.

6th House—Virgo Archetype

This area describes the way acquired knowledge is used to manage daily existence and the level of function and productivity in this regard. It describes personal control skills and the ability to correct, align, and perfect personal creative effort in order to keep improving the way one functions. The sixth house describes personal effort, labor capacity, and general work related issues including the nature of one's work, the work environment, as well as maintenance requirements to ensure that life runs smoothly. The sixth house also describes health concerns and how the body is managed as a resource. As the last house in the lower hemisphere of a chart, this house reflects the level of mastery one acquires as an independent being through the refinement of personal skills. The signs and the planets in the sixth house describe how these matters are addressed.

6th house themes

Management of daily life, function, health management, hygiene, work, professional environment, skills, refinement.

7th House—Libra Archetype

This area describes what the person seeks in other people because of a feeling of inner lack. It describes the needs that stimulate relationships and partnerships, and the nature of relationship interactions. The seventh house points to the necessity of finding balance in life by exploring polarities in order to find the middle way. The signs and the planets in the seventh house describe how these matters are addressed.

7th house themes
Relationship and partnership dynamics, choice of partners, attraction to differences, need for balance.

8th House—Scorpio Archetype

This area describes dynamics pertaining to the need to grow into higher levels of being. The eighth house is where the person recognizes he or she may be limited or weak in some areas and, as a result, where more power is sought through personal transformation. Thus when feeling limited, it describes where more consciousness and effort must be invested in order to outgrow weaknesses, expose shadows, and evolve. The eighth house points to the need to exchange resources and absorb from others what one may lack in return for something equally valuable. The exchange may be on material, emotional, or spiritual basis. Thus dynamics associated with this house revolve around attraction, rejection, emotional attachment, love, dependence, and the need to sexually merge with another. It also describes endings and death, reflecting the need to change and let go of what doesn't work anymore. The signs and the planets in the eighth house describe how these matters are addressed.

8th house themes
The experience of limitation and the growth impulse, inner change and transformation, endings, vulnerabilities and shadows, intimacy with others, sexuality, exchange of resources, power and powerlessness.

9th House—Sagittarius Archetype

This area describes the process of truth seeking to realize a larger life potential and find meaning on both a personal and a collective level. The ninth house describes one's perception of truth and one's belief system and experience with cultural, religious, and spiritual issues. This house refers to the expansion impulse that may apply on material, creative, or spiritual levels—outgrowing existing boundaries and conquering new horizons. In this regard, it also refers to the dissemination of knowledge and resources, and higher education. The signs and the planets in the ninth house describe how these matters are addressed.

9th house themes

Expansion, faith, belief system, religious, philosophical or spiritual knowledge, teaching, higher education, travel, open spaces and nature.

10th House—Capricorn Archetype

This area describes the impulse to establish a structure based on what is believed to be true. The tenth house represents the need to acknowledge and implement universal and social laws in order to develop, mature, and perform in a healthy way on both a personal and a collective level. In this context, the tenth house refers to the need to be mentored and guided by reliable authorities, and in turn describes how the person matures to become an authority and train novices in areas of expertise. It points to the necessity of gaining credibility, taking responsibility, and gaining status in order to function in the larger framework of society. On these bases, the tenth house describes one's approach to ethics, laws, authority figures, the establishment, and life's principles in general. One's relationship with parents, educators, bosses, and society is detailed here. The signs and the planets in the tenth house describe how these matters are addressed.

10th house themes

Moral references, authority figures, guidance, conditioning, society, laws, structures, societal status, credibility, ambition, leadership.

11th House—Aquarius Archetype

This area describes the need to increase and refine the quality of life on both a personal and a collective level. It points to the necessity for progress and emancipation in order to better master life's challenges and enhance human potential. Intellectual creativity, research, and the higher self are developed through this house providing one with the ability to become more objective about life matters. The eleventh house also describes social and group dynamics resulting from bonding with like-minded others—this includes friendships and community involvement. The signs and the planets in the eleventh house describe how these matters are addressed.

11th house themes

Progress, objective perspective, innovation, community, friends, higher potential, civilization.

12th House—Pisces Archetype

This area describes the influence and function of powers operating in life that are greater than the individual and all encompassing—these powers include nature, fate, the divine, or the masses. Through this house, the person faces what is impersonal and cannot be owned as well as what is beyond one's knowledge and cannot be predicted. On the one hand, the twelfth house refers to the individual's ability to connect with the masses or the collective through a public function or profession, and the potential for public appeal. On the other hand, it points to the danger of victimization, chaos, neglect, and dysfunction because one has no control over matters ruled by this house. Because this house reflects what is all encompassing, it inspires surrender and acceptance through spiritual development. This house also refers to dream states, unconsciousness, and the mysteries of life left to be discovered. The signs and the planets in the twelfth house describe how these matters are addressed.

12th house themes

What cannot be controlled or owned, surrender, victimization, higher forces, untamed nature and animals, the divine, spirituality, unconscious motivations, dream state, public exposure, public function, career, self-dedication, potential fame and the relationship with public figures.

Synthesizing the Meanings of the Signs, the Planets, and the Houses

In a chart, each planet is positioned in a particular sign, which in turn lands in a particular house. For example, we may have a chart where the planet *Mars is in Capricorn in the third house*; thus we have a combination of three archetypes at play: Mars (Aries archetype) in the sign of Capricorn (Capricorn archetype) in the third house (Gemini archetype)—see figure 21.

Figure 21: Mars in Capricorn in the third house

Analyzing a Sign, Planet, and House Configuration

Using the above example, in a simplified way we can analyze a sign, planet, and house configuration as follows:

- *The planet* is a function of our consciousness (*what*). In this example, Mars relates to the function of consciousness concerning *action, individuality, and defense.*

- *The house* is the area of influence in our life *and* consciousness (*where*). The third house relates to the area of influence concerning *navigation, knowledge, and communication.*

- *The sign* is the way the matter is handled (*how*). The sign of *Capricorn* refers to proceeding *with authority based upon what is perceived as reliable and ethical.*

Synthesizing all of the above information, people with Mars in Capricorn in the third house tend to approach life in the following ways:

- They actively seek (Mars) knowledge (third house) that is tested and reliable (Capricorn).

- They are very defensive (Mars) about their knowledge (third house) in a rather authoritative way (Capricorn).

- They defy (Mars) information sources (third house) that are not perceived as coherent and reliable (Capricorn).

- They actively seek (Mars) to learn and adapt to the environment (third house) in a responsible fashion (Capricorn), for example, through planning trips or studies ahead of time.

An Astrological Chart

Looking at a chart with all the factors included can at first appear overwhelming, but like learning a new language, with some practice it becomes easily accessible.

It is at first a visual exercise to identify all the factors and see how they interrelate. We will use the example of the performer Madonna's chart to familiarize ourselves with a chart (see figure 22).

Looking at her angles, we can see that the rising sign on her

Ascendant is Virgo, and more precisely the 8th degree of Virgo. Her Descendant is consequently 8 degrees Pisces. Her MC is 3 degrees Gemini and her IC, exactly opposite, at 3 degrees Sagittarius. In this example, the Koch house system was used to calculate the rest of the houses.

Because her Ascendant is not exactly 90 degrees from her MC, the size of the houses is slightly uneven. Since her first house begins at 8 degrees Virgo, it means that part of the sign of Virgo will be in her twelfth house (from 0 to 7 degrees Virgo) and the rest of the sign of Virgo will be in her first house (from 8 to 29 degrees).

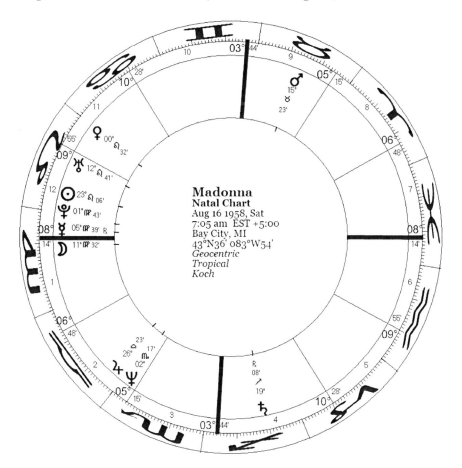

Figure 22: Example chart: Madonna

Consequently, planets that are positioned between 0 and 7 degrees Virgo will land in her twelfth house, and those positioned between 8 and 29 degrees Virgo will be in her first house. We can see the planets Pluto and Mercury respectively at 1 and 6 degrees Virgo indeed in her twelfth house, and the Moon at 11 degrees Virgo in her first house.

The way the planets are positioned in her birth chart shows an emphasis on the *eastern hemisphere*—she has eight planets in this part of the chart, from Venus in Leo to Neptune in Scorpio. Generally, this emphasis means that the person will face existential forces larger than him or herself and consequently learn to improvise and respond to emerging circumstances, rather than have more control over the unfolding of events. However, these planets in the eastern hemisphere are positioned in western hemisphere signs (Leo to Scorpio); therefore, the need for control and the desire to create her destiny surely is present. The contradiction of eastern hemisphere houses and western hemisphere signs can create a good balance between knowing what is in her power to change and when she must surrender. If she fails to integrate this balance, she may experience frustration when trying to control everything and ending up having plans constantly deviated.

Within the eastern hemisphere, *the fourth quadrant* is the most populated with five planets in the eleventh and twelfth houses (from Venus to Mercury). The fourth quadrant represents public involvement and the need to align her personal life with larger collective or spiritual principles. It means the person is pressured to adapt to impersonal dynamics and integrate into a greater scheme of things. If well managed, the person can succeed in receiving from and influencing collective matters. If mismanaged, the person may feel anonymous and overwhelmed by larger circumstances.

Because she has personal signs populated (Leo and Virgo) in these impersonal houses, it means that her personal sense of purpose and way to manage life (Leo and Virgo) are oriented toward collective matters and needs. It is well documented that from an early age, Madonna aspired to become famous and wanted to touch the masses (twelfth house)—she did so through becoming a performer (Leo). It is also well documented that she leads an active and involved spiritual lifestyle and has gone through considerable soul-searching phases in her life: first rejecting her traditional religious upbringing and then becoming controversial by mixing sexuality with the sacred.

The most emphasized elements in her chart are fire and earth with eight planets in Taurus, Leo, Virgo, and Sagittarius. Fire-Earth people are immensely creative, resourceful, self-driven, self-reliant, resistant and strong—they shy away from weaknesses.

The most prominent mode is the *fixed mode* with five planets in Taurus, Leo, and Scorpio, describing a strong focus of energy, an abundance of creativity, the use of internal resources, pronounced individuality, and the aspiration to leave a mark.

Much more can be analyzed and delineated from this chart if getting further into details, but the purpose here is to look at the general chart disposition and train the eye to identify the general themes.

How and Where to Create a Chart

A chart can be calculated using software now readily available online, sometimes for free. One can purchase an astrology program and enjoy many additional interpretation and calculation features.

I personally recommend that you also purchase a book called *The Ephemeris*, which consists of a table that describes the daily position of the planets by sign and degree. Despite the fact that all astrology software calculates the positions of the planets at any given moment, it is advisable to acquire an ephemeris book, in addition to a computer program, so that you can observe the progression of planets over the course of several months at one glance.

Chapter Five

The Moon in Signs and Houses

The Moon rules the sign of Cancer—accordingly, it describes the function of consciousness that relates to personalizing our existence. We are born into a vast world that contains endless components; the Moon reflects the need to personally associate with particular elements, and not others, so that we can relate to existence through those elements. Without a feeling of personal connection, we can end up in a diffused or indifferent state of being—a condition that might eventually compromise our sanity. When finding people or things to emotionally associate with, we connect with life. Through the function of the Moon, we find a home in the vastness of existence.

The personalizing role of the Moon reflects our need as an individual to have a separate identity and unique experiences in life. Each person naturally identifies with something specific to his or her nature and develops a unique life orientation relative to that. For example, one may know about all the existing countries in the world but will form a connection with just a few, usually starting with one's country of birth. Such a process extends to all areas of life from associating with particular friends to developing particular tastes and preferences. As we make these connections, a whole identity and lifestyle emerges.

The Moon relates to our personal vision and experience of life; it is *the subjective filter* through which we perceive and process existence. Generally describing our personal perspective—the kind of glasses through which we see life—the Moon describes the foundation we generate life circumstances from. Through the Moon, first and foremost, we find our personal way to relate to existence and develop a life of our own.

In a birth chart, the Moon symbolizes *the ego*. There are many definitions and misconceptions associated with the ego, especially in spiritual literature where it is often perceived in a negative light. But the ego is simply our individual sense of self; it is the individual sense of consciousness that allows us to define ourselves and serves as the filter through which we process and eventually assimilate each encountered experience into our system. Through the ego, we form *emotional attachments* to people, things, or ideas. These attachments become our identity, and we become invested in what we are attached to—*through emotions, experiences are marked in our system*. We can call the ego our personal processor, and the soul operates through the ego to foster its evolutionary purposes.

Beginning with infancy, the first people we personalize and become attached to are our parents, particularly our mother. There are many mothers in the world, but our mother is the one who counts the most for us—through our Moon, we personalize her. In a healthy way, attachments allow emotional identification and investment. When a parent-child attachment is mutually created, a nurturing relationship is established.

Since the Moon represents the personalizing process, it refers to everything we take into our system. Just like the stomach, we need to digest what is ingested so that it can become part of us. As we take in, digest, and assimilate life experiences, our sense of being expands and gradually includes new elements. Thus the Moon refers to growth and the *continual process of becoming* on all levels: biologically, emotionally, as well as spiritually. The constant need to process and personalize what life exposes us to requires time and protection from stress or threats. The Moon represents all the needs and conditions required to foster healthy emotional processing; when we digest an experience, we isolate from the external rhythm into a more intimate and nurturing space. Once the experience is digested, we feel more secure with it and are able to reengage with the outside world.

Relating to developmental processes, the Moon also represents what is not fully mature and ripe: it describes vulnerabilities, neediness, and the necessity for support. For example, this dynamic refers to parent-child relationships where parents protect and guide their children who are involved in their growth. However, even as adults, there are always experiences that put us in a position of needing emotional guidance and protection, just like a child. Therefore, the Moon points to the eternal *inner child* in every being—the part of us that keeps developing and becoming something regardless of our age.

The Moon symbolizes the essential need to have *a support system*. Since we all have an inner child, no one can always remain strong and beyond vulnerability—the Moon describes the need to rely on others, to receive support and nurturing in time of need, and to also provide this type of support to others. In this sense, establishing a support system relies on allowing a healthy dependence when needed and making sure that a support net is in place if a crisis occurs. Having a family is the first gesture in establishing a support system, providing the family is functional. A support system—whether through family, friends, or society—is a requirement for a healthy emotional life and in the long run necessary for our mental health.

With the Moon there is a paradox—on the one hand, it points to the need for security through familiarity so that we are able to process experiences in a safe way; on the other hand, it describes the need for growth and the fact that the continual process of becoming relies on encountering foreign elements. When a person alternates between embracing what is new and retreating to what is known, this eternal paradox generates mood swings. It is a push-pull effect that can at times be confusing, especially to the environment. The Moon reflects the fact that it takes time to warm up to new things and familiarize oneself with them—hence the back and forth motion.

Since the Moon points to emotional processes, it refers to *the time needed* to emotionally process experiences—digestion cannot happen instantaneously. The assimilation of life elements occurs gradually, and for this to happen personal contact with the encountered elements is required. For example, when a child begins school, the assimilation process starts when the child visits the school, discusses the programs, and gets acquainted with the teachers and eventually his or her peers. In the course of days, as the process of association unfolds, school gradually becomes an integral part of the child's reality—an attachment is formed and he or she eventually feels more secure.

However, life does not always provide "easy food to digest." For example, we may lose a dear one and be pressured to assimilate what happened and the new reality that ensues. In this case, grief results from the emotional attachment to the deceased prompting one to learn first hand about difficulty, the finality of life, and the necessity of death. As painful as it can be, our emotions allow us to have a direct and personal experience with the event. Sometimes excessive attachment, in this case to the deceased, leaves us unable to let go and digest the experience. Unresolved emotions can induce post traumatic stress symptoms such as anxiety, chronic insecurity, or mood swings.

Beyond difficult events to digest, one may have to face the fact that life does not always allow the necessary time to assimilate an experience. Stress, obligations, and survival needs can force one to move on with life and adjust rapidly without having the opportunity to dwell in emotional processes. For example, time for emotional processing may be a luxury for a person who has to provide for his or her family. It is not always viable to express needs and vulnerabilities. This dynamic can apply to maternity leave; for example, many systems require new parents to return to work three months after delivery, usually way too soon for both the baby and the parents to adjust emotionally.

→ The placement of the Moon in the birth chart describes the person's ability to connect with life and find elements he or she personally relates to. Through the Moon, the person chooses, consciously or unconsciously, what to become emotionally attached to or involved with. Thereafter, the person becomes part of what he or she associates with and gives and receives nurturing and support through these bonds—one's identity is shaped by these emotional associations whether a home, one's family and friends, or an idea.

→ Symbolizing the need for a support system, the Moon represents the need for shelter and safety when processing emotions. Life experiences are processed through the emotions so they can be personalized and assimilated into one's system. Once an experience has been assimilated, it allows the person to grow as his or her identity changes accordingly.

→ The Moon represents the relationship with the person one first connects with and personalizes: the mother. From the womb through the early years of life, this connection sets the tone for one's general sense of belonging and development. Such a dynamic gradually comes to include all family members.

Moon keywords and phases of development

- *The personalizing process, the nature of one's personal connection with life, emotional associations, the management of emotions, the orientation of the growth process.*

- *Security needs, the management of intimacy, the approach to vulnerabilities, one's support system.*

- *One's family life, sense of belonging, nurturing needs, the relationship with one's parents—especially the mother, the mother's personality.*

The Moon in Aries ♈, in the 1st House, or in Aspect to Mars ♂

— *The personalizing process, the nature of one's personal connection with life, emotional associations, the management of emotions, the orientation of the growth process.*

— *Security needs, the management of intimacy, the approach to vulnerabilities, one's support system.*

With the Moon in Aries, in the first house, or in aspect to Mars, a person establishes a personal connection with life on the basis of the need to be, to independently take charge of one's life, and to promote causes that are perceived as important. Consequently, one's personal approach and perspective of life is colored by an engaging, and yet, defensive instinct. There is a need to gain strength, promote worthy causes, and freely express oneself. A person will emotionally relate with elements in life that support this orientation.

The very experience of existing is a feat—emotions are expressed as they emerge without any inhibition. Having a very potent emotional nature, the person marks his or her presence and experiences everything in a relatively raw fashion. The defensiveness intrinsic to the Aries archetype directs the emotional nature of the Moon—individuals with this placement react strongly toward any inhibiting factor that poses a threat to their security and independent orientation. Evolutionarily speaking, there is a need to develop a new identity and sense of self that cannot be conditioned by external factors; therefore, a rebellious attitude can be anticipated when pressured to conform to something they do not completely emotionally identify with. This defensive attitude may be a reaction to conscious or unconscious memories of emotional violation or loss of self. Now the focus is on initiating a new beginning where no external factor intervenes or controls personal associations and choices. Under these influences, choice is of paramount importance, and when choosing something to emotionally associate with, the connection is usually passionate and complete. Consequently, the person experiences intense emotions such as fervent and dedicated love, anger, and passion.

Aries is oriented toward change and renewal, and when the Moon is involved one aims to totally reorient emotional needs and attachments. The aspiration for change and renewal usually stems from a reluctance to go back to old patterns that do not serve the person anymore. But the transition between old and new choices can be lengthy; until older patterns are completely surmounted the person will keep meeting circumstances that reflect the past and react defensively toward these situations. For example, the person may have been emotionally invested in unhealthy relationships and now have the desire to break away from such a past; yet until these past patterns are really resolved, he or she will keep meeting people who reflect these unhealthy dynamics consequently causing a strong defensive reaction.

Under these influences, emotions are relatively untamed and instinctual, bypassing apparent logic. They can manifest in spontaneous attractions or repulsions to people or other elements, sometimes without an apparent tangible reason. However underneath it all, these strong reactions are not random; they are tied to survival needs, protective instincts, and an aspiration for renewal. Yet the way these reactions comes across, it can seem as if the person is responding only to immediate gut feelings. Touchiness, fast emotional infatuation, confrontational expression, excitement, and passionate demonstrations of affection are examples of such an approach. Generally, emotions are transparent. Through such emotional intensity, a person has a direct and close connection with life, as if experiencing everything on bare skin. Experiences are powerfully and immediately processed, providing one with a feeling of being alive and present in each moment.

Emotional growth is oriented toward developing one's sense of self. The individual is cultivating independence and learns to take charge of his or her life by defending personal rights and his or her sense of justice. As a result, there is usually a strong emotional association with elements that represent honor, justice, and courage. If the growth process unfolds positively, leadership and entrepreneurial qualities are enhanced as well as the courage to be authentic, reliable, and honest. One may also encourage others toward self-empowerment.

When obstructed and mismanaged, the growth process may flounder in exaggerated defensiveness and bad temper. Excessive emotional reactions can be rooted in a victim mentality whereby the person perceives threats everywhere. In extreme cases, a constant feeling of threat and an incapacity to channel emotions constructively can lead to rage and violent outbursts. In a different way, mismanagment can occur when going through recurrent false starts in life because of a lack of confidence and then overcompensating through a daring attitude that in reality camouflages a fear of failure.

A person with an Aries, first house, or Mars aspecting Moon yearns for emotional security through feelings of strength and courage. Knowing that one can take care of and defend oneself in a time of need is a source of comfort. The risk of being controlled or victimized by others deters one from overly relying on anyone else. Interestingly, the dedication to independence and the affirmation of personal power may lead the person to cyclically rebel against his or her own emotional attachments. A fear of staying attached for too long to anything or to anyone can haunt one. Therefore, as much as there is a tendency to be totally immersed in one's emotional involvement, a point may be reached when the need to disengage emerges. The rupture may not necessarily be radical; it can simply reflect the need for time on one's own to reaffirm one's independence and sense of self. Yet others can feel quite confused by this behavior since the person moves from being firmly engaged to being guarded. Confusion in this regard mostly stems from a lack of communication, but more often than not, even the individual him or herself does not consciously understand the reasons for the change of mood and therefore cannot explain what is happening to others.

The paradox of emotional investment and disengagement manifests in intimacy as well. On the one hand, there is a strong presence, a constant need for emotional expression, and an aspiration for a complete commitment that is expressed in a protective and passionate way. On the other hand, this is contrasted, at times, by a need for solitude, rebellion, and separation. While security is found through independence and self-motivation, establishing a support system that nurtures these needs is critical. At heart, the individual longs for encouragement and loyalty, and wants to be able to rely on others to stand behind his or her cause in time of need.

  — One's family life, sense of belonging, nurturing needs, the relationship with one's parents—especially the mother, the mother's personality.

Under these influences, the family atmosphere may encourage the spirit of independence. Parents may themselves be self-employed, artistic, and self-motivated, with dinner conversations focused on sharing new ideas, ventures, and life chapters. Without necessarily being negligent of maternal duties, the mother may have leadership qualities and a powerful spirit that defies the stereotype of a submissive housewife. The child may feel protected from external hostility by her defensive nature—just like a cub feels protected by the lioness fending off predators.

The bond with the mother and the family may be symbiotic as each person in turn defends the other against injustice or external threats. Nonetheless, because the evolutionary lesson is to develop one's own spirit and might, one may feel the need to break away from the family at some point. But this does not necessarily mean that there will be a sudden rupture or even a physical separation. For example, the child with this signature may break away from family expectations and traditions or simply need space to cultivate his or her individuality. At times, the push-pull motion can be extreme—the child may leave home and then feel compelled to return, and then again feel the need to separate because of emerging differences. These circumstances reflect an identity problem with the child feeling conflicted between wanting to belong and wanting to forge his or her individuality.

In more extreme cases, we may find a family atmosphere that is highly emotionally charged. Parents may rival each other or express their defiance toward injustice, generating an overall feeling of antagonism and strife. If conflict arises between the parents, the Aries Moon child may take sides hoping to empower the parent he or she identifies with the most. The rejected parent may harbor negative feelings toward the child, and in extreme cases, jealousy and competition for loyalty may lead to outright hostility.

In other circumstances, the mother may rebel against the role of motherhood, feeling that her children take her away from her sense of self. She may fluctuate between engaging and disengaging from her role, generating confusion among family members. For the children, this situation inevitably generates nurturing deficiencies and misplaced emotions that can result in reactive behavior, uncontrollable emotional outbursts, and emotional withdrawal. This condition can be eased when the mother gains confidence with her own identity and finds the right balance between meeting her own needs and family commitments.

These configurations can also lead to abrupt separations. It may be that the family is constantly moving and uprooted, and has to reestablish a new identity time and time again. In another way, the family may dissolve with the parents moving away from each other. In extreme cases, the child may be separated from a parent, possibly even through death.

The child may defy any form of injustice and expose perceived dysfunctions that occur in the family. With a desire for renewal, he or she may not hesitate to challenge a parent who is considered to be out of place. Such a child is usually mature, confrontational, and strong spirited.

Evolutionary Lesson

The Moon in these positions describes an evolutionary lesson to forge one's way through potential resistance so that one may authentically and freely express emotions and identify what to emotionally attach to (or not). Choosing what to take in and associate with is the first step toward creating a separate sense of identity. One can have strong presence in life, but over time, there is a tendency to be embedded in an identity crisis because the need for renewal and the reassessment of one's personal orientation is constant. When emotionally engaged, a person with these signatures must learn to maintain perspective and consider personal needs as well as those of others so he or she can avoid getting blindly carried away by emotion. While emotional release is fundamental, it must remain appropriate.

The Moon in Taurus ♉, in the 2nd House, or in Aspect to Venus ♀

— *The personalizing process, the nature of one's personal connection with life, emotional associations, the management of emotions, the orientation of the growth process.*

— *Security needs, the management of intimacy, one's approach to vulnerabilities, one's support system.*

With the Moon in Taurus, in the second house, or in aspect to Venus, a person establishes a personal connection with life on the basis of the need to stabilize existence, use reliable resources to sustain oneself, and find a sense of peace. Consequently, one's personal approach and perspective of life is colored by the need to develop inner resistance, get in touch with internal talents and resources, and foster self-sufficiency. The person will emotionally relate with elements in life that support this orientation.

Aspiring for reliability and stability, the person is selective when becoming emotionally involved but committed once having chosen. Attachments are usually profound as one is focused on grounding one's sense of identity. Like the Aries Moon, the emotional nature is driven by primal needs; however, with Taurus the motivating factors are security, longevity, and dependability, instead of freedom of expression and defense. Here the pace of emotional assimilation is slower because the person strives to have the time to process and adjust to life's development. Loyal to one's personal rhythm, the individual isolates him or herself from disturbing or stressful external factors. It is common for individuals with this signature to periodically withdraw from social interaction so they can enjoy the peace of solitude where a sense of freedom can be found. Unaffected by external incentives to achieve or conquer, patience is found in allowing each thing in life to gradually fall into its right place.

The need for strong attachment and a slower pace can lead to a resistance to change because the Taurus Moon person is more oriented toward gradual and constructive development. Through emotional attachment, the inclination is to stay put despite eventual storms and tribulations. In a positive way, inner strength, commitment, and consistency allow one to build a solid foundation—as a survival instinct, the person does not give up easily.

When mismanaged, the desire for stability and security can lead one to hold on to the status quo and adapt to unhealthy situations. The reluctance to change is not always apparent to the outside world because on the surface the person may seem to be mobile, open minded, and flexible. In some cases, one may appear to change but in the end come back to the same place, holding on to deeply rooted habits.

The Moon in these placements reflects a desire to find a stable and lasting support system. The person gravitates toward what stands the test of time. To minimize the unpredicability that comes when relying on external factors, the person often finds a stable support system through self-sufficiency. A safe nest is built as one makes sure it is equipped with the necessary resources. A support system may also be established through securing financial means resulting from personal work or family assets.

Because the Taurus archetype reflects the material dimension, there is a strong emotional association with the tangible world and whatever symbolizes solidity, beauty, and endurance. For one, we may see a strong connection to the earth, soil, and vegetation in general. Nature's wealth of resources and cyclic regularity provides a sense of harmony and grounding. In another way, the person may have a distinct artistic inclination rooted in an emotional association with harmony and beauty. Artistic qualities can manifest through music, carpentry, or design. Connection to the physical body and sensuality is also likely to be emphasized: touch, smell, taste, and sexual pleasure are common avenues of emotional expression. Association with the material dimension may also be expressed in being strongly attached to physical possessions whether the sentimental value of childhood items, pieces of furniture, art work, or financial assets. Security is usually found through ownership consequently encouraging one to establish solid financial ground.

With the Taurus archetype, the nurturing cravings intrinsic to the Moon may be constant. The person cannot delay his or her hunger and yearns for immediate relief because stability and survival depends on it. Consequently, personal needs, security, and hunger are usually consistently addressed with the intent to satisfy them at every given moment.

When mismanaged, one may feel chronically insecure and constantly "hungry"—this "starvation mentality" may come from an early life or possible past life trauma related to deprivation. At times, this sense of insecurity can manifest in the obsessive consumption of food. The slow metabolism intrinsic to Taurus combined with the tendency to overeat may induce excess weight gain.

With the Moon in these placements, one's intimate world is usually rich and of paramount importance. Naturally inclined to cyclically withdraw, an inner world is created that usually remains very private and warm: one's house can serve as a fortress that protects one from the rest of the world. However, this intimate world is not necessarily physical but can be within the depth one's own soul where comfort is found in self-reliance. Few people are included in this intimate world, yet when trust is established the emotional connection is personal and strong.

— *One's family life, sense of belonging, nurturing needs, the relationship with one's parents—especially the mother, the mother's personality.*

With the Taurus archetype coloring the Moon function, childhood may center around family dynamics where peace and security are a priority. For example, the person may grow up in a rural environment, close to the simplicity of nature and less exposed to outer stimulation. Parents may be physically and emotionally sound, providing everything necessary for immediate needs. They may be inclined toward physical labor and very skillful, but not necessarily intellectually sophisticated.

In some cases, the hold on harmony may overshadow the necessity for honest and uncomfortable discussions. When problems need to be addressed, parents may be inaccessible, especially if expressed emotions are perceived as disruptive. A fear of conflict and disturbance may create this form of denial so that a peaceful atmosphere can be maintained, even if it is artificial. In other circumstances, problems may be discussed within the family but the changes necessary to solve them soon forgotten. Sometimes a child may experience rather tumultuous family dynamics but find peace through isolation and building a safe inner world. These circumstances are likely to strengthen the child's inner core and reduce emotional dependency.

In other circumstances, financial security may be a central familial theme. The focus on material matters is sometimes due to financial struggles that require the family's attention. Parents may be frugal and often refer to what they have versus what they lack. For example, a single mother may struggle to make ends meet. In other circumstances, love and affection are expressed through material generosity and presents. The mother may be a compulsive shopper, surrounding herself with art and luxuries. Needs are addressed through material gratification, sometimes manifesting in a family that accumulates assets and wealth to make sure that lack will never occur. However, while never lacking for anything materially, the child may sometimes feel lonely and emotionally neglected.

Because Taurus relates to sexuality and the Moon to emotional expression within the family environment, there can be boundary problems that in extreme cases lead to sexual abuse in the family. Sometimes this manifests as inappropriate body language or allusions. In more severe cases, it results in actual molestation. To see if such a scenario is relevant, the whole chart has to be examined relative to the Moon.

In more constructive ways, the family environment reflects wealth and generosity in a physical as well as emotional way, while the aesthetic flavor of the house adds to a sense of safety.

These signatures may manifest in parental figures who possess strong character and integrity. Possibly self-made, artistic, and or independent, they may inspire others in their anchored spirit, consistency, and endurance. When excessive, they may lack communicative skills becoming inflexible, prejudice, and rigid.

Evolutionary Lesson

The Moon in these positions describes an evolutionary lesson to establish a reliable base so that the person can safely process his or her emotions and guarantee constructive development in life. There is a need to build a foundation that provides sustenance and stability, a place where emotions and vulnerabilities can be expressed and worked on. If taken too far, this can lead to an imbalance that manifests in excessive withdrawal or a lack of emotional communication. Positively, a framework of stability can be found in the reliability of a family environment or a physical place to which one feels strongly connected.

The Moon in Gemini ♊, in the 3rd House, or in Aspect to Mercury ☿

— *The personalizing process, the nature of one's personal connection with life, emotional associations, the management of emotions, the orientation of the growth process.*

— *Security needs, the management of intimacy, one's approach to vulnerabilities, one's support system.*

With the Moon in Gemini, in the third house, or in aspect to Mercury, a person establishes a personal connection with life on the basis of the need to understand the diversity of existence and successfully navigate its currents. Consequently, one's personal approach and perspective of life is colored by a yearning for learning, an openness to a wealth of experiences, and an aspiration to connect seemingly separate phenomena. The person will emotionally relate with elements in life that support this orientation.

Learning begins within one's personal world; the individual tries to intellectually understand his or her emotions so they can be better processed and directed. Knowledge provides a sense of security; thus with these configurations one moves from a purely instinctive and untamed emotional expression to a more regulated and conscious approach. Emotions are observed and analyzed so they can be understood within the context of everyday life. Sometimes this learning process occurs through extended conversations about feelings or the nature of people in general; at other times, it occurs through simply watching the way people interact and identifying their patterns of behavior. Each sequence of life becomes a study, and over time a broad perspective of human nature is acquired through these observations. Such a perspective helps one better manage one's own emotional responses and gain a better sense of direction in life. Security is obtained in finding logic and common sense in the way life runs and how people interact; through understanding the particularities of emotions, one begins to understand the wide-ranging dynamics of culture and existence.

Since the person is more attuned to environmental dynamics, cultural and world events significantly influence personal development and maturation; one's identity is colored by external events and the circumstances of one's geographical location. Synchronizing one's personal rhythm with the external rhythm, growth and development are enhanced by emotionally absorbing the diverse dynamics intermingling in the environment—everything is taken in and processed.

Sometimes, when failing to synchronize with the environment, feelings of awkwardness emerge. One may not communicate or behave in ways that are understood by others and as a result feel emotionally insecure. The pressure to adapt to the environment and integrate into its flow can at times be very stressful. However, usually the person learns quickly, mostly through observation, and eventually transcends the feeling of awkwardness.

When mismanaged, overly adapting to external dynamics can lead to an identity crisis whereby one develops a public persona that does not reflect one's true self. Copying others in order to feel a part of the environmental interplay, one may turn into a chameleon, lose his or her center, and become fragmented. Often the identity crisis heightens a fear of shame. For example, a person may hide or deny his or her background from the public for fear it is not considered sophisticated enough or in line with the current trend. In more balanced scenarios, the person is able to learn from encountered diversity while staying grounded. In this case, authenticity is not compromised by continual exposure, but rather enriched by it.

Because one's inner rhythm has to synchronize with the outer rhythm, these influences also require a person to speed up the emotional assimilation process. When involved with outer dynamics, there is no opportunity to stop the course of life and take time off: everything happens simultaneously and is often outside of one's control. These circumstances can be compared to a person attempting to catch a train in a foreign and busy train station; the need to compute diverse information and simultaneous events requires a personal adjustment. If one is not up to speed in grasping the information, the train is not going to wait. Similarly, emotions have to be processed faster for a person to feel ready for a sequence of events—the mind pressures the emotions to accelerate processing time.

A better understanding of emotional mechanisms helps to accelerate emotional processing. Possessing a mental awareness of emotions prevents one from dwelling too long on difficult situations. For example, in the event of a trauma, the mind thinks through better ways of coping; thus the mind becomes a tool that faciliates working through potential pain and difficulty. Discussing, reading about related matters, and educating oneself helps the person gain insight into emotional quandaries. Once logic is found behind the reasons for the pain, it often makes it easier for the person to overcome a situation and move on.

Positively, the mind's influence on emotions allows a person to become more emotionally aware, sophisticated, and perceptive, increasing his or her ability to navigate more successfully through life's diversity. Negatively, discrepancies between the pace of the mind and the emotions causes a split between these two dimensions of consciousness. When this happens, acquired knowledge is not integrated into one's system and the person ends up emotionally incapable of applying what he or she has learned—intellectual reasoning is detached from emotional insecurity. Typically the person ends up overrationalizing emotional experiences without truly feeling them. Sometimes this dynamic manifests in talking compulsively because every casual experience triggers a lengthy conversation. As the mind tries to control the emotions, the emotions end up controlling the speech.

Under these influences, emotional associations occur with elements that represent knowledge, openness, culture, liberalism, and diversity. For example, individuals may identify with new ideas or trends and update their personal identity with the symbols of modern times.

Differently, they may become eternal students "living" in bookstores or university hall benches. In general, they are fascinated by people and life, constantly observing movements in an effort to understand people's underlying motivations; in this process they find answers to their own personal life dilemmas. This "anthropological" outlook often includes exposure to foreign environments and the necessity of integrating into multiple cultural rhythms.

Periodically, the person may need to travel and explore the diversity of life. Strongly inclined toward urbanism and modernity, one may want to relocate to a larger metropolitan area. However for others, the fascination is oriented more toward primal cultures that portray an authentic facet of life. Learning and expanding one's own egocentric structure opens up a wide variety of cultural experiences.

Establishing a support system that nurtures both freedom of movement and spirit is essential. One requires an environment that provides the opportunity to continue learning whether through books, cultural experiences, or observing life. Having an open and liberal environment, as well as the financial freedom to explore life, is fundamental.

– One's family life, sense of belonging, nurturing needs, the relationship with one's parents—especially the mother, the mother's personality.

With a Gemini, third house, or Mercury aspecting Moon, the child tends to learn more by interacting with the environment rather than solely being influenced by the parents. Usually the child is sensitive, absorbing many impressions from school and or social dynamics. In some cases, the parents are liberal and open in their approach, encouraging individual exploration and learning. The family may travel frequently and expose the child to a wide variety of experiences and cultures.

In other cases, the parents may place too much importance on the outside world, lacking the confidence and consistency to serve as role models. A child may go as far as losing respect for his or her parents, feeling alienated or embarrassed by them. Compared to what he or she is exposed to environmentally, the parents may be perceived as being out of sync with modern times, creating mentality gaps between the two generations. Feeling misunderstood as a result of these gaps, the child may refrain from sharing experiences with the parents.

Being open to external dynamics can lead to an identity crisis and a feeling of rootlessness. For example, this may occur when a family moves a lot or immigrates to a foreign country and the child is exposed to a totally new culture. The pressures of assimilation can create identity confusion as the new culture overshadows the connection to personal origins leaving the child feeling torn between different worlds. Until differences are integrated, the child may feel that he or she doesn't belong anywhere. In spite of being socially active, this feeling of rootlessnes can lead to nervous tension, a tendency to disassociate from the family, and a feeling of alienation.

In other situations, the family itself may embody cross-cultural dynamics. The parents may come from different ethnic or mentality backgrounds, exposing the child to different customs and languages within the household. Right from the start, he or she is exposed to the vastness of the world and learns to assimilate input from a wide variety of sources. Often this generates a nomadic feeling of being at ease with everyone everywhere, but unable to personally identify with any specific place, culture, or family.

The core need of a Gemini Moon person is to learn and grow by assimilating new concepts. Quite often, the child with these Moon placements is the one bringing new knowledge home and educating the family about different ways to face life's challenges. The parents may provide financial security and a structure, but the child brings content and new ideas. If the parents are not open minded, the chasm between the two generations can grow ever wider because of the mentality differences. When the parents are liberal and inspiring in their wisdom, a creative channel of communication can be established between the generations with the child feeling both emotionally secure and mentally stimulated by family interactions.

Education, sophistication, and intellectualism may be emphasized in some families. A cerebral mother, busy coordinating numerous social and professional events, may be quite inspiring in her managerial capabilities and social skills. The mother may be in touch with modern trends: cultivated, socially knowledgeable, and consumer-oriented. If she is overly intellectual, criticism and wit may overshadow emotional nurturing.

The Gemini archetype also represents siblings. In some cases, it may mean that a sibling serves as a parent or that he or she parents younger siblings. These configurations may portray a strong emotional bond between siblings, or depending on the rest of the birth chart, a necessity to purge and process sibling issues on an emotional level.

Evolutionary Lesson

The Moon in these positions describes an evolutionary lesson to synchronize the personal inner rhythm with outer circumstances and environmental motion. As a matter of survival, increased awareness and intellectual understanding help the individual bridge with the world, upgrade emotional processing, and adapt to ever changing life circumstances. However, it is important to understand that after being widely exposed to external dynamics, one may need periods of isolation to find oneself again. Positively, increased emotional awareness significantly enhances egocentric development and emotional intelligence.

The Moon in Cancer ♋ or in the 4th House

— *The personalizing process, the nature of one's personal connection with life, emotional associations, the management of emotions, the orientation of the growth process.*

— *Security needs, the management of intimacy, one's approach to vulnerabilities, one's support system.*

With the Moon in Cancer or the Moon in the fourth house, a person establishes a personal connection with life on the basis of founding a personal world within existence where he or she can safely develop. Consequently, one's personal approach and perspective of life is colored by a yearning for intimate connections with people or things, the need for a support system, and the desire to attune to one's internal rhythm. The person will emotionally relate with elements in life that support this orientation.

The Moon in these positions describes an evolutionary need to create supportive conditions so that one's development unfolds in a healthy way. Each life experience is emotionally processed so that it can be integrated into one's system and foster maturation. As emerging needs are addressed to support development, one learns to get in touch with weaknesses so they can eventually be overcome as growth takes place. Development must be gradual and sequential: proceeding too fast, neglecting needs, or skipping steps can lead to blockages and misplaced emotions. Like a growing child, the completion of one developmental phase sets the stage for the next—the timing cannot be rushed.

More attuned to one's internal rhythm, the person is likely to be more self-accepting instead of trying to prove anything or addressing external pressures. There is a strong need to be sheltered from stress in order to cultivate optimum conditions for a healthy emotional development; thus one strives to create an environment that is as supportive as possible. Like a baby in the womb, disturbances are best avoided. Therefore, there is less interest in success and achievement under these influences, instead the focus is on establishing intimacy and warmth so that the inner child can be nurtured.

In a healthy way, the person leads an authentic life and is in touch with him or herself, preferring more modest and intimate experiences. Through legitimizing inner processes, maturation unfolds in a healthy way and one matures from dependence to independence rather gracefully. Qualities such as emotional warmth, accessibility, trustworthiness, acceptance, and a willingness to provide support become second nature.

Negatively, the person can over process every emotion and stagnate because challenges are avoided at all costs. Overly sheltered, he or she may attempt to emotionally control the environment so that personal neediness is unconditionally supported. With a childish attitude, one may cultivate an unhealthy dependence on others, becoming manipulative and shying away from responsibility. This orientation is likely to result in an inability to cope and perform successfully in life.

On another level, the Moon in these placements describes an inclination to strongly emotionally associate with elements that resonate with one's sense of being; what is perceived as foreign and distant is considered utterly irrelevant. Everything is related to in a personal way; likes and dislikes are clearly defined. In this same vein, there is often a strong attachment to one's sense of identity such as one's family, country, or roots. Security is found through a sense of belonging and depends on being able to trust the environment when feeling vulnerable. Support, nurturing, and dedication are best found among one's own.

However, the paradox intrinsic to a Cancer or fourth house Moon is that while there is a tendency to shy away from foreign elements, at some point the need to reach out emerges. One's approach shifts according to tides and phases—timing is everything. Drawing a comparison to the pregnancy process, a baby in the womb is kept warm and sheltered to concentrate on its development. But once the time has come, reaching out and exploring new dimensions of being becomes instinctively relevant. Thus one moves from security needs to developmental needs—in and out of the shell.

Accordingly, when encountering something new, a "courting dance" is set in motion for the sake of establishing a feeling of familiarity with the new subject. Typically this "courting dance" manifests as getting close then withdrawing—two steps forward, then two steps back—until one becomes familiar, more acquainted, and secure. If the courted subject happens to be a person, that person is likely to get confused by mixed messages: feeling invited on the one hand and then later ignored by the Cancer or fourth house Moon person. What must be remembered is that it is just a process of familiarization—processes cannot be rushed!

Once intimacy is successfully established, the person can also provide nurturing, comfort, and security for others. As much as the person is involved with personal needs, he or she may also be protective of others and immediately reach out to support those in a vulnerable position. The Moon's influence in these positions makes one very human, stripping one of any pretense.

Life, however, does not always provide the latitude to process and mature without any disturbance. It is not possible to be completely sheltered from stress and necessarily so. We do not live in a linear world where everything happens gradually and sequentially; there are many cross-currents that one must simultaneously cope with. Personal growth processes may get interrupted by unexpected events—yet when this is the case, skipped steps can be recaptured at a later stage in life. Personal development must adapt to the pressure of facing unexpected challenges so that healthy coping mechanisms can develop. However, if personal processes are frequently interrupted during developmental years, unresolved emotions can result. A childhood filled with ruptures and sudden changes may cause misplaced emotions. The person may subsequently spend years recapturing what was missed. In extreme cases, excessive trauma can lead to arrested emotional development. While the body continues to grow, the emotions are stunted, manifesting in chronic existential insecurities. Healing comes in reestablishing a safe haven and a relatively stable life where emotional processing can resume in a healthy way.

With the Moon in these positions, establishing a support system is essential. One realizes it is not always possible to be on top of everything; when experiencing weakness, it is important to be able to rely on someone else. In turn one may assume the sheltering role and provide support for someone else in time of need. This is why the support system of a family is so important. One's family does not always consist of blood relatives but may, for example, include trusted friends.

> – *One's family life, sense of belonging, nurturing needs, the relationship with one's parents—especially the mother, the mother's personality.*

With a Cancer or fourth house Moon, the family environment may radiate acceptance and support. The parents may be relatively simple spirited, accessible, and modest. Without being consciously aware of it, the parents may shelter their children from outside stress and emphasize family values above achievement. Family members may be unconditionally accepted, but strangers frowned upon. The strong sense of family may, for example, manifest in having a grandparent live in or through maintaining close contact with extended family. The permissive tendency within the family may have its downside when problems are not adequately confronted. For example, circumstances such as low school grades, excessive weight, or fears of driving may linger and never be properly addressed because there is no pressure to overcome them. Conversely, when too much pressure is imposed, the child is likely to shut down and become irresponsive. Finding the right balance between support and challenge is the key. The mother may be a classic housewife: dedicated, nurturing, protective, and strong spirited within the household, but weak outside of it. The child may feel safe and in absolute trust yet lack guidance and backbone when having to confront external pressure because the parents themselves lack this experience.

In a more difficult scenario, one or both parents may be weak, anxiety prone, and childish to a debilitating extent. Dreading the day the child becomes mature enough to leave, the parents may end up overprotecting the child and keep him or her weak and dependent to maintain their personal feeling of safety. Excessive attachment and overidentification may create circumstances where the parents expect the child to be an extension of themselves, wanting him or her to like what they like and fear what they fear. In other circumstances, their weakness can lead to a role reversal where the child takes on most of the parental responsibilities. A sick, needy, or irresponsible parent may require constant care and attention and in such a way keep the umbilical cord uncut.

Similarly, the family environment may be emotionally dysfunctional with one or both parents constantly consumed by shifting emotions. Because of their own emotional wounds, the parents may be self-absorbed and fail to properly care for the child, emotionally neglecting him or her. A climate of inconsistency, fragility, and unreliability can heavily stress the child's own emotions and project developmental problems on to the next generation.

In healthier ways, these configurations manifest as a deep bond with the maternal figure and a healthy family intimacy. Accessible parents offer support without preventing the child from exploring life. The child in turn expresses warm and protective emotional qualities. In this regard, having a pet can be a healthy outlet to process nurturing needs.

Evolutionary Lesson

The Moon in these positions describes an evolutionary lesson to allow the ego to fully form in an authentic and organic way—through healthy emotional attachment, the person's sense of identity and connection to life is established. Developmental processes must be allowed to unfold as naturally as possible while understanding that stress and crisis are also a part of life. Thus a balance must be found between permissiveness and support versus healthy boundaries and challenges. When this balance is established, a truly integrated, wholesome, self-motivated, and affectionate person can emerge.

The Moon in Leo ♌, in the 5th House, or in Aspect to the Sun ☉

— *The personalizing process, the nature of one's personal connection with life, emotional associations, the management of emotions, the orientation of the growth process.*

— *Security needs, the management of intimacy, one's approach to vulnerabilities, one's support system.*

With the Moon in Leo, in the fifth house, or in aspect to the Sun, a person establishes a personal connection with life on the basis of acknowledging one's role in nurturing and enhancing life. Consequently, one's personal approach and perspective of life is colored by creative desire, the association with one's lineage and progeny, and the need to make each moment meaningful. The person will emotionally relate with elements in life that support this orientation.

There is an evolutionary need to nurture and foster one's creative potential. Resources and attention are invested toward fulfilling one's personal sense of purpose with the intent of eventually seeing it bloom and inspire the environment. People with this signature perceive their personal world as important, not only for their own growth, but also for its relevance to the environment.

The person possesses a strong emotional nature and can move other people or in turn be moved by life circumstances. Every emotion is given a stage, and in such a way a feeling of being alive and involved prevails. Strong attachments are created with people and experiences— the details of each encounter heightened. Everything is experienced and expressed rather strongly.

Concentrating on intimate needs and personal expression, one demands a lot attention from the familial or social environment, but usually the favor is returned through a generous spirit and one's self investment in life. Positively expressed, a vibrant personality conveys warmth, generosity, playfulness, and respect. The person exhibits a healthy sense of ambition motivated by creative initiatives. However when mismanaged, emotions are excessively dramatized and narcissism takes over when a bottomless need for attention overpowers healthy motivations. As a result, dramatic crises and problems are created without a true basis, unnecessarily complicating existence. Jealousy and competitiveness emerge and are directed toward anyone who naturally draws attention.

With the Moon in these placements, one gradually cultivates personal creative capacities, giving oneself the necessary time to potentially mature and grow into positions of influence and inspiration. Aspiring to lead a meaningful life, the person is naturally inclined to emotionally associate with elements symbolizing respect, heroism, and talent. As a result, people who have achieved important deeds and manifested their creativity—such as artists, leaders, or mavericks—are likely to draw admiration.

On another level, these configurations may encourage the rise of women's role in society. The symbolism of motherhood attributed to the Moon combined with the natural leadership qualities of Leo can lead to the promotion and veneration of women's spirit and causes. Consequently, one may identify with women whose nature is inspiring.

The Leo fixation to leave a legacy is not solely based on the need to secure one's sense of validity in existence; it is also rooted in the survival instinct to defy extinction and promote the continuity of life. When the Leo archetype colors the Moon, it emphasizes the need to nurture life and pass the torch on to the next generation so that the legacy can continue in full splendor. Accordingly, children may be an important focus because they represent the continuation of life. An individual may, as a result, strongly associate with children, especially his or her own, and invest significant emotional energy into their development. Nurturing life may also manifest in personal care and attention for the animal world. On a professional level: one will care for successors who continue the business or line of work. The strong emotional association with the successor can at times bring about excessive expectations and overprotectiveness. Generosity and attention can camouflage emotional control as the individual may expect absolute loyalty in return for his or her generosity. High expectations are bound to lead to disappointment.

Under these influences, security is found in living a meaningful life, whether it is established through glorious achievements or simple deeds, and seeing that life has at least somewhat improved because of one's efforts. Living can be a daily celebration as one feels joy and takes pleasure in the little details that constitute one's life. Thus a playful approach can foster fun and positivism. Failing to find intimate meaning can induce depression. When feeling insecure, the person may become jealous of other people's success. In order to transcend this negative approach, there is a need to be proactive; engaging in life and having goals or hobbies can provide a healthy sense of meaning. Similarly, security and meaning can be found in seeing one's children or legacy develop and prosper; an important concern is knowing that life will continue.

A support system is necessary to develop personality and creative potential. Support may result from encouragement, vocational guidance, financial funding for projects, or respect for personal life choices. One needs a strong wind pushing from behind to spring forward in life with the best chances for success. This form of support can be returned when one nurtures other people's potential.

— One's family life, sense of belonging, nurturing needs, the relationship with one's parents—especially the mother, the mother's personality.

The Moon in these positions can describe a family environment that provides special attention and caring as each child is perceived as a treasure to cherish. Beyond emotional nurturing, attention may be focused on developing the child's creative potential, for example, by enrolling him or her in all kinds of artistic courses. In many cases, the mother is the leading figure in the family, the one who is dependable and possesses the character to manage the family. Sometimes the mother is glorified because of her strong spirit. The family dynamics may be supportive and emphasize togetherness and unconditional trust in each other.

In other cases, the person may come from a respected lineage, adding a sense of pride to one's belonging. With or without a prestigious heritage, there is often an undercurrent of expectation in the family, usually leading to pronounced parental involvement in the child's life, even into adulthood. From the choice of profession to the choice of a spouse, opinions are stated, and in extreme cases, the child is strongly pressured to meet family expectations. In more ideal circumstances, the parents are involved without applying such pressure.

When expectations are exaggerated, one or both parents may control the child to an extreme degree because of their excessive emotional identification. The child's privacy may be totally invaded, supposedly for the parents to monitor what is in the child's "best" interest. A parent, usually the mother, may also project her unfulfilled fantasies on to the child, for example, through enforcing piano and violin lessons, or perhaps ballet classes. Every lover the child dares to present to the parents undergoes scrutiny. Unless rebellion kicks in, the child may become his or her parents' clone.

In other circumstances, the mother may be intensely involved in her own emotions or self-actualization needs to the point of neglecting her child. The mother may be extremely narcissistic and even compete with the child for attention, with the child's reality revolving around the mother's desires and tantrums. When taken to further extremes, the mother may even sabotage the child's own development because of her jealousy; this is usually more pronounced when the child is a girl because the identification and competition are more obvious.

The potential for jealousy not only exists between the mother and the child, but also between siblings. Parents may play a game of favorites and unconsciously stimulate these dynamics when assessing which child has the "best genes" and is most likely to bring honor to the lineage. Sometimes, one child possesses remarkable talent and overshadows the others without the parent's initial desire to discriminate in any way. In this circumstance, favoritism and jealousy may be the natural outcome, even if unintended.

At its best the Leo, fifth house, or Sun aspected Moon describes an approach to life that comes from the heart. It represents an ego that is strong and grounded thus able to pour its wealth into existence with gratitude and love. This love comes from appreciating life and manifests in self-love, faith in existence, and kindness. This heart-centered approach is sometimes the result of motherly devotion to the children in the family.

Evolutionary Lesson

The Moon in these positions describes an evolutionary lesson to nurture creative development and purpose, and in such a way nurture the life impulse inside every person. Learning to provide care and attention naturally fosters generosity. There is a lesson in expressing emotions—giving them the full volume they deserve to help make life a celebrated experience while maintaining a balance so that excessive drama is avoided.

The Moon in Virgo ♍, in the 6th House, or in Aspect to Mercury ☿

— *The personalizing process, the nature of one's personal connection with life, emotional associations, the management of emotions, the orientation of the growth process.*

— *Security needs, the management of intimacy, the approach to vulnerabilities, one's support system.*

With the Moon in Virgo, in the sixth house, or in aspect to Mercury, a person establishes a personal connection with life on the basis of the desire to support the function of life and improve the use of resources. Consequently, one's personal approach and perspective of life is colored by a yearning for healthy development and refinement, and a need to properly direct how life is managed. The person will emotionally relate with elements in life that support this orientation.

There is an evolutionary need to foster healthy emotional development and processing. Similar to Gemini's influence, also ruled by Mercury, the mind typically intervenes in emotional processes. With the Virgo archetype, the purpose is to monitor, regulate, and manage emotions in order to ensure that one develops efficiently and productively. Closely supervising every phase of development, the person tunes into every nuance of feelings and emerging emotions. As one becomes progressively aware of problems—such as emotional excess, debilitating weakness, or dysfunctional family dynamics—one gradually learns ways to readjust.

Concerned about proper function, knowledge is used to improve emotional nurturing, general life management, and intimate environmental conditions. As a result, the person may, for example, analyze psychological interplay in the family, regulate dietary habits, or create an aesthetic home environment, seeking conditions that support healthy emotional function and development.

Positively, emotional analysis enables one to better understand processes and heal potentially unbalanced tendencies, increasing emotional intelligence, awareness, refinement, sensitivity, and caretaking capabilities. This approach helps a person better manage potential stress and find the appropriate balance between the need for security and the need to embrace new challenges. As performance levels and the quality of one's life improves, dysfunction gradually decreases. Efficiency, order, and organizational skills help elevate the spirit through promoting a healthier lifestyle on all levels.

Negatively, excessive emotional analysis and control can end up disrupting natural cycles instead of enhancing them. Fearing problems and dysfunction, one may become overly self-conscious and obsessed with trivial details. Accordingly, the inability to tolerate any form of irregularity may increase an acute sensitivity to disorder, even physical dirt. Control needs and low tolerance levels make one less adaptable and more easily upset when things do not turn out as planned. A fear of losing control may induce frequent "allergic" reactions to a range of diverse factors. For example, when aspiring for order and perfect function, the person may create a sterile environment and become obsessed with cleanliness, or become intolerant of natural things such as sand, bugs, or exuberant children. Similarly, the need for predictability can generate anxiety issues. To feel safe, the person yearns to control everything and in the process ends up losing trust in the natural process of life. In extreme cases, fears can escalate into obsessive compulsive behavior until trust in life is reaffirmed.

On another level, these influences describe an emotional association with elements that embody the highest level of function, balanced proportions, order, refinement, productivity, clarity, cleanliness, and safety. For example, attention may be invested in giving and receiving high quality service or in improving one's health through working out and eating nutritious food. Aesthetics can play an important role in the person's life because beauty is perceived to reflect balanced proportions. Great attention may be directed toward enhancing one's physical appearance or in developing a taste and talent for design. Feeling beautiful or surrounding oneself with beauty and serenity helps one feel secure. In another way, feeling functional or useful through having a job and an active life are key factors that contribute to a feeling of emotional balance.

Emotional attachment to high standards and balanced proportions may, however, have its limitations. Beyond the potential for anxiety, as previously described, one may become very critical of perceived flaws and seek security through perfection. The person may fear weakness in general. Anything that is considered inappropriate such as poor performance, physical unattractiveness, or emotional weakness may become the subject of derision and sarcasm. Accordingly, the person often possesses a pronounced sense of humor—the jokes usually at someone else's expense. This attitude camouflages a dread of ridicule and shame, and shows that underneath it all the person with the Moon in these positions can be hard on him or herself.

With organizational skills, a person is often a support system for other people. Managing, caretaking, and logistical planning are helpful for others who may not be as detail oriented. However, learning to receive support is no less important; this may be as simple as accepting encouragement or compliments for one's work. With the Moon in these placements, one needs a support system to enhance performance and live in a healthier way. Support may be found through healthcare guidance, logistical planning, or by learning practical skills.

> *— One's family life, sense of belonging, nurturing needs, the relationship with one's parents—especially the mother, the mother's personality.*

The Virgo, sixth house, or Mercury aspected Moon can describe a family dynamic where the parents are highly functional and busy producing. A sense of duty may be emphasized, pressuring each member to perform particular tasks for the sake of a larger endeavor. The mother may be a "super-mom"—gifted at multitasking, multitalented, tireless, and dutiful. She may closely take care of every family member's problems and excel in all domestic tasks, or work hard professionally and take care of all the domestic duties during her "spare" time. However, goals of efficiency and productivity may overshadow the need to accept vulnerabilities; in fact, guilt may be projected toward family members deemed incapable or unproductive. Aimless days at the beach may be perceived as waste of time or even parasitical. The child may receive close attention and care, but end up overprotected with every movement monitored in fear of making a mistake.

In some cases, it may be that only some family members are highly functional while others are totally dependent and less capable for varying reasons. Perhaps a family member is dysfunctional, mentally challenged, or disabled and requires constant attention. The contrast between efficiency and dysfunction may be strongly emphasized within the family dynamics.

In other circumstances, the family atmosphere may emanate sophistication and grace. The child may grow up in an environment where modernity, civility, and culture are emphasized, persuading the child to be mild-mannered, serious, and appropriate. A beautiful or elegant and refined mother may be admired for her style and taste, but possibly be "too refined" to touch. Emotional needs may be contained because of a concern about being disruptive. This may be particularly critical when the child is in early infancy and needs to be able to express him or herself more freely and be emotionally understood. The mother may easily feel overwhelmed and panic at the unpredictible and even chaotic aspect of raising a child, preferring when possible to leave the child in the care of nannies while she attends professional or social duties. In this case, the home atmosphere is relatively sterile while public esteem is sought after—shame becomes the one thing to be avoided at all costs.

In the long run, the family's strong attachment to perfection is likely to create a crisis if apparently civilized behavior covers emotional distress. Within the family, emotional repression is likely to erupt in various dysfunctions such as alcoholism or mental health issues. In a similar way, families may not necessarily emphasize aesthetic and sophisticated qualities in a modern sense but rather extol the virtues of purity, righteousness, and exaggerated modesty. Emotional or sexual chastity may be expected often coming from heavy religious conditioning within the family.

Family dysfunction may also manifest in heavy criticism or possible humiliation. The criticism may be expressed seriously and sharply or through constant humoristic sarcasm and ridicule. Jokes about "fat" or "stupid" people may float around the house and while they are "funny" end up generating an atmosphere where everyone becomes self-conscious for fear of being the subject of the next joke. A chronically dissatisfied mother can make the child feel his or her natural expression is always inappropriate. Whether her criticism is about hair not being in its "right place," lovers not coming from "good enough" families, or the child's taste never being refined enough—reasons are never lacking.

As if civilizing a wild indigenous being, the mother may try to completely control every choice and direct the child's future, training him or her to excel in a rather industrial fashion. Enforcing sophisticated codes of conduct and dress, insisting on high levels of education, and asking for perfect performances may indeed serve her children in some ways. But while intentions may be pure with a genuine desire to help, the child ends up denied of his or her authentic expression; in order to keep healthy proportions, flexibility is an absolute necessity.

Scenarios may be reversed when the Virgo, sixth house, or Mercury aspected Moon child is living in a chaotic family where the parents are barely functional. In this case, the child may take the role of restoring order.

In a healthier fashion, the mother may use her strength and expertise to enhance the child's development in a supportive and loving way. Patient enough to address problems and come up with strategies to overcome them, she may be a tremendous help to the child. Instead of repressing natural behavior for the sake of order, organizational skills are used to bring the best out of the child in an authentic way.

Evolutionary Lesson

The Moon in these positions describes an evolutionary lesson to direct emotional processing in ways that enhance one's development. Emotional health means learning to harness emotions yet doing so in a way that doesn't nullify their natural expression. The purpose of the Virgo Moon archetype is to heal areas of dysfunction and or trauma, and improve function. In addition, lessons include understanding that knowledge and control have their benefits but must be used in a holistic context; leading a healthy lifestyle also includes learning to be spontaneous and to trust the flow of life.

The Moon in Libra ♎, in the 7th House, or in Aspect to Venus ♀

- *The personalizing process, the nature of one's personal connection with life, emotional associations, the management of emotions, the orientation of the growth process.*

- *Security needs, the management of intimacy, one's approach to vulnerabilities, one's support system.*

With the Moon in Libra, in the seventh house, or in aspect to Venus, a person establishes a personal connection with life on the basis of wanting to find balance through the unification of opposites. Consequently, one's personal approach and perspective of life is colored by the need to learn about others, develop new perspectives, and identify what components are missing in order to create harmony. The person will emotionally relate with elements in life that support this orientation.

There is an evolutionary need to pursue one's personal growth through experiencing life's polarities. The person strives to understand issues from a variety of angles and gains a sense of security when balance is attained. For example, one's parents may come from different backgrounds, and when exposed to each of their unique orientations, the tendency is to first identify with one parent's perspective and then after a period of time switch to the other's for the sake of eventually finding balance. After having absorbed and processed each parent's influence, he or she may seek to emotionally identify with something else altogether.

Not wanting to firmly take sides, one strives to remain emotionally neutral. Such an approach usually fosters emotional maturity and wisdom because depth and understanding is gained by exploring different perspectives. In search for a more unifying outlook on life, at some point the person is likely to detach from parental influence and explore what other people or cultures have to say and offer. Different views are considered in every area of life, whether trivial things such as the way to cook an entrée, or more fundamental issues such as where to belong and what priorities to associate with.

Commonly, the person tends to shy away from patriotism and searches for a sense of identity that includes elements foreign to one's biological origins. This orientation is not always conscious and immediate. As a child, the person may not question his or her identity right away, but following travel or social exchange he or she may start to become aware of other ways of being and doing things. Exposure to diversity makes one realize that something is lacking in a single-minded perspective. This lack creates a feeling of restlessness, alienating one from one's origins.

Naturally different approaches, backgrounds, or cultural ways strongly appeal to the person with these chart configurations because of the desire to learn from opposites. Security is eventually found when harmonizing between different or polarized ways, but until coming full circle and finding balance, the inclination is to reach out to the "other side" and focus on what is outside of oneself. Through this process, a lot of power is given to "the other." Trust is usually granted quickly as one easily identifies with people and their stories. As a result, the individual is able to emotionally understand others and their points of view.

Positively, emotional growth is accelerated as the person constantly integrates new elements into his or her personal world and gradually becomes more aware, knowledgeable, and wholesome. Fairness, compassion, and inner balance, as well as openness, accessibility, and humility are pronounced. Equipped with a broader perspective that considers all sides, the person acts wisely and is less likely to get emotionally carried away or react on a whim.

Alternatively, difficulty can manifest if a person overidealizes what others have and rejects his or her own sense of self. Such an approach is likely to induce confusion and emotional abuse because the person is not emotionally grounded and loses a sense of internal balance. Typically when operating in such a way, an identity crisis becomes inevitable because of a chronic sense of dissatisfaction with oneself.

Upon experiencing an identity crisis, emotional scattering can occur. One may move from relationship to relationship, ideal to ideal, cause to cause, or get lost in the extremes in the search for what is wholesome and right. Each time one attempts to settle for a particular choice, a sense of emotional lack emerges reminding one of what is missing. While continually exploring life's multiple facets, a point of clarity may eventually be reached when the person realizes that the search for external balance is an escape from oneself. Consequently, the need may emerge to return full circle and embrace one's origins. Ultimately, the yearning for balance can lead one back "home" because this is the bit of oneself that was disregarded and originally caused internal polarization.

Similarly, the aspiration to find security through balance may create an attachment to perfection to the point where one is not satisfied with anything less than absolute harmony. These high standards can make one reluctant to emotionally identify with anything, seeing incompletion in everything. This state of mind fosters indecision, wastes potential, and leads to a feeling of chronic alienation and frustration. A more flexible approach must be adopted including accepting life as a process and journey instead of seeing it as still harmony.

With the Moon in these positions, the person emotionally identifies with elements, opinions, and ways that reflect holism, social harmony, and union. There is also a strong tendency to embrace controversy. Always assessing all sides, the person may identify with any position that is perceived as undervalued or misrepresented by the consensus. For example, one may emotionally associate with a minority culture if that culture happens to be invalidated; the nature of that culture is less important because what emotionally affects one is the fact that there is neglect and imbalance. As a result, one's orientation and choices can often be unpredictable and shock people when taking an unpopular side.

In more ordinary cases, the Moon in these positions reflects a strong emotional need to be in a relationship and have the experience of togetherness. Romanticism, generosity, grace, and a willingness to compromise personal needs may come naturally. From observing people and listening to them, greater psychological insights are gained. The person often takes the role of the counselor offering perspective and direction to others.

A solid support system can be established by creating a sense of union and an atmosphere of tolerance. Being there for others and having patience and a sincere interest in people's stories serves as a comforting presence, especially for those at a disadvantage in life. In return, relationships and partnerships provide security and support— togetherness helps one feel stronger in a challenging world.

— *One's family life, sense of belonging, nurturing needs, the relationship with one's parents—especially the mother, the mother's personality.*

A Moon in Libra, the seventh house, or in aspect to Venus may reflect family dynamics where parents live in a codependent relationship and a sense of harmony is sustained by the complete compliance of one side, usually the mother. The attachment to their relationship may keep the parents from asserting their individuality in fear that it may trigger disruption and a separation. A parent may lose him or herself in the partner; sometimes when the second parent is not even emotionally available but instead busy flirting around. The Libra Moon child internalizes the imbalance, unhealthy dependence, and loss of identity in others.

The parents may also constantly compare their situation with other families and idealize the success they see outside. Because of these comparisons, the child may constantly feel inadequate and end up doing the same thing—invalidating him or herself and perceiving the grass as greener elsewhere.

In some cases, the child may feel alienated from the family because he or she is aware that the family environment is dysfunctional and internally knows that there are healthier ways of interrelating. The child may be relatively mature and possess a naturally broad awareness that allows him or her to identify the parents' mismanagement. He or she may confront the parents and try to educate them about a more balanced and appropriate way of dealing with each other and life. This dynamic can even go as far as the child fantasizing about being adopted by other parents. It may be that he or she feels more comfortable with a friend's parents instead of his or her own, again reflecting the idealization of what others have. Upon becoming an adult, typically this child will aspire to do exactly the opposite of what his or her parents did and create entirely different family dynamics.

In other circumstances, the child's parents may be polarized, either regularly fighting with one another or actually divorced. Typically, the tendency is for the child to play the parents' counselor and try to negotiate between them. Acquiring psychological insights from the battleground, the child becomes highly perceptive and mature, and tries to be fair in accommodating both parents, usually at the price of personal compromise. Sometimes the child takes one parent's side and fights the other, then later on changes sides and identifies with the other parent. This dynamic may expand beyond the actual relationship between the parents and come to include new relationships formed with the parents' new partners before or after a divorce. The child witnesses the parents going through the motions of excitement and separations in relationships and grows up with mixed feelings about relationships in general. The family may come to include half siblings. In some cases, despite the changes and disruptions in the family structure, a sense of community and tribe may be created by extending the family unit and welcoming differences and mixture. In these scenarios, the mother is usually social, liberal, and has an open spirit.

In more balanced scenarios, parents are highly aware and conscious, offering the child greater life perspectives while respecting his or her individuality. Grounded and yet open-minded, they may successfully establish a balance between finding a sense of belonging as a family unit and embracing an inclusive approach to diversity. Values of tolerance, kindness, and support are presented as foundations for healthy emotional expression.

Evolutionary Lesson

The Moon in these positions describes an evolutionary lesson to broaden one's sense of identity and establish a more holistic sense of self. This process may lead to confusion because the individual is simultaneously processing a wide range of emotional impressions. The key to successfully managing this dynamic is to remain grounded and refer back to fundamental values when assessing new and diverse approaches so that emotional scattering and identity crises are reduced. The way to stay grounded is to avoid overidealizing what one lacks and maintain a more neutral approach in the search for balance.

The Moon in Scorpio ♏, in the 8ᵗʰ House, or in Aspect to Pluto ♇

— *The personalizing process, the nature of one's personal connection with life, emotional associations, management of emotions, the orientation of the growth process.*

— *Security needs, the management of intimacy, the approach to vulnerabilities, one's support system.*

With the Moon in Scorpio, in the eighth house, or in aspect to Pluto, a person establishes a personal connection with life on the basis of the need to enhance growth processes and increase power. Consequently, one's personal approach and perspective of life is colored by a hunger for a more complete sense of fulfillment, a more confrontational approach toward limitations, and the courage to see the hidden truth. The person will emotionally relate with elements in life that support this orientation.

With these configurations, the evolutionary intent is to enhance one's personal development and realign the ego with the growth requirements of the soul. Because the soul operates through the ego, in this phase one's ego must evolve so that it can better serve the soul's evolutionary purpose. In everyday life, this means that one's personal approach to existence needs to be worked on to foster deeper levels of expression. This can consist of, for example, deepening one's emotional nature and redefining how personal security needs and attachments are managed. The purpose is to create an emotional metamorphosis whereby one can become deeper, healthier, and emotionally stronger.

To stimulate growth, limitations intrinsic to one's emotional reality come to the surface—either through natural introspection and self-analysis or through crises that pressure the person to become aware of emotional dysfunction. For example, the person may experience rejection and be forced to reexamine his or her ways. Through this redefinition process, he or she becomes more emotionally conscious and can change unhealthy emotional patterns. No longer able to live in denial, the person seeks ways to outgrow limitations and heal problems. Some may choose to use the help of a therapist while others do the work on their own. In one way or another, an emotional rebirth is sought and tremendous psychological energy is invested in that process.

With time, the person gains emotional self-awareness and often becomes a natural psychologist who identifies other people's emotional blockages as well. Knowing pain, naivete is lost, and one becomes highly perceptive often spotting cues in other people's behavior that reveal their psychological inclinations—emotional dishonesty or hidden insecurities are fast uncovered. Once issues are identified, there is usually little tolerance for maintaining things as they are or allowing them to stagnate through repeating problematic patterns. This approach is also directed toward others; consequently, the person may appear confrontational or intense when wanting to change things and refuse to accept other people's denial issues. Yet because change is required in the most emotionally sensitive spots, it cannot be rushed.

Conversely, if a person with these Moon placements chooses to remain in denial when personal dysfunctions emerge, the intensity of limitations is likely to increase until measures are taken to correct them. Emotional shocks may be experienced as a reaction to denial. Feeling disempowered through the pain, it is no longer possible to escape or avoid taking action toward healing and behavioral change.

The pressure to evolve one's emotional nature intensifies the pace of one's development; an individual may outgrow situations and people faster than others and therefore break away from attachment in surprising ways. At times, this approach can be highly threatening to the environment. For example, the person may feel the need to sever ties with a loved one because of an unhealthy dynamic, but the partner may not be ready for that. There is a paradox with this Moon placement. On the one hand, there is a need to deal with very deep insecurities and therefore sensitivity and patience are required. On the other hand, the need for change can force one to be firm and uncompromising.

The need to evolve is constantly contrasted by the need for security; finding the balance between strength and weakness is not always obvious and can put one through emotionally trying situations. In order to resolve emotional problems, one may end up uprooting or cutting ties by choice or circumstance and experience emotional distress as a result. Yet the intent is to do what is intuitively sound to support growth and evolution. It is important to note that the person with these signatures may experience both ends of this dichotomy: either the one inducing a separation, or the one experiencing abandonment.

Positively, emotional introspection and inner work can render one highly conscious, insightful, and courageous in challenging situations. Survival instincts are refined over time, allowing one to be more resistant and capable of emotionally handling existence. The person masters the balance between emotional strength and sensitivity, and being deeply committed and emotionally supportive yet accepting of necessary changes. With a mature, honest, and direct approach to life, one tends to refrain from pleasing others by adopting politically correct attitudes and instead opts to get to the core of the matter. Upon making a choice, one's emotional investment is usually sincere with the intent of giving the best of oneself.

Negatively speaking, recurrent emotional trials may take their toll and render the person emotionally fractured. Post-traumatic stress may be experienced to varying degrees of severity. One may become consumed by chronic insecurities and abandonment fears that take the form of possessiveness, obsession, distrust, and an insatiable need for reassurance. Insecurities can manifest as a need for a lot of emotional discussions and processing, but in further extremes can result in manipulative behavior and emotional blackmail. The reason for these emotional conditions can be identified in one's early life experiences of separation or rejection, or even past life traumas.

Alternatively, the desire for growth and development may take the form of a chronic hunger for more in life; the need for more affection, more money, more sexuality, or more power may become all consuming if one feels stuck in existing conditions. Emotional security may never stabilize unless constant increase and growth is guaranteed. The relentless hunger is usually a compensation for self-worth problems and possible memories of emotional abuse whereby one felt deprived, abandoned, and or defenseless.

In extreme cases, a person's chronic hunger may lead to dishonesty and using others for hidden agendas. To satisfy personal needs, the person attracts people and situations that appear to answer these cravings and forms a commitment without revealing hidden opportunistic intentions. Once the need is met, commitments are then severed leaving the partner with unfulfilled promises. This vampirism and opportunism creates negative karma based on the misuse of emotional power. Such a person never feels satisfied and cannot experience true affection and love because of emotional corruption; consequently, he or she can cause a great deal of emotional damage to others. The person with the Moon in this position may also be the one who is preyed upon by this kind of parasitic character.

With the Moon in these configurations, strong attachments are created with people who have a transformative effect and help one overcome weakness. Sexuality can play an important role in one's emotional world because it serves as a means to form an emotional attachment to another. If feeling unloved or insecure, sexual needs may intensify relative to the hunger for affection. Positively, a powerful intimacy can result from deep sexual communication and bonding.

The person knows what it means to be vulnerable, rejected, or in pain and may, as a result, become a support system for those who are facing similar circumstances. For example, he or she may choose to adopt abandoned children. In other ways, one can offer support through becoming a therapist and guiding others toward emotional empowerment by healing trauma.

— One's family life, sense of belonging, nurturing needs, the relationship with one's parents—especially the mother, the mother's personality.

With a Scorpio, eighth house, or Pluto aspected Moon, strong and even symbiotic family ties may exist resulting from members relying on and supporting each other—sometimes in contrast to perceiving the external world as untrustworthy. A sense of insecurity or danger may be projected toward anything on the outskirts of the family nucleus. This attitude often originates from a fear of loss or abandonment rooted in the parents' early life experiences: they may have survived a war or been orphaned and thus infiltrate the memory of loss into the family atmosphere. Different scenarios result from these circumstances. In some cases, because of the emotional wounding, the parents may shut down emotionally and be extremely private and secretive, not explaining to the child what goes on in their world. In other cases, the parents may be emotionally manipulative because their fear of loss prevents them from letting the child grow naturally and leave the household. While the parents are reflecting a sense of emotional stagnation in these examples, the child is challenged to change these dynamics and with time outgrow the emotional dysfunction.

In some cases, strong attachment needs and insecurities may not be equally intense with all family members and thus generate misunderstandings. For example, a child may be born with unconscious past life memories of loss and cling to the mother almost obsessively while she does not understand the root of such obsessive attachment and pronounced insecurity. Obviously, such a child needs considerable support to overcome existential fears, but the mother may in her own reasoning try to resolve the situation by pushing the child away in order for him or her to learn independence. The mother may have good intentions but is subject to generate more emotional damage if she acts too abruptly and fails to identify the deeper emotional needs.

Similarly one parent, usually the mother, may be insecure in her relationship with the other parent and fear adultery or abandonment.

These fears may be validated or not, but in either case the child grows up witnessing one parent with low self-confidence and insecurities and the other parent as often unsatisfied. In the same vein, one parent may go through a transformative process from being dependent and weak to becoming self-assured, independent, and creative. Such a transformation sometimes results from a divorce between the parents. In this case, the child assimilates a positive image of renewal and realizes the possibility of positive change and overcoming debilitation.

In more extreme cases a parent, most likely the mother, emotionally rejects the child early on. Reasons vary: she may have not been ready for motherhood, suffered from post-partum depression, or simply felt no chemistry with the child. The consequences of these rejections are obviously devastating, yet not always doomed to a bitter end. It may be that a rough start pressures both sides to become more introspective and readjust; thus initial difficulty becomes a transformative experience. Failing that, the child grows up feeling insignificant, antagonized, and unloved, transporting these feelings in other areas of his or her life. For the child, the challenge remains to re-empower him or herself through a personal renewal. Understanding that the rejection is the parents' problem, and not one's own, may be a first step toward healing and creating healthier emotional dynamics in adulthood. Such an extreme scenario may also occur through the death of a parent and circumstances that abruptly expose one to the extremes of strength and weakness.

In more balanced circumstances, the parents are equipped with psychological insight and wisdom that help them manage family dynamics in a supportive and loving way. Children may learn from watching the parents go through their own changes and evolution, and thus be inspired to renew and empower themselves as well. With a deep emotional bond, the children may venture into the world knowing that the connection to the family is unshakable.

Evolutionary Lesson

The Moon in these positions describes an evolutionary lesson to accept that emotional security includes the need for change—security relies on growth. Since evolution through emotional transformation is a strong aspect with these placements, one learns that attachments in life are not permament because change is often "around the corner." When expanding his or her consciousness and feeling empowered, the person can see the benefits of change. Notwithstanding, even though attachments are bound to impermanence, they must still be nurtured and cultivated for the duration of their existence.

The Moon in Sagittarius ♐, in the 9th House, or in Aspect to Jupiter ♃

— *The personalizing process, the nature of one's personal connection with life, emotional associations, management of emotions, the orientation of the growth process.*

— *Security needs, the management of intimacy, the approach to vulnerabilities, one's support system.*

With the Moon in Sagittarius, in the ninth house, or in aspect to Jupiter, a person establishes a personal connection with life on the basis of the need to search for meaning behind every occurrence and perceive a greater potential yet to be realized. Consequently, one's personal approach and perspective of life is colored by an adventurous spirit, a yearning for authenticity and freedom of action, and a more philosophical way of thinking. The person will emotionally relate with elements in life that support this orientation.

The evolutionary need to associate a greater sense of meaning behind one's personal existence is often stimulated by a sense of limitation, especially when dealing with the immediacy of existence where everything can seem trivial and small. Sometimes the search for meaning can be a reaction to a painful crisis that served as a trigger; the individual looks for a higher spiritual reason for the pain and in such a way uncovers additional dimensions to his or her personal existence or life in general. In other circumstances, the desire for more meaning is not necessarily oriented toward spiritual understanding, but simply toward wanting a more abundant and promising life. One may have visions, goals, and hopes of living more passionately and meaningfully through mundane things such as wanting more financial freedom, desiring to travel, or having more fun. Whether materially, intellectually, or spiritually motivated, a sense of lack must be overcome through an increase in meaning. Typically, the person has an optimistic spirit that is fueled by the desire for expansion.

Positively expressed, this orientation manifests in initiatives, the creation of opportunities, and an openness to adventure and risk. One's sense of security is founded on faith in a greater potential instead of the immediate circumstances. Faith provides the emotional strength to cope with uncertainty when new projects are not yet realized; the big picture is what matters, less so the details. Equipped with an uplifting and inviting presence, the individual is usually intimately warm and upbeat.

When mismanaged, there is a strong inclination to get emotionally carried away. One can become overly attached to the desire for increase, even when there is not a substantial foundation in place to support such prospects. Frustrated by the limitation of everyday reality, one may overcompensate through fantastic projects or visions that cannot be materialized. One may also associate with spiritual meanings that are farfetched and based on wishful thinking instead of the Truth. Since one's emotional security relies on rather abstract beliefs and meanings, it can be difficult to admit inconsistencies.

Emotionally attached to personal beliefs, stubbornness and serious communication problems with the environment may result because a person is not willing to doubt him or herself. In extreme cases, the gap between personal projections and reality is so wide that everything ends up mismanaged in one's life; the delusional attitude contaminates daily survival issues resulting in failure and debt. The need for meaning must be based in truthfulness. When realigning the ego with Truth, exaggerations, self-righteousness, and unfounded optimism diminish.

When inspired by religion, personal spiritual experiences, or intuition, a person can gather the courage to change his or her life according to what is perceived as truthful. For example, if a job is not true to the person anymore, he or she may find the courage to leave the secure job and face the prospect of financial insecurity if needed. The same applies to the person's choice of friends, living environment, and intimate partners; they have to resonate with one's nature and offer meaning. Accordingly, the person emotionally associates with elements and people who have a positive, enhancing, and stimulating influence leaving behind anything perceived as restrictive, artificial, or depressing.

To emotionally process experiences in a healthy way, there is a strong need to be in an environment that encourages authentic expression and exploration. Failing to find or establish this, the person may have emotional outbursts or compensate through excess and self-indulgence. Food addictions are a common way of compensating as well as excessive spending or talking.

The need for authenticity can draw one to anything that inspires the natural and untamed. Open natural spaces and wildlife may have a purging effect on one's psyche and emotions. Similarly, the need for emotional transparency can be important; one yearns to externalize and discuss emotional experiences as a way to gain insight and a greater understanding of life—honesty and transparency is also expected from others though not always fulfilled. Establishing a support system that allows a more casual, straightforward, and playful approach is important. The person tends to shy away from what may be too reserved, tamed, and regulated. However, there is a danger in overindulging in such a direction and becoming emotionally invasive without regard for boundaries. The potential to overdramatize personal feelings and involve everyone in one's constant rationalizations and dilemmas can become overbearing.

Support can be offered to others by helping them believe in themselves and adopt a more daring approach to life. The person can lift others' spirits and encourage them to seize opportunities instead of giving in to insecurities. One's faith-bound attitude can be positively contagious.

– One's family life, sense of belonging, nurturing needs, the relationship with one's parents—especially the mother, the mother's personality.

With a Moon in Sagittarius, in the ninth house, or in aspect to Jupiter, the family atmosphere may encourage faith and optimism. The parents may be religious or spiritually inclined and find comfort and hope in higher meaning, thus remaining positive despite life's challenges. Consequently, all important decisions and lifestyle choices may be inspired by religious and or spiritual associations. One's upbringing may be colored by associating meaning and philosophical explanations with life details; an explanation or rationalization is offered for different actions and circumstances. Faith can provide emotional security, confidence, and a sense of well-being given that it is not dulling the mind and critical thinking. Yet when this dynamic is misused, the parents, especially the mother, may be so attached to their beliefs that a sensible conversation is not possible and every argument is resolved with a philosophical, religious, or spiritual rationalization. The child may feel invalidated and misunderstood when not heard or when his or her emotions are confined to a philosophical label.

This dynamic may also manifest in nonreligious families where the parents are prejudiced and argumentative. Communication in the household may be unproductive as each person tries to win an argument by out screaming the other. In some circumstances, the parents may also be quite unrefined or even vulgar because of a lack of measure, proper education, and attention to detail.

The focus on opinions and beliefs may also originate from a cross-cultural family environment. The parents may come from different origins, races, or religions and expose the child to diverse approaches to existence. Depending on the case, the culture of one parent may be more predominant than the other's by mutual choice or emotional manipulation. For example, one parent may have converted to the other parent's religion.

In other circumstances, the parents may have strong beliefs and ideals that are not necessarily cultural or religious in nature. The parents may have visions and big plans that generate an optimistic atmosphere rooted in faith that a greater potential lies ahead. The optimism can be exaggerated and possibly induce delusions of grandeur or a lack of proportion. For example, a lot of money may be spent on lavish vacations while plastic chairs fill the living room. Expectations for easy success may also be projected on to the children and disappointment expressed when they do not respond with similar enthusiasm and ambition. The child may feel invaded and embarrassed by the parents' outgoing, overconfident, and exaggerated tendencies, and yearn for more down time and privacy.

In more balanced circumstances, the Moon in these positions can manifest in a warm and playful family environment. The parents, especially the mother, may have a strong personality and view, but in this case, express it through wisdom and understanding instead of self-righteousness. The child may be provided with support for authentic expression and creative freedom as the family generates abundance and fosters opportunity—a permissive approach provides a sense of security and optimism.

Evolutionary Lesson

The Moon in these positions describes an evolutionary lesson to lead one's personal life in a truthful and authentic way. A yearning to know more of the Truth naturally incites the individual to search for life's greater potential and in such a way create abundance and expand the content of his or her personal life. Accordingly, a lesson of honest emotional communication and free self-expression is in order yet without trespassing other people's emotional boundaries.

The Moon in Capricorn ♑, in the 10th House, or in Aspect to Saturn ♄

— *The personalizing process, the nature of one's personal connection with life, emotional associations, management of emotions, the orientation of the growth process.*

— *Security needs, management of intimacy, approach to vulnerabilities, and one's support system.*

With the Moon in Capricorn, in the tenth house, or in aspect to Saturn, a person establishes a personal connection with life on the basis of needing to find what has been proven to be reliable, ethical, and or right, and serving as an example of such principles. Consequently, one's personal approach and perspective of life is colored by higher behavioral standards, maturity, and a desire to prove personal competence. The person will emotionally relate with elements in life that support this orientation.

With the Moon in these positions, there is an evolutionary need to establish healthy boundaries for emotional development so that growth can unfold in the most natural way. The person is learning how to manage emotions and find the balance between softness and rigor; there is a need to provide enough time and nurturing for natural growth processes to occur yet without overindulging so that emotional stagnation and dysfunction is minimized. One learns about the danger of overprocessing emotions which can prevent one from moving on to more advance stages of becoming. Consequently, there is a tendency to avoid being emotionally overprotected for fear that it would hinder one's capacity to become independent and resilient enough when facing life's challenges.

Adjusting to appropriate boundaries allows the person to better regulate his or her development and improve coping capacities. Emotional development is analogous to the natural cycle of pregnancy where nine months are required to come to term—less time than that is hazardous, but so is going beyond it. One of the most fundamental concerns of this Moon position is to tune into the natural timing of maturation cycles.

Typically at first there is a tendency to be too lax or too stern when managing emotions and vulnerabilities—it takes time to find the right balance. As much as the person exhibits evident maturity in certain areas, there may be blockages and immaturity in others. For example as a child, one may find little interest in playing with toys, instead preferring more serious activities such as mastering the violin while at the same time fearing to go to sleep with the lights off. Until the balance between emotional maturity and immaturity is better regulated, the potential for skipping developmental steps is likely. For example, these configurations may be present in the chart of premature births where pregnancy phases are skipped and subsequently have to be recovered through an incubator. In other ways, skipping steps may manifest as shying away from weaknesses or denying their existence altogether, yet experiencing breakdowns under pressure. Trying to force maturation inevitably leads to setbacks.

The individual is also pressured to be emotionally strong in order to align with higher duties and responsibilities. The Capricorn archetype opens one to realities larger than oneself, where private needs must be transcended in order to respond to collective requirements. Circumstances may require the person to be up to greater tasks and put aside concerns about personal discomfort. For example, the person may be the first born in the family and therefore be the one in the position to help take care of younger siblings. One's maturation process may be enhanced or even rushed because greater needs are calling and require reliable behavior. Consequently, the person may become a strong and nurturing figure for others. This dynamic can also apply on a professional level when assuming a management, coaching, or directing position. If this tendency is excessive, personal needs can end up completely neglected and suppressed to one's detriment. Once again, the right boundaries must be identified between addressing personal and larger matters.

Often perceived as strong and capable, other people easily come to rely on the individual. Fulfilling positions of authority can make the person feel secure because it provides a feeling of doing something right. The fear of not being taken seriously is a fundamental source of insecurity that incites one to want to have something concrete to show for one's efforts, yet when at times failing to perform successfully, judgment and contempt may ensue. Thus being in positions of authority is not only a result of necessity and duty, but also fulfills a security need.

When guiding and leading others, a natural dependence is formed between the authority and the subject. Such a position can escalate to the point where the person ends up being a defacto parent for others. While benefiting from the authority in such a role, the person may also resent the dependence because it can be interpreted as weak behavior. Subsequently, he or she may unexpectedly become completely unavailable; thus double messages are given and cause confusion. On the one hand, the individual takes on all the responsibility when identifying with the authority role; on the other hand, he or she pushes people away or reprimands them when their neediness is considered upsetting. This dichotomy often reflects one's own internal struggle to be able to accept personal needs.

Positively expressed, these configurations depict someone who manifests strength of character, reliability, leadership qualities, wisdom, and maturity. Equipped with an innate ability to address challenges and cope with stress, one may fulfill important roles that require endurance, expertise, and the capacity to sacrifice personal needs when duty calls. Deep wisdom may intuitively be accessed when the person naturally discriminates between what is truthful and what is unreliable—making the right decisions in the right time.

These qualities can render the person a remarkable educator who provides apprentices with the right amount of support and challenge. A healthy expression of maturity results from establishing healthy priorities and boundaries; a balance is found between addressing vulnerabilities and overcoming them, between attending private needs and professional ones. When such a balance is attained, maturation unfolds in a more gradual way without rushing or skipping important developmental phases.

When mismanaged, the person may experience serious disruptions in the growth process, resulting in emotional deprivation and misplaced emotions. It is not uncommon for the maturation process to be rushed and create setbacks as a result. Under pressure to prove personal capacities, one may undertake tasks that are too hard to manage and fail for not being truly ripe for them. Accordingly, one's emotional system may end up overly charged and appear strong when in fact it is on the verge of breakdown.

When needs and weaknesses are repressed, misplaced emotions can cause depression and cynicism. Misplaced emotions may also manifest in an unhealthy combination of infantilism and unforgiving or cruel behavior. One may repeatedly fail in life, trying too hard to prove one's competence, and compensate through diminishing other people for their shortcomings. The person must learn that weaknesses need to be addressed and healed rather than suppressed. Healing comes when one is able to let go of harshly judging shortcomings and can open up emotionally.

Because insecurity rises when not being taken seriously by others, the person may overcompensate by trying too hard to act strong and wise—this creates pressure whereby the person ends up leading a double life: the one seen by others and the other one kept religiously private where shortcoming are concealed. The fear of being judged can render one emotionally shy.

Other difficulties can erupt when manifesting exaggerated feelings of guilt that arise when failing to meet performance standards or making mistakes. Trying to always act with mastery, a person can end up being too harsh on him or herself. Guilt is not necessarily negative in all cases because it reflects the need for self-adjustment; however, problems become real when it is excessive and hinders development for feeling undeserving.

In another way, the Moon in these placements inclines one to emotionally identify with people or elements that represent strength, success, ethics, and wisdom. Comfort can be found in old traditions because they have passed the test of time and appear reliable; there is a yearning for something that works while ideas that are considered fanciful are often scorned.

With a strong need for proper guidance, one can find a support system in structures that provide clear and reliable definitions of what is right and wrong in life. Moral codes can be absorbed through personal soul-searching or through the guidance of an external authority. The need for structure can also manifest in an appeal for architecture, design, and music, especially melancholic or classical pieces—violin is often the chosen musical instrument.

> – *One's family life, sense of belonging, nurturing needs, the relationship with one's parents—especially the mother, the mother's personality.*

With the Moon in Capricorn, in the tenth house, or in aspect to Saturn, family dynamics may be rooted in solid foundations or older traditions. The parents may aspire to provide the best education and support system they can in hope of preparing the child for the complexities of life. Consequently, they implement values that have passed the test of time such as respect, humility, and duty. While having good intentions, the parents may on some occasions be too confident about the reliability of their education and general views, and resist adjusting to new ways of doing things. The child may face a wall when wanting to introduce new concepts, for example, when choosing clown school over law school. The parents' conservatism may be rooted in their own fear of failing as parents, hence their reluctance to take risks.

In other cases, the parent, usually the mother, has much more authority than the other parent and directs the whole family. The mother may be a "supermom" who takes all the responsibility on herself while the other parent emanates weakness or unavailability. She can be a source of security and comfort but tends to always feel guilty for one shortcoming or another; therefore, she thinks she must justify her existence through duty, self-sacrifice, and demonstrations of strength. The child relies on this "unbreakable" figure and yet may be emotionally deprived because the mother is consumed by duties.

Conversely, there may be a family pattern in which one or both parents are absent, dysfunctional, incapacitated, or infantile, pressuring the child to mature relatively quickly. Roles may also be reversed when the child becomes the caretaker and the one to implement boundaries toward the parents. The intensity of this experience may vary from case to case; it may be that the parents are incompetent and reject all forms of responsibility or that circumstances, such as an illness or postpartum depression, make them unavailable for a period of time. In this case, the child learns to develop an inner authority and a strong sense of boundaries. For the sake of balance, the need to make up for a compromised childhood emerges in later stages of life.

For others, the search for boundaries may manifest in a tendency for the parents to be too stern and adopt a "tough love" approach such as not attending to their crying baby "to teach him or her the virtues of independence," or sending children to boarding schools where little personal attention and affection is provided. The child may feel guilty for never quite matching parental expectations and suffer from bouts of depression or compensate for emotional repression through outbursts of wild behavior.

In further extremes, the parents may exhibit sadistic tendencies and expect absolute submission through intimidation and punishment. If this is this case, the child is obviously psychologically harmed.

In more balanced scenarios, the parents may be serious individuals who sometimes try too hard to do the right thing, while remaining forgiving and supportive in their approach. The need to expose the child to solid values and morals does not hinder experimentation and an openness to new ideas, yet the need to test the credibility of these ideas through results usually remains. The parents may, however, perceive the child's maturity and trust his or her judgments, allowing him or her the freedom to make personal decisions. The child feels respected and supported in this fashion.

Evolutionary Lesson

The Moon in these configurations describes an evolutionary lesson to align one's personal life with what is truthful and right to the best of one's understanding. Unethical or dysfunctional emotional patterns must be adjusted; accordingly, one learns to identify what works and what is just. Usually emotional adjustments are made by implementing healthy boundaries, either through relaxing the existing ones or by establishing firmer ones. The Moon in these positions may also reflect an evolutionary need to purge negative karma brought from past lives where one may have deserted responsibilities. A sense of guilt may be rooted in these unconscious memories and serves to orient one toward correction and release.

The Moon in Aquarius ♒, in the 11th House, or in Aspect to Uranus ♅

- *The personalizing process, the nature of one's personal connection with life, emotional association, management of emotions, and the orientation of the growth process.*

- *Security needs, management of intimacy, approach to vulnerabilities, and one's support system.*

With the Moon in Aquarius, in the eleventh house, or in aspect to Uranus, a person establishes a personal connection with life on the basis of the aspiration to elevate living standards and unite with like-minded people who resonate with ideals of progress. Consequently, one's personal approach and perspective of life is colored by forward thinking, social interaction, and a desire to speed up processes. The person will emotionally relate with elements in life that support this orientation.

There is an evolutionary need to upgrade one's emotional system in order to refine the way that all growth processes unfold. The motivation behind upgrading can sometimes be rooted in an early or past life memory of emotional crisis or dysfunction. The person is now geared toward finding new ways and solutions to cope with and resolve emotional complexes. This orientation induces a more cerebral and reflective approach to emotions so that one can develop a broader perspective and gain emotional understanding.

When emotional, the person simultaneously observes his or her own behavior, including reactions and outcomes, and analyzes ongoing dynamics as if a spectator of his or her own life. Subsequently, conclusions are drawn about the best way to proceed. Personal awareness, intelligence, and insights are used to enhance emotional development and manage life. Consequently, emotional intelligence is developed, and one becomes further aware of one's own psychological dynamics as well as others'.

The logic behind emotional patterns is gradually uncovered providing further clarity. This approach helps one process life experiences faster and more efficiently; for example, if going through a difficult breakup, understanding the reasons that led to the crisis helps one transcend the pain faster than if deprived of that lucidity. With a broader perspective, the person can internalize that healing options exist and thus avoid stagnating in pain. With more emotional insight, the person refines his or her response to life circumstances becoming more progressive, civil, considerate, and gracious; for example, conflicts are courteously debated rather than allowed to escalate to the point of potential hostility.

However at times, the environment may fail to respond to the more sophisticated and mature approach. People may overreact emotionally and get carried away in negative directions; one must learn that not everyone remains civilized and proper when emotions are triggered. As a result, a sense of alienation from the environment can grow because of the feeling that there are mentality gaps between oneself and others. Witnessing a lack of consideration, coarseness, gratuitous violence, or the intolerance of differences, the person may see others as less aware and even primitive in their way of managing their emotions and personal lives. This outlook can create circumstances where the person feels isolated and alienated from the environment.

Looking for a sense of identification with like-minded people, one may feel the need to relocate to environments that are more progressive or liberal and change the nature of people to interact with. Commonly, one associates with more urban and progressive environments where people are generally better educated. However, since the individual is constantly upgrading his or her emotional approach, gaining new insights may again create gaps with the environment. The accelerated pace of processing and assimilation recurrently generates gaps and feelings of alienation.

When feeling alienated, the lesson is to pursue one's natural pace of development without snobbery or emotional distancing. Refinement and sophistication can lead to arrogance often manifesting in sarcasm and disdain for those who are perceived as less refined. A way to stay more humble is through understanding that while relatively more aware emotionally, one may be a novice in other areas: everyone has strengths and weaknesses. Besides, being more cerebral and analytical can render one overly contained and self-conscious. One may have something to learn from people who in their simplicity are more spontaneous and emotionally expressive.

Positively expressed, these influences manifest in an open-minded, emotionally intelligent, and inclusive approach. Refined qualities of respect, tolerance, humanism, and civility are emphasized. When addressing emotional issues, a gentle and considerate attitude can help reduce unnecessary drama and encourage healthier emotional function. The person may become a good counselor, providing an objective perspective and emotional clarity. This dynamic can apply on a larger social scale when helping deprived or discriminated sectors of society elevate their standards of living and overcome existing quandaries.

Negatively, the person can become overly cerebral and consequently sharply critical and dismissive of anything perceived as malfunctioning; there is a tendency toward derision, a lack of patience, and nervousness. The mind may override the emotions to the extent that one loses touch with personal vulnerabilities. Every feeling is thoroughly analyzed but not truly experienced; inevitably, emotions end up suppressed as theory replaces feeling.

The individual may talk about higher virtues, but be incapable of relating emotionally on an intimate level. The fast-paced forward thinking mind may leave the slower processing emotions behind; thus one's wisdom fails to be truly integrated. One may know every solution to existing problems but fail to implement these solutions when faced with the actual circumstances in his or her own life. This can be, for example, the person that gives self-righteous advice to everyone about relationships but fails to resolve issues in his or her own relationships.

Another expression of the gap created between the mind and the emotions can manifest when the person habitually and systematically rationalizes pain and becomes attached to logic instead of the actual experience. This approach becomes an escape whereby one remains removed from emotions so that pain is avoided. For example, when facing rejection, rationalizing the event and understanding why the partner "had to leave" allows one to stay neutral and above the wound. However, removing oneself from the pain does not truly mean that the pain is processed and healed. Solutions are truly integrated when negative patterns are not repeated and healthier dynamics result.

In extreme cases, gaps between the mind and the emotions become too important and affect behavioral patterns. This can lead to serious dysfunction such as unexpected emotional outbursts, panic attacks, or acute emotional numbness and apathy. In further extremes, this condition may escalate to dissociative behavior and split personality disorders. In this case, the lesson is to assess the origin of one's fear of feelings and to identify an earlier trauma that may have triggered the escape of the emotions through the mind. Eventually, the person may reengage with his or her emotions and get in touch with a more primal form of expression. The mind can still help one understand dynamics but without completely neutralizing primal emotions anymore.

Although typically there is a natural inclination to reduce dramatic outbursts through a reflective approach, the opposite outcome may ensue; overanalyzing and overprocessing emotions may actually generate unnecessary drama. Every transitory emotion ends up being discussed and counseled about, even when trivial. The aspiration to be aware and find solutions to quandaries can be exaggerated and create problems where there are none. Here the lesson is about gaining real perspective and knowing when to let go; one may need to turn a blind eye to some issues if need be, for the sake of a better flow.

The Moon in these positions can generate identification with groups and social circles that reflect one's personal values. This way, the person can find a sense of belonging with like-minded others and create an alternative family. Biological ties may become less important when the priority is on sharing mutual values and views of life. Even when committed to an intimate relationship, one may still feel the need to maintain an active social life, cultivate friendships, and be involved in a community. Similarly, the person may associate with groups, organizations, and parties defined by a common interest, ideology, or vision.

With these configurations, one may associate with elements that represent modernity, class, broader awareness, and quality. Interest in advanced technology and gadgets can keep one updated with innovative products, or in a different way with alternative energy technology. In another way, the emotional focus may be oriented toward social activities whether enjoying group exchange and activities or involvement in humanitarian causes.

Group association may provide a support system when fulfilling the role of an alternative family. Creating communities promotes a feeling of belonging that may not initially be obvious. A support system may also result from helping, or being helped, to upgrade standards of living. For example, the person may receive guidance on using computers or provide counseling to others to resolve problems.

— One's family life, sense of belonging, nurturing needs, the relationship with one's parents—especially the mother, the mother's personality.

With the Moon in Aquarius, the eleventh house, or in aspect to Uranus, the family environment may be relatively sophisticated and refined. The parents may belong to a higher socioeconomic class, lead a progressive lifestyle, and be involved with elite circles. Usually, getting a good education and maintaining a level of quality is emphasized. There may be a sense of pride within the family and relative to that, expectations that the children perform highly. The parents may appear open minded and accessible but underneath the surface be quite judgmental and attached to their elitist values. The pressure to be appropriate and civil may impede answering more primal emotional needs, sometimes even refraining from touch. Even when the family does not belong to a higher echelon, there may be criticism toward any form of behavior that is considered grotesque, overly dramatic, or dense, making the child and other family members feel like "primitive beasts" when daring to get carried away.

In other cases, the parents are aware of emotional needs and try to do everything to provide the best for their children. Open-minded and considerate, they listen and are attentive to each child's individuality and support their creativity. There is an inclination to associate with progressive ideals such as having the children attend alternative schools or consume organic food; every dynamic is handled very "consciously." The mother in particular may be youthful in spirit and sometimes addressed as a friend instead of an actual parent; she may be admired for being relatively special, trendy, and wise.

Alternatively, it may be that one parent has a higher awareness while the other parent is not as sophisticated, leading to mentality gaps between the parents. This contrast creates struggles around emotional issues and the best way to deal with existence. The children may identify more strongly with the progressive parent and feel embarrassed by the other one.

In the same vein, the person may be born into a family that is relatively dysfunctional with parents who are naive about how to adequately manage existence. They may aspire to be sophisticated and imitate their trendy neighbors, but fail to be truly mature emotionally. The child may feel alienated from the parents for that reason and instead rely on intuition or external role models to more appropriately address life challenges. This dynamic can lead to ruptures between the child and the parents, sometimes to the extent that the child feels disdain for his or her family. In extreme cases, the child may abuse his or her parents through verbal criticism and fundamental disrespect because they are considered "stupid" or "backward." While the child needs to be in touch with his or her unique personality, there is a need to learn about emotional vulnerability and inclusion. There is a lesson in accepting the parents for who they are; given that despite their lack of sophistication, they probably do have love for the child.

When well balanced, the family reflects caring parents who constantly upgrade their way of educating their children, not only through expanding their culture but also by consciously addressing their emotional needs. A bond of respect and friendship may be created between the two generations that is founded on both mutual affection and inspiration. The mother may emanate nobility, dignity, high ethical behavior, and wisdom, drawing respect and admiration from the child and the environment.

Evolutionary Lesson

The Moon in these positions describes an evolutionary lesson to bridge between the higher mind and the emotions so that new and more effective ways to handle existence are developed. Through observation and education, the person acquires wisdom and insight, and uses it to better manage his or her emotions. The purpose of the Aquarius Moon archetype is to harmonize the mind and the emotions, rather than create an imbalance where one overpowers the other and results in dysfunction. Another way to encourage emotional security and development is to create communities and bring people together where resources and insights are shared. Ultimately, the goal is to elevate standards for healthier living.

The Moon in Pisces ♓, in the 12th House, or in Aspect to Neptune ♆

— *The personalizing process, the nature of one's personal connection with life, emotional associations, the management of emotions, the orientation of the growth process.*

— *Security needs, the management of intimacy, one's approach to vulnerabilities, one's support system.*

With the Moon in Pisces, in the twelfth house, or in aspect to Neptune, a person establishes a personal connection with life on the basis of the need to find commonality among the diverse forms of life and see unity in all. Consequently, one's personal approach and perspective of life is colored by flow, greater acceptance, and a yearning to simplify everything. The person will emotionally relate with elements in life that support this orientation.

With the Moon in these placements, there is an evolutionary need to associate one's personal ego with larger meanings and needs, realizing that one's true identity extends beyond the immediacy of the current time and space and includes everything that is part of Creation. One gradually learns to dissolve factors that separate one being from another and realizes that beyond form, time, and space, all beings come from the same source and share a collective identity. To actualize this evolutionary intent in a healthy way, the person needs to find the right balance between his or her personal identity—that which pertains to intimate needs and processes, and the collective identity—that which pertains to others' needs and collective associations. Prior to attaining that balance, there is a common tendency to swing between the extremes with external or collective needs overshadowing personal ones.

The individual may neglect or sacrifice his or her own nurturing, processing, or security requirements and unconsciously expect to be just fine. Following the stream of life without getting in touch with personal need or desires, one may passively adapt to life circumstances and other people's needs. It may appear that there is always something more important or urgent than oneself that requires one's attention. On a mundane level, long work hours may come at the expense of family life, and then the family needs may take the remaining time, leaving one with little time for self-care. Sacrifice may come naturally—often because one's sense of self is not fully constructed and the person feels he or she *is* work, society, the children, or the spouse—the sense of self is fused with everything and everyone.

A lack of boundaries between oneself and others can manifest in every world event tremendously affecting one emotionally. One may feel everyone's pain including animal's or absorb what goes on in life like a sponge. Being so exposed to life can overwhelm the person because there is no filter or effective immune system to discriminate what comes into one's system. Over time, this condition can cause the person to shut down emotionally because one's system is unable to process the influx and gets flooded.

The excessive emotional exposure often results from naïvete whereby the person expects life to be a given medium of peace, love, and justice for all, and with this positive and trusting spirit fails to develop a protective mechanism. This approach may be overly simplistic because personal vulnerabilities are disregarded and this induces the neglect of self-maintenance, as if one is able to handle and take everything.

Before gaining clarity on the need for healthier boundaries, a common way to keep the positive and trusting attitude is to deny pain and trivialize details—staying emotionally unattached keeps pain at bay and everything positive. Such freedom from attachment may come at the expense of self-neglect, such as skipping meals, never going for a medical checkup, or always being "fine" even when facing emotional trials. Attending personal needs may seem burdensome because it confirms that one has vulnerabilities. Yet when pain eventually becomes unavoidable and the cost of denial overwhelming, one may swing to the other extreme and completely shut down emotionally.

Hiding from life and people and becoming utterly unavailable at that point, the person tries to somewhat get the pieces back together.

A common cause for getting hurt is being taken for granted or getting taken advantage of by others. Having attended everyone else's causes but one's own, one may experience abuse and a lack of gratitude. Disillusionment throws one completely upon oneself. Beyond the immediate hurt feelings, one may feel cheated when personal ideals fail, potentially rendering one bitter and henceforth distrustful. One may subsequently perceive people as wicked or become angry at life because "it is not fair."

These circumstances all come from an internal imbalance between personal needs and external ones. Once the person realizes that self-maintenance is required and that he or she cannot expect to stay safe by the grace of people or God, measures are taken to better handle essential needs and nurturing.

On another level, because the sense of self expands beyond form, one may tap into individual and collective unconscious realms—for example through having an active dream life. Emotional dynamics may be purged through dreams as one taps into dimensions that are beyond space and time. Under these circumstances, sleepwalking is not uncommon.

Sometimes the escape from pain and the lack of proper self-maintenance may result in a relatively ungrounded lifestyle with frequent relocations and recurrent sudden separations. In this case, each time a problem arises, one may feel victimized and choose to sever attachments without looking back, starting anew time after time with the hope of finding "the" perfect haven somewhere else. This pattern is bound to induce recurrent disillusionment.

When healing is considered and the person makes the effort to reconnect with his or her emotional self, an intimate world is created where security and nurturing are accessible. In order to better manage intimacy, there is a need to accept that emotional attachments are necessary even if they pose a risk of pain, or even if emotional commitments limit one's free spirit to a degree. One learns to value the gain coming from these attachments.

Positively through these configurations, the person finds the right balance between his or her public and personal life. Dedication to larger dynamics—such as one's professional life, humanitarian causes, or spiritual involvement—is harmonized with personal needs, intimate relationship needs, and psychological introspection. The person is compassionate and generous yet implements healthy boundaries so he or she does not become overwhelmed, depeleted, or abused. Without being naïve about challenges and potential corruption, one may see goodness in all—yet goodness is not taken for granted.

The individual may also develop healthy adaptation and improvisational skills—such as knowing when to be flexible and when to release attachments, and yet commit and invest him or herself when appropriate. With natural simplicity and transparence, one may radiate charm and accessibility.

Negatively expressed, one may be chronically overwhelmed by life circumstances and feel crushed by existence when personal ideals keep failing. A fatalistic "black and white" vision of existence colors the way everything is addressed whereby the perceived pure, innocent, and good is contrasted by the perceived corrupt and villain. Entangled in naïve idealism, there is a strong tendency to identify with the victim's position because victims appear innocent.

In other ways, an overly simplistic approach to life can generate an opportunistic approach that only relies on "good fortune" for success. Benefiting from strikes of luck, the person may take these moments of grace for granted and hope to overcome all challenges this way— eventually one is brought back to reality when mismanagement crises surface. Through emotional shocks, a reality check may be imposed to remind one to have an emotional body! Events such as abandonment, abuse, or lifestyle dysfunction may surface and force one to adopt healthier coping mechanisms. For example, substance abuse may take its toll and make one realize a more conscious approach is in order.

Eventually when addressing life and emotional needs more carefully, the need for "wake up calls" through shock and pain is minimized.

The person is inclined to emotionally associate with elements that are reminiscent of innocence and plainness; simplicity in people or the purity of the natural world are often cherished and provide a sense of comfort. Nature allows one to reconnect with the origins of existence as it offers a point of reference in life. In this same vein, one may associate with religious rituals and symbols or spiritual concepts that serve as a connection to a greater sense of personal identity.

Associating with public causes or institutions is also possible such as being involved with hospital care, social services, municipal activities, or caring for public causes. A support system may be established when offering care for the needy and the deprived without discrimination. In return, the person may benefit from the support of the community and or larger institutions that offer social programs or from complete strangers who offer help in the spirit of brotherhood.

— One's family life, sense of belonging, nurturing needs, the relationship with one's parents—especially the mother, the mother's personality.

The Moon in Pisces, in the twelfth house or in aspect to Neptune can describe a family environment in which one parent, usually the mother, is a devotional person that identifies with values of self-sacrifice. The mother is completely dedicated to her family and other people in need, often neglecting her own personal needs—as if she doesn't have any. Children are raised in a trusting and loving atmosphere, sheltered from harm. Sometimes the parents may try to keep their children innocent and pure, removing as many difficulties and challenges as possible. The mother's devotion is usually taken for granted because she may unconsciously identify with the martyr role, often proudly so. It is not uncommon that the mother, or both parents, are not adequately equipped to effectively cope with life's struggles. Resources may be mismanaged and provoke survival crises. As a result, the parents are chronically overwhelmed by problems that affect the household atmosphere.

In other cases, the mother may be overwhelmed to the point where she cannot address her children's nurturing needs. Depression, emotional immaturity, oversensitivity, difficulty in the marriage, childhood traumas, or other factors can cause a shut-down of her system and lead to emotional unavailability. Children witnessing the chaotic situation fear adding more burden through their personal needs and opt to be as good and quiet as possible while denying their own nurturing needs. The level of dysfunction varies from case to case.

In other cases, it may be that the mother is overly simplistic about her parental role and relies on delivered pizzas, nannies, and TV programs to attend to the children's needs. The children may refrain from expressing their emotional needs because it may burden the parent, so they prefer to sublimate their issues. In more problematic circumstances substance abuse, a carefree attitude, and lack of consistency by the parents may considerably accentuate neglect.

In further extremes, the level of neglect may seriously threaten the child's safety. The dysfunction usually transpires to physical levels when most of the house amenities are not working, meals are poor or lacking, and hygiene is compromised. The child may be exposed to the parent's decadent behavior such as hard-core addictions or sometimes prostitution. Lacking boundaries and common sense, abuse may add to neglect and accentuate the child's victimization. In one way or another, the level of chaos and dysfunction may be important enough to draw a social worker's urgent attention.

Similarly, the child may be abandoned and put in an orphanage because the parent is unreliable, absent, or unable to care for him or her. Being raised in an orphanage for at least a period of time, the child's needs are not addressed personally but rather on a collective basis. Consequently, the sense of self is fused with the larger institution and other children.

Differently, the Moon in these positions can describe a family environment that is religious or spiritually oriented. Faith and ideals serve as a foundation for values and everyday management. At times, this scenario may also reflect naivete when the parents prioritize spiritual involvement at the expense of survival needs. However, when well managed, the child is raised by parents who are motivated by spiritual meanings when addressing everyday matters.

When well balanced, parents offer their children unconditional support and implement values of compassion and dedication. Values of self-sacrifice—but with dignity, adaptability, and wisdom—may guide the child toward contributing to making the world a better place.

Evolutionary Lesson

The Moon in these positions reflects an evolutionary lesson to accept life as it is, both the beauty and the difficulty, and personally contribute to further promote goodness in it—replacing simplistic idealism with a more conscious form of compassion and devotion. A healthy approach allows one to find a personal place in the world in the midst of both beauty and difficulty, and inspire others through unifying diversity and encouraging inclusiveness. Such an approach is possible when a balance between self-care and attending larger needs is found—this implies knowing when to become emotionally attached and when to let go based on what the circumstances require.

The Moon in Synthesis

In this section, Moon placements are analyzed to illustrate how to synthesize configurations that include a planet, a sign, and a house. The way to proceed with any astrological analysis is to first understand the general themes and attributes that pertain to a given configuration. For example, when you are interpreting the meaning of the Moon in a birth chart, you have to consider the sign, the house placement, and any aspects the Moon is making to other planets (aspects will be discussed further in future volumes).

Before getting into the details of the specific meaning, it is important to have a general idea of *what is common* between all of the factors involved. To determine the general themes, first assess if there are repeating signatures. For example, if the *Moon is in Aries and also in the first house* of a chart, then there is a "double signature" because both the sign of Aries and the first house belong to the same archetype of Aries, meaning that we have double dosage of Aries themes with that particular Moon placement.

Using another example, if the *Moon is in Gemini in the eleventh house*, we see that both Gemini and the eleventh house (the Aquarius archetype) are cerebrally oriented; therefore, in this case, we can anticipate a pronounced use of the mind to manage emotions. There is always something that unites the different factors of a configuration even if at first they appear contradictory.

For example, if the *Moon is in Aries in the tenth house*, there seems to be two conflicting forces operating: Aries is emotionally reactive and unrestrained while the tenth house (the Capricorn archetype) is about responsibility and containment. However, what unites both the Aries and the Capricorn influences is a strong will, determination, and endurance. Hence the Moon in Aries in the tenth house describes a strong emotional nature that is capable of handling challenges and holding leadership positions while tending to abstain from expressing vulnerability.

After defining the common denominators, understanding the possible *contradictions* or *excesses* intrinsic to the placement provides a more complex grasp of the influences at play and the possible paradoxes the person may live with. This phase of the analysis is still about gaining a general perspective for the sake of having a first impression about the configuration. Going back to the *Aries Moon in the first house* example, there is a double dosage of reactive energy with powerful emotions that are strongly personalized and expressed without restraint; it might lead to excessive temper and accentuated touchiness, and result in scenarios where the person gets carried away with defensive and reactive behavior.

In the second example, the *Gemini Moon in the eleventh house*, there may be an excessive control of one's emotions through the mind because the person may be too sensitive to environmental (peer group) pressure and constantly attempt to appear "cool" or composed. This tendency may lead to accumulated nervous energy and a possible detachment from one's feelings.

With the *Moon in Aries in the tenth house* example, the person may live with an inner contradiction between emotional release (Aries) and restraint (tenth house) and therefore fluctuate between the extremes. When going too far with emotional expression (Aries), he or she may subsequently feel guilty (tenth house), and yet when holding back to adapt to external circumstances (tenth house), feel frustrated (Aries). These excesses and contradictions can be resolved through conscious work and behavioral adjustments.

All placements, without exception, have their positive and destructive potential. There is no perfect placement denuded of challenge and stress because there is always an evolutionary lesson involved that compels the person to learn new things. Until the lessons are learned, one may experience imbalances or excesses in regard to the particular influence of a planet. The purpose of this tension is to learn more about life and master these evolutionary lessons in order to be able to manifest the positive potential and overcome negative expressions of a planetary placement.

Some planetary placements may be more stressful than others, especially when particular aspects to other planets are involved, but the key is to understand the theme embodied in that placement and find a healthier way to express it rather than classify it as good or bad. This is the value of a spiritual approach to astrology—one configuration has many layers of expression instead of being only one dimensional. No configuration represents a fixed and finite potential; there is always room for more growth and depth as a person becomes more evolutionarily conscious.

The next layer to add in the synthesis process is to understand the nuance between the sign and the house as described in Chapter Four: "The Planets in Signs and Houses." *The house* is the area of operation while *the sign* is the way of operation. The following examples illustrate these gradual steps in a brief and concise way.

Example One: The Moon in Cancer in the 7th House

- *Unifying factors:* The Cancer and seventh house (Libra) archetypes are both oriented toward the acceptance of personal vulnerabilities as well as others'. A person with this placement tends to be more patient and compassionate, aware of needs and processing requirements.

- *Contradictions:* Cancer is more individual and personal, whereas the seventh house (Libra) is oriented toward others and their needs. At first glance, it appears that the person fluctuates between identifying with personal needs and other people's needs.

- *Excesses:* When dealing with emotions, there may be an excess of neediness because of undefined boundaries. Accepting vulnerabilities may lead to overprotective behavior and the avoidance of challenges.

- *Sign and house integration:* The seventh house represents the *area or context* of relationships. Through this house, we experience a personal sense of lack and yearn to complete ourselves often through other people whether on a social, professional, or intimate level. Through union, a greater sense of self can potentially be attained. In simple words, the seventh house refers to relationships needs and dynamics, and to facing the forces of duality.

The sign of Cancer describes, in this case, *how* the relationships are to unfold and *the way* a person approaches this theme. With a Cancer Moon active in the seventh house, there is a strong need to create a securing intimacy (Cancer) with a partner (seventh house) and to create a sense of familiarity. A nurturing and supportive approach can be expected, but it can potentially cause neediness in relationship exchanges—the person may either attract rather needy partners or become needy in relationships.

In some cases, one person may take a more mothering role (Cancer) in the relationship (seventh house) while the other may take a more childlike role. In this scenario, an imbalance may be created because the person fulfilling the mothering role may not have his or her personal needs addressed. It is not possible to know from the chart alone who takes which role. A person may play both roles, moving from one role to the other (child to parent) in each relationship.

The Cancer Moon in the seventh house reflects a need to gradually become accustomed to another person. A sense of security must be built over time (Cancer). Rushing to create an intimacy can create a false sense of security that is bound to collapse soon after. The person may, consequently, give mixed messages—being readily available and then becoming self-protective and distant. If the relationship persists, time can help one feel genuinely safe, whereby vulnerabilities are gradually exposed through discussing and sharing mutual needs.

The Evolutionary Purposes and Dynamics of a Cancer Moon in the 7th House

— The personalizing process, the nature of one's personal connection with life, emotional associations, the management of emotions, the orientation of the growth process.

— Security needs, the management of intimacy, the approach to vulnerabilities, one's support system.

With the Moon in Cancer in the seventh house, the evolutionary intent is to establish a sense of security in relationships and use that medium to process emotions, assimilate new dynamics, and enhance growth. In this effort, the aim is for the dynamic to be mutual and for each person in the relationship to support the other. In doing so, each person reveals their weaknesses and exchanges their insights about the best way to manage emotions; new insights gained through the exchange promote support, growth, and development for each person involved. The purpose of this configuration is to establish trust and a healthy dependence in relationships. Marriage or partnerships serve as a very important support system through which one finds the emotional resources to cope with life's challenges.

Positively expressed, the person may have a very nurturing and compassionate nature (Cancer) that attracts people with an equally humane and supportive approach (seventh house) Together, a sense of companionship provides unconditional love and assistance. The person may very likely possess counseling skills (seventh house), helping people feel at ease because he or she is emotionally accessible (Cancer). Tenderness and gentleness can become a powerful means to penetrate deep emotional insecurities and heal them (Cancer).

Negatively, there may be an excessive dependence in relationships that leads to an unequal distribution of roles. One person may take the parenting role (Cancer) while the other surrenders in an infantile way and expects to be unconditionally taken care of (Cancer). The stronger individual becomes the defacto parent and is likely to have a savior's complex, feeding the dependence in failing to establish healthy boundaries while supporting the other (seventh house). This dynamic can be emotionally draining and utterly unproductive for all involved. Instead of growth, an excessive focus on neediness generates emotional stagnation.

In reality, it is likely that the person with this configuration experiences both some of the positive and the negative expressions of this configuration. Going through the extremes, one may eventually regain center and with time learn to better manage and regulate these dynamics.

– One's family life, sense of belonging, nurturing needs, the relationship with one's parents—especially the mother, the mother's personality.

The family atmosphere may emanate hospitality and a general sense of trust. Strangers may be welcome and extra food kept for unexpected guests. The parents may, however, be overprotective (Cancer) and pleasers (seventh house) if they compulsively try to make everyone safe and happy. Being soft, one or both parents may emanate weakness and excessive dependence. When confronted with existential challenges, the parents may reflect a sense of helplessness; naïve and relatively childish, they may rely on stronger figures such as other family members or friends to help them out (Cancer).

Positively, the parents maintain a healthy balance between giving personal attention to the child to secure healthy emotional development (Cancer) and exposing the child to different perspectives and approaches so that he or she may feel secure with people or realities that are different from his or her origins (seventh house).

Conclusions

If appropriate boundaries are not set when defining roles and tasks in relationships, the person with this configuration is likely to remain either too dependent or an accomplished pleaser who overly identifies with the caretaker role. Neediness may become excessive to the point of never being satiated, inducing a potential for excessive attachment to people.

To better regulate the balance between personal needs and relationship dynamics, one learns to establish healthier boundaries whereby time is dedicated for self-care and then for others. When feeling internally nourished and safe (Cancer), one may open up to learn from others and different life approaches (seventh house).

Example Two: The Moon in Pisces in the 5th House

- *Unifying factors:* The Pisces and fifth house (Leo) archetypes are both inspired and possess a positive outlook on life. The glamour of Leo combines with the idealism and vastness of Pisces.

- *Contradictions:* Pisces is impersonal, unattached to matter and time, and prefers to passively adapt while Leo is very personal, involved, in touch with emotions, and in need for control.

- *Excesses:* The person may be excessively extravagant and emotionally involved with plans that are too vast and not really tangible; there is a general tendency to get carried away in fantasy.

- *Sign and house integration:* The fifth house represents *the area and context* of self-actualization. Through this house, a person feels the need to personally participate in the greater play of life and have an impact on the flow of things. It is a house where the ego gets in touch with its creative power and feels a sense of personal destiny. The fifth house also describes themes around children including relationships with them.

The Sign of Pisces, in this case, describes *how* one's self-actualization process unfolds and *the way* a person will make it happen. It will also describe how children issues are addressed. With a Pisces Moon, the individual may feel that his or her personal actualization must be inspired by collective dynamics, possibly touching people on a large scale. For example, one's personal creative expression may be spiritually inspired. This configuration may even point to a feeling of being chosen by higher powers to accomplish something meaningful in the current life. There is a strong emotional association and identification with a sense of purpose and the need to fulfill personal ideals. Because the combination of Pisces in the fifth house (Leo) is very inspired, immense creativity can be expected. The person may have natural artistic talent and or a rich imagination.

The Evolutionary Purposes and Dynamics of a Pisces Moon in the 5th House

- *The personalizing process, the nature of one's personal connection with life, emotional associations, the management of emotions, the orientation of the growth process.*

- *Security needs, the management of intimacy, the approach to vulnerabilities, one's support system.*

With the Moon in Pisces in the fifth house, the evolutionary intent is to personally associate with a personal meaning for life and to align one's creativity (fifth house) with collective needs (Pisces). The person is inclined to freely express emotions and have a generous approach to life while expecting to be validated and supported because there is a sense of importance and meaning to his or her creative expression. Creative outlets may touch and inspire people, possibly through artistic channels or spiritual wisdom.

One is also likely to be personally involved with the emotions of the collective, for example, by emotionally identifying with the plight of deprived populations (Pisces). The person may find personal meaning in nurturing people from all walks of life or promote creative projects (fifth house) for charitable causes (Pisces).

With this configuration, children may also be a focus. Different outcomes can manifest, starting from being focused on one's own children (fifth house) to being inspired to adopt children (Pisces); in both cases, one may have naïve expectations (Pisces) that children (fifth house) are easy to handle. As a result, one may be too lenient with children and end up overwhelmed when their behavior becomes unruly (Pisces).

Positively expressed, the individual may possess a very compassionate and generous nature emotionally oriented toward promoting just causes and creative endeavors. Deeply inspired, talents and creativity may blossom to the point of gaining public acclaim, potentially raising one to relative fame and recognition (Pisces). One may also possess an uplifting and encouraging nature—believing in life, love, and caring for children.

Negatively expressed, one may get carried away and fail to manage one's life productively. Having high ideals and taking on projects (fifth house) that are too vast (Pisces) may lead to emotional instability and fluctuation between sharp highs and lows; becoming overwhelmed, one's emotions may become volatile and excessive. Conditions such as manic depression can manifest because of the swing between high expectations and low results. Feeling victimized when naïve ideals do not materialize, one may try to gain sympathy and nurturing by crying wolf and then becoming overwhelmed and consumed by personal dramas when losing perspective.

— One's family life, sense of belonging, nurturing needs, the relationship with one's parents—especially the mother, the mother's personality.

Family dynamics may represent a sense of glamour; for example, the mother may have leadership qualities and be venerated for her personality, creativity, and generosity. Similarly, the parents may be artists or freelancers who emanate freedom of spirit. Nonetheless, family prestige (fifth house) may be lost at some point in time perhaps because of the naïve management of life (Pisces). Consequently, one or both parents may feel sorry for themselves (Pisces) and fail to accept the conditions of a decreased status lifestyle. In extreme cases, self-pity may generate emotional dramas (fifth house).

Positively, the parents offer the child an abundance of personal attention, supporting his or her creative inspiration and inborn talents (fifth house). The parents may serve as reliable role models who are both accomplished in their own right (fifth house) and generous to society, providing the child with healthy values of compassion and dedication (Pisces) while directing the child so that he or she is not overly naïve when addressing life's complexities (Pisces).

Conclusions

The fragile balance between meeting personal nurturing needs (fifth house) and the collective calling (Pisces) is not easily attained. The person is likely to swing from being overly consumed by personal ambition to sacrificing oneself for others or larger causes. The evolutionary lesson is about letting go of dramatic expectations and remaining authentic to the simplicity of one's true nature. In this fashion, one can naturally inspire others without losing him or herself and can also better manage his or her emotions. There is a need, first of all, to attend to personal needs in order to establish a solid foundation on top of which larger needs can be addressed. When this balance is established, emotional involvment may nourish creative outlets in ways that inspire and help others. For example, the person may feel personally connected (Moon) with creative projects (fifth house) to help deprived (Pisces) children (fifth house).

Chapter Six

The Sun in Signs and Houses

The Sun rules the sign of Leo—accordingly, it represents the function of consciousness that relates to actively participating in life's creative development. The Sun symbolizes our role in the bigger play of life and our unique way of making a contribution. Through the Moon, we connect with life by forming personal attachments to particular elements. Through the Sun, we find a personal sense of meaning and purpose—our personal role within the vastness of existence.

Under this influence, we manifest the capacity *to create* and make things happen; creativity is an empowering ability that provides us with the means to affect destiny instead of merely reacting or adapting to circumstances. Creativity is a sacred capacity because, for better or worse, it accedes us to change the direction of life and fundamentally affect developmental courses, capturing the possibility of influencing and altering the original setup of life and nature. In a way through creativity, we get in touch with the ability to be godlike—to breathe life into form and *make something where there was nothing.* The gratification that results from creativity is orgasmic, but the responsibility therein tremendous.

Mastering the Sun's power enhances our *leadership capabilities*. The ego yearns to fulfill a significant role, yet significance is not measured according to a level of popularity but rather according to whether we positively affect life in some way; what matters the most is the quality and intent of our contribution. Leadership stems from the capacity to launch processes and confidently assume the responsibility for the goals to come to fruition. Consequently, it requires determination, willpower, and strength of character. Leadership is the direct result of managing creative effort; it may or may not involve leading other people because first and foremost it is about assuming a role in life.

The placement of the Sun also illustrates the *character and personality* emerging from our personal aspirations, principles, goals, and capacities. The person's presence and influence on the environment is described through the Sun's placement in the birth chart. Therefore, the Sun is not only about creativity and having an impact, but also about the nature of the personality behind the actions; it describes how a person naturally draws attention and overcomes anonymity.

The creative process accedes one to immortality—when creating something we give life. When facing the fact that nothing in life is permanent, we defy death through creativity. Knowing that our personal creations carry on after our passing provides us with a tremendous sense of *potency and vitality*. This concept first applies to the reproduction instinct because *having children* guarantees that life will go on after our death. The Sun represents *the battle against extinction* whereby the torch of life must be passed on to keep the flame burning, defying the end of time. Hence the Sun represents issues related to fertility and one's lineage.

Through the Sun, life is sustained by *love* because one results from the other—loving life stimulates the creative impulse—and as we love, we are able to give life. Fundamentally, creativity is our unique and personal way of giving something back to the divine; we received life on this planet and in this universe, and our gratitude and appreciation are measured by our willingness to maintain and enhance it. Through creativity, we give something back to existence and the Creation.

When passing the torch to the next generation, there are great expectations that they will face life with grace and virtue, and proudly carry the heritage on. Similarly, the new generation expects the previous one to serve as a reliable and inspiring role model.

Issues of *respect* are strongly emphasized with the Sun. Since defying death is an important task, respecting life and living beings is a way to express appreciation for all invested effort toward this aim, honoring those who manage to live and create. Additionally, respect comes from being *inspired*. A person immersed in a creative process is very attentive to figures, symbols, or causes that are considered worth carrying on for. The Sun represents the experience of being moved, impressed, and affected in a way that enthuses and motivates the spirit.

Relying on role models, whether parental or iconic figures, can at times create an unhealthy dependence; the person can easily be engulfed by the *expectation* to continue a tradition or a lineage the way the previous generation did to the point of denying his or her personal uniqueness. The person can almost become a "clone" of the role model and be controlled to act only according to expectations. The role model may manipulate followers or successors through conditional generosity and support—only granting praise and support when expectations are fulfilled, or in other words only when others do what the role model wants.

The pressure to fulfill expectations can manifest in the classic parental hope that children continue the parental lifestyle and line of work; it may be particularly emphasized through the father's influence, for example, in carrying the father's name or continuing the father's business. The child may also be expected to do things that the parents failed to achieve in their own lives such as playing the piano or becoming doctors. In these circumstances, the parents are emotionally attached and invested in what the child represents, and such a subjective orientation can, at times, blind them from gaining a true perspective of the child's authentic nature and uniqueness. A child may carry the torch and continue the lineage, but the purpose is to do so in his or her own unique way. There is an evolutionary pressure for the child to break away from expectations that precisely fit the parental mold. This is one of the reasons why it takes two people to have a child; the child's nature is never exactly like either parent but instead a mixture of both, in addition to environmental influences.

Similarly, expectations can also extend to teacher and apprentice interactions or any other situation where a succession is pending. The teacher may expect the apprentice to exactly follow his or her lead, but nature does not intend it this way. Different environmental conditions and the individuality of the apprentice are bound to generate a different twist to the way things end up being done, prompting a change in the course of development.

The role of parents, teachers, and leaders is to inspire the next generation, not to force their agenda on it. When bringing life to this world, one has to nurture and guide it and then at the time of its ripeness release it with love and faith. Hence as the torch is passed from one generation to the next, it changes in form—this is part of life's development.

→ The placement of the Sun in a birth chart describes the relationship between the parent and the child, or the mentor and the apprentice, from the perspective of defining how they mutually inspire and shape each other's character. In particular, the Sun represents the relationship with one's father and one's own children. Fertility issues and the capacity to have and raise children are also described by this influence. The Sun also represents the expectations from one generation to the next relating to issues of respect, admiration, and inspiration. Accordingly, the necessity to individualize and find one's own unique way of pursuing one's destiny is an intrinsic part of the Sun's influence.

→ Since the Sun is the life giver, it also describes the willingness to care for all living beings and life—human, animal, and vegetal. The person is empowered through the vitality and potency intrinsic to the creative process, but he or she can also empower other people through inspiration and generosity—the life-force energy can be shared. Without generosity, life does not thrive and the future is in danger; at some point, reaping what one sows and the reward of one's generosity and investment comes in larger doses.

→ As the Sun represents the life force, it also represents the love force; there is strong emotional involvement in the endeavor to keep the torch of life burning; it requires tremendous personal attention and thoughtfulness. Creativity is an opportunity for the person to give something back to God or the divine—this motivation may be unconscious for most people, yet under this influence it is fundamental—the Sun symbolizes the labor of love and what we create in order to keep life going.

Sun keywords and areas of development

- *The creative impulse emerging from one's love for life.*

- *Character and personality, leadership qualities, the ability to initiate and promote goals, the capacity to take the forefront and perform.*

- *Self-actualization, creative qualities and insights, the need to have an impact and leave a legacy.*

- *Caring, generosity, one's personal investment in life and the living, issues of respect.*

- *The relationship between one generation and the next, the relationship between the leader and the follower with mutual expectations to perform, inspire, and carry the torch. The relationship with the father, the description of his personality.*

Note: The relationship dynamics between the child and the parents apply whether the Sun is in the child's chart, describing his or her familial and paternal interactions, or in the parents' charts, describing their approach to their children.

The Sun in Aries ♈, in the 1st House, or in Aspect to Mars ♂

— The creative impulse emerging from one's love for life.

— Character and personality, leadership qualities, the ability to initiate and promote goals, the capacity to take the forefront.

— Self-actualization, creative qualities and insights, the need to have an impact and leave a legacy.

— Caring, generosity, one's personal investment in life and the living, issues of respect.

With the Sun in Aries, in the first house, or in aspect to Mars, a person's love for life manifests in the willingness and effort to take personal charge and fight for life against potential threats of oppression or extinction. Creativity is awakened and emerges like a new sun, vital and potent, ardently piercing its way through to gain new ground and conquer darkness.

There is an evolutionary need for the person to play an active role in creating and protecting life against contradicting forces, and to forge one's way through space and time. Strength is developed by standing up to potential defiance or any factor that attempts to control or suppress what one is about; the driving force is the impulse to be and the need emerge victor against the odds of defeat or death. In some cases, the Sun in these placements describes a memory of having been denied, disregarded, or stripped of rights, rendering one defensive and protective of justice and freedom of action. Consciously or unconsciously, one may be consumed by the need to prove one's right to exist and to do things independently; therefore, creative capacities are heightened as a way to mark one's presence and inspiration.

Sometimes the struggle for existence expands beyond one's private scope and includes fighting for the rights of minorities or underprivileged populations. The person may engage in a battle to restore respect in hope of abolishing different types of oppressive systems. A defensive, alert, and emotionally charged attitude can be expected as the person is easily triggered by perceived injustice. Inadvertently, the person may spontaneously attain leadership positions while defending principles, rights, or causes: through various forms of activism, the courage to take a stand can inspire others.

The Sun in this position represents the beginning of the process of becoming; in this budding phase, considerable effort and perseverance must be invested to conquer obstacles and eventual opposition. Without voicing oneself and consciously pushing goals and causes forward, one risks fading into anonymity. For example, an individual may pioneer a new project and completely identify with it, spending hours and resources to develop it, and then engage in an effort to prove its relevance to critics. Once a new project takes off, there is a tendency to shift one's attention to new endeavors rather than maintain existing ones.

Under these influences, the person is usually reluctant to have to depend on other people in order to promote personal goals and ambitions. There is a desire to follow one's own inspiration and compromise on nothing; hence working alone or leading others is the preferred mode of operation. There is a need to feel personally involved and passionate about one's goals: doing something out of obligation or against personal firm principles is doomed to failure. Once engaged in a creative process, the person becomes like a powerful engine—the investment is total and he or she "trail blazes" forward until the goal is attained.

Impatience is common if disturbances or obstructions erupt and divert the course of events, and yet when they occur, these obstacles are frontally addressed. A desire for quick results renders one uncomfortable with states of limbo; if things stagnate, new ways are employed to try speeding up the actualization of personal goals. Sometimes, the person may come on too strong and override other people's objectives, even crush them. In some cases, this happens because of one's blind passion and innocent loss of perspective, but in other circumstances, an overly defensive streak can manifest in pronounced competitive inclinations. The passion to win is stimulated by the rage to exist.

Generally speaking, these configurations point to a generous approach to life and people. Personal engagement and dedication is transparent and obvious. However, easily offended and prone to causing adversity, the person tends to rebel and break away from any engagement if feeling disrespected or unjustly treated; when this happens, working things out diplomatically is sometimes the last thing on his or her mind.

The Sun in these positions describes recurrent new starts with the capacity to reinvent oneself a few times during one's life. Evolutionarily speaking, the person searches for his or her sense of purpose and plants seeds in different directions to eventually see what takes and blooms. Even though the determination to own one's destiny and to be loyal to oneself is strong, finding out what that destiny actually is and what one is truly about is a work in progress; the person may feel tremendous passion and creative inspiration but struggle to actually give it a defined form. Every new direction can appear to be "the one," but eventually enthusiasm wanes when reality does not support personal expectations. One may have to come to terms with having a few new starts in life instead of following a single long-lasting direction.

The recurrence of new beginnings does not necessarily result from wrong choices but more from an internal process of self-discovery whereby one cyclically redefines personal goals and values. It can manifest in feeling "done" with a particular project and then having a new inspiration to self-actualize in a way that better fits one's new state of being. Each moment brings a new revelation that can change the person's direction. While deeply embedded in the effort to be and exist, one's identity and direction is still in the making and subject to redefinition.

With distinctive creative capacities, there is a fundamental need for freedom to pursue personal inspiration. Creativity reflects one's effort to fend off death; consequently, it holds sacred meaning and is something one is protective of. As a result, the person usually fares best when self-employed or when given the latitude to independently develop projects. He or she has the power to energize people or projects and infuse enthusiasm in others. Whether an entrepreneur or an artist, one's personal contribution may be found in developing projects and promoting pioneering ideas. Similarly, one may become an activist, using fervor to support those in need and help them come into being.

> *— The relationship between one generation and the next, the relationship between the leader and the follower with mutual expectations to perform, inspire, and carry the torch. The relationship with the father, the description of his personality.*

With the Sun in Aries, in the first house, or in aspect to Mars, the family may serve as an encouraging force for the child. Representing a strong force behind the child's struggles and ambitions, the parents may offer unconditional support. There may be expectations to accomplish important things and take projects seriously, sometimes to the extreme of projecting expectations of heroism on the child; the child may be pressured to achieve extraordinary feats in life and feel anonymous when failing to do so.

In this context, the relationship with the father may rely on mutual inspiration and dedication; however, this bond can sometimes be emotionally overcharged to the point of overidentification. For example, the father may fail to grasp the child's individual nature or opinion and expect him or her to agree with him on everything. He may be a kind, proud, generous, active, and yet stubborn and temperamental man. Eventually, the child will feel the need to uncover his or her unique sense of self, and if the father fails to accept this process, the child will likely rebel and separate from the father.

In other circumstances, adversity may reign between family members to the point of serious antagonism. It can be a struggle for the child if he or she feels misunderstood and has to fight his or her way through in order to have choices legitimized. Arguments, anger, strife, and resulting dramas can be common in this case and are usually accompanied by jealousy and a constant feeling of discrimination that is shared by one or more family members. The child may strive for attention and recognition as a proof of existence, but end up gaining that only through rivalry. The father's character may be dominated by his temper and an overwhelming presence because of his desire to win and impose his way. He may be volatile and swing from being an ally to a rival. In extreme cases, his emotional outbursts can manifest in physical violence.

These configurations can also point to an abrupt separation from the father because of a dispute, a parental divorce, or even death. It may also be that the child and the father choose to sever their connection for various periods of time in order for each side to regain their sense of individuality, instead of either party compromising their sense of individuality.

Positively, these configurations describe a family that promotes individuality and the unique qualities of the child, and grants independence and freedom as a form of family support. The parents themselves may have entrepreneurial or artistic tendencies and encourage the child to develop in this direction. With a strong familial support system, the child may inspire the courage to forge through life's challenges and accomplish a meaningful sense of destiny.

Evolutionary Lesson

The Sun in these positions describes an evolutionary lesson to survive nature's natural selection process through the means of one's own creative effort. Consequently, one's sense of purpose and existence can be recurrently challenged, but each victory renders one stronger and more confident; the principles that one stands for are subject to existential tests. The personal evolutionary objective is to keep creating and producing in order to defy the odds of defeat and exist; yet there is also a lesson in learning to dissolve adversity and win together when possible.

The Sun in Taurus ♉, in the 2ⁿᵈ House, or in Aspect to Venus ♀

- *The creative impulse emerging from one's love for life.*

- *Character and personality, leadership qualities, the ability to initiate and promote goals, the capacity to take the forefront.*

- *Self-actualization, creative qualities and insights, the need to have an impact and leave a legacy.*

- *Caring, generosity, one's personal investment in life and the living, issues of respect.*

With the Sun in Taurus, in the second house, or in aspect to Venus, a person's love for life manifests in an effort to solidify the life force and gather all of one's resources within and without to secure supply and continuity. Creativity increases tremendously as one integrates it into the realm of matter through using the senses and available resources to build foundations and beautify the experience of life.

There is an evolutionary need to preserve the life impulse by creating a solid and stable foundation with the hope that this foundation remains to serve future generations. The individual aspires to create conditions that support and nurture a consistent flow of creativity—one's sense of being must not only exist, but subsist.

Creativity and personality develop from within instead of being influenced by external dynamics. Inner foundations are established and dependence is reduced to solidify and remain as authentic as possible to one's sense of self. Values, principles, and purposes are defined within this internal immersion, and they help one stand firm and grounded when proceeding with personal objectives.

The person is naturally self-motivated and inspired to create things that have lasting value. Being one's own leader and following an individualistic and sometimes solitary path, the call for praise and admiration is often secondary: contentment and independence matter most. Inspired, resourceful, resistant to pressure, and trustworthy, one may have leadership capacities, but the odds of assuming a leading role are reduced by a general reluctance to be disturbed by other people. Striving to be unaffected by external trends and pressures, one may appear stubborn and headstrong because only personal experience and inner conviction serve as guiding references.

People living with this person might struggle because they may not be included in his or her life as much as they would like to be. The intensity of this dynamic varies from person to person, and yet when excessive, it can induce extreme isolation or manifest in an inflexible will. In other circumstances, the person may be social and interactive but prefer to act alone and need a lot of space when undertaking projects.

Possessing a wealth of inner resources, the person may enjoy an abundance of artistic capabilities and or self-taught knowledge. There is an inclination for music, pottery, sculpture, drawing, and design. In other ways, self-deductive faculties may take the form of scientific and mathematical prowess. Creative efforts are used to connect to one's essence, give form to feelings and ideas, and foster survival. One may use personal talents as a currency of exchange to secure an income. For example, if not able to afford a higher education, the person might use his or her physical capacities to make money, perhaps through modeling, construction, or agricultural jobs; the body and physical strength are often recognized as the first available resource.

There is a need to define and ground one's sense of self and purpose. Getting acquainted with available means that could foster production and creativity is a step in that direction. There is no appeal in ephemeral success; instead, the person desires to have a strong and enduring impact. Seeking longevity, prosperity, reliability, and influence, the aim is to produce things of quality that stand the test of time.

At times, the strong attachment to consistency and harmony can cause laziness. On the one hand, there is a need to take whatever time is necessary without rushing for quick results when creating something.

On the other hand, if the goal is to always neutralize external pressure and hold on to stability, one's slower pace can become unproductive. Self-indulgence can lead to a waste of potential. Without having to be aggressively ambitious, it is important to maintain a healthy and renewed creative flow.

There is a strong need to involve the senses in one's creative expression. Therefore, one may aspire to create things that appeal to vision, taste, and ear. For example, natural ways of self-expression may include architectural design, landscaping, massage therapy, cooking, or music. The senses reflect a need to experience life through feel, touch, smell, and sexual expression—stimulation through sex is a form of connection to life. However, the senses may be overly indulged sometimes resulting in various forms of excess.

As one aspires to give form to creative expression, productivity can be measured through financial or asset gain. Efforts must lead to tangible results in order to be considered worthwhile; thus accumulating goods may be a way to determine one's sense of power and influence. Alternatively, making money and gaining assets can be perceived as a means of guaranteeing consistency and solidity. Financial security may even become a creative purpose of its own; in this context, creativity may be oriented toward business and asset management. The Sun in these positions potentially describes a capacity to bring about financial prosperity.

Despite the tendency to be territorial and self-contained, the person may exhibit generous qualities, especially through material forms of offerings. For example, one may support others financially and provide them with opportunities to make money, or give people presents. However, there may be a need to trust the other before being generous. Generally inclined to be in a survival mode, generosity is sometimes calculated.

— *The relationship between one generation and the next, the relationship between the leader and the follower with mutual expectations to perform, inspire, and carry the torch. The relationship with the father, the description of his personality.*

The Sun in Taurus, in the second house, or in aspect to Venus can reflect a parental expectation to achieve stability, usually by emphasizing the importance of financial security when assessing the child's creative potential. In the family, success and worth may be measured by financial gain. Thus the child's authentic personality is sometimes overlooked when all the attention is focused on the future material worth of his or her achievements. The family may be affluent and consequently embody these material values. The father may be a reliable and consistent figure but rigid and often poorly communicative, sometimes lacking in a proper education or a broad awareness of diversity. He may be a self-made person who started with meager means and worked hard to gradually attain a higher socioeconomic status.

In other circumstances, the family expectations are minimal and ambition is perceived as secondary. The family lifestyle may be centered in simplicity and regularity, or sometimes the family lives in a rural setting. A lack of stimulation may emphasize the more stable and peaceful aspects of existence but limit growth and opportunities for progress. The father may embody these dynamics and focus on the sensual and physical aspects of life. The child may continue this somewhat uneventful lifestyle or else choose differently through developing his or her inner unique creative potential.

In other ways, the family atmosphere may encourage creativity and authenticity. Refinement, harmony, and culture may be emphasized and provide a sense of stability and peace that is not necessarily materially oriented. The parents may dislike discussing and exposing the unaesthetic aspects of life and avoid delving into issues such as violence and vice, and in such a way shelter themselves and the children from negativity. The father may be strong spirited and possess a wealth of artistic talent allowing him to lead an independent lifestyle. He may be admired for his unique and rich character but possibly remain relatively reclusive and difficult to access.

Evolutionary Lesson

The Sun in these positions describes an evolutionary lesson to realize internal capacities that can be used for creative purposes. The person sees him or herself as a rich mine to excavate goods from. Moreover, the intent is to give form to creative outlets and in such a way allow the life impulse to be more securely channeled. Integrating creativity into the material dimension also provides a tangible way of assessing its worth.

The Sun in Gemini ♊, in the 3rd House, or in Aspect to Mercury ☿

— The creative impulse emerging from one's love for life.

— Character and personality, leadership qualities, the ability to initiate and promote goals, the capacity to take the forefront.

— Self-actualization, creative qualities and insights, the need to have an impact and leave a legacy.

— Caring, generosity, one's personal investment in life and the living, issues of respect.

With the Sun in Gemini, in the third house, or in aspect to Mercury, a person's love for life manifests as the need to learn about its complexity and multiple expressions so that it can be properly navigated and further enhanced. Accordingly, caring for life manifests in educating others about possibilities and ways the diversity of life's elements complement each other. Creativity is stimulated by a desire to expand the mind, discover new forms, and synthesize separate elements into one paradigm.

There is an evolutionary need to better understand the way the environment and life works in order to adapt one's personality and creative expression accordingly. There is a greater chance of success and well-being if one is aware of and in sync with external dynamics.

Integrating into the environment involves coordinating one's rhythm of production with the external rhythm. Consequently, the person learns about life's diverse character and the multiplicity of existing orientations in order to find his or her place in the midst of it all. Finding the balance between personal expression and the environmental requirement is a work in progress. When well-adjusted, the individual expands the impact of his or her creative outlets through networking and remaining open to diversity.

Adaptation requirements generate an observing nature when one enquires about the external and internal world. However, a split can occur between the two realities if the person develops a persona to respond to the external world while keeping the inner self more concealed. The persona is a more presentable version of the self that displays taste, erudition, manners, wit, and poise. When becoming more socially and culturally exposed, one may feel it is not necessary or advisable to be completely transparent to others—there is a self-protective instinct to guard weaknesses and insecurities from potential derision. The individual may, consequently, appear more self-confident than he or she actually is. Nonetheless, through accumulating diverse experiences, one's personality becomes more refined, cultivated, conscious, and colorful. A broader perspective is developed that includes different ways to express creativity and proceed with life.

When mismanaged, the pressure to adapt can induce a loss of self in the environment as one's personality becomes overly associated with social and cultural expectations. The person may end up copying what others do, forgetting what he or she is inwardly about. Succumbing to role models with unique character and wit, one's identity and sense of purpose may get lost and scattered.

Eventually, when mediating between one's authentic self and the outside world, one becomes well trained in dealing with a variety of simultaneous pressures. Better navigation skills are developed that foster the capacity to successfully manage the complexity of existence. For example, a more objective approach and broader perspective helps one quickly decide whether initiatives can thrive or not. The ability to launch multiple projects at once and coordinate between the different factors involved is also enhanced. Having a broader awareness also enables one to connect with the right people and know how and where to proceed when wanting to promote ventures or causes; consequently, information and knowledge help one proceed quickly and efficiently. The Sun in these positions is well equipped to survive in the "jungle of modern life" and interact with different environmental factors. Stress and stimulation levels may be high, but the capacity to confidently handle challenges can be acquired.

These configurations can describe pronounced creativity in all mental and intellectual avenues including information, communication, education, navigation, language, and speech. Social and networking skills may also be well developed and manifest in coordinating, mediating, or networking skills. Accordingly, it is likely that cross-cultural experiences are encountered; one may move from a rural setting to a city or from one country to another, possibly because of self-actualization incentives. If born in a relatively small-minded environment, one may eventually feel the urge to relocate in order to have more opportunities and meet people who better relate to one's broader ambitions. The person learns that life is so rich and has so much to offer that it inspires him or her to move to other places if an environment is not supportive or limiting. Such a need for exposure and accomplishment is not necessarily motivated by an ambition to achieve; it is more rooted in a need for exposure and a hunger to personally experience life. Once knowing about existing diversity, one may create networks between different environments and facilitate projects founded on cultural exchange or international trade.

There is a strong affinity for the foreign, which usually makes one welcoming and generous with immigrants and supportive of their rights. A dedication to promoting tolerance and accepting cultural diversity is common under these influences as one usually looks forward to learning from different traditions through art, food, or language. Generally speaking, an important cause is found in educating others and promoting awareness in order to overcome existing ignorance—this may apply to different areas in life, not only social causes.

- *The relationship between one generation and the next, the relationship between the leader and the follower with mutual expectations to perform, inspire, and carry the torch. The relationship with the father, the description of his personality.*

The Sun in Gemini, in the third house, or in aspect to Mercury may describe a family atmosphere that is relatively liberal and supportive of a child's need for learning and experimentation. The parents may encourage cultural exposure and stimulate discussions that reflect on life's dynamics, common knowledge, and culture. The family itself may have cross-cultural exposure either because the parents come from different backgrounds or because the family has relocated to different countries. The father may be social, well-connected, restless, and possibly critical. He may be often absent because of travel, but yet have many stories to share. The relationship between the father and the child is usually relatively easy-going and friendly; however, the child may feel that the absence or permissiveness of the father leaves him or her without a clear sense of direction. In a way, this liberal approach may offer too much freedom without clear direction.

In other ways, the family environment may be weak in character if the parents are overly self-conscious and heavily influenced by external opinion when defining their sense of purpose. Overidealizing trends and gossiping about other people's success, they may fail to provide the child with a sense of direction and the confidence to express creative capacity. Sometimes, the loss of identity happens because the parents are new immigrants and pressured to adopt new customs. No longer belonging to their old identity, and yet not fully familiar with a new one, they may experience an identity crisis that affects the children. In one way or another, the child may feel alienated from the parents' mentality as it is perceived as more limited or even backward—instead, the child may find role models in the environment. The child may, in this case, feel embarrassed by the father and sometimes only come to accept him in later years. Both sides can transcend the fear of shame as they become better integrated within themselves.

Alternatively, the parents may be very mental and sophisticated, possibly coming from a rich academic background with a scientific inclination. The child may be highly cultivated and expected to succeed through intellectual achievement. Criticism or even sarcasm may make the child immediately conscious of any faux pas. While providing the child with a wealth of learning opportunities, there may be a lack of a heartfelt connection. The father may be socially respected for his intelligence but fail to relate to the child if he or she isn't "mentally polished" according to his personal expectations. Learning to listen and accept each other's differences is part of the evolutionary lesson between the father and the child.

Evolutionary Lesson

The Sun in these positions describes an evolutionary lesson to understand that life takes many forms because each time and space uniquely colors environmental factors. Accordingly, there is a constant need to adapt one's creative expression to the nature of the current time and space. Positively, the person becomes more aware of life's intricate mechanism and adapts to it by synchronizing his or her creative output with environmental factors while maintaining authenticity in the process.

The Sun in Cancer ♋, in the 4th House, or in Aspect to the Moon ☽

— The creative impulse emerging from one's love for life.

— Character and personality, leadership qualities, the ability to initiate and promote goals, the capacity to take the forefront.

— Self-actualization, creative qualities and insights, the need to have an impact and leave a legacy.

— Caring, generosity, one's personal investment in life and the living, issues of respect.

With the Sun in Cancer, in the fourth house, or in aspect to the Moon, a person's love for life manifests in a protective and nurturing instinct, and an understanding of the importance of one's role in monitoring and enhancing life's development. Caring for life shows through offering a support system based on mutual reliance. Creativity grows and is nurtured by time and attention without compromising authenticity and reliability.

There is an evolutionary need to emotionally secure and support one's creative self-actualization. The person aspires to fully get in touch with his or her sense of purpose and takes whatever time is needed to model creative outlets. Supportive conditions to facilitate this process include freedom of creative expression and experimentation, encouragement for efforts and talents, and time for endeavors to ripen into their intended form. There is a need to feel intimately connected with chosen purposes in order to cater to their development. Intimidating or inhibiting factors are avoided in order to remain authentic and preserve supportive conditions.

When well-managed, efforts invested in caring and nurturing bring about a confident, generous, and accessible personality that is gifted with highly unique creative ideas. Feeling very personal and intimate with the creative process fosters imagination and inspiration, and gives a personal touch and twist to the way of doing things. When producing things, there is a preference for more intimate settings and a reluctance for larger public exposure based on the concern that collective pressure may divert one's course of action. The person usually prefers to keep things intimate and draw people inside his or her personal world instead of adjusting to external demands; in the person's private kingdom, his or her personality usually shines bright.

Even when compelled to deal with the outside world to publicly promote personal objectives, there is an attempt to establish an atmosphere of friendliness, warmth, and security with the people involved. When creating a sense of familiarity, the person's underlying desire is to maintain a certain amount of control within the environment to make sure that personal needs and conditions are met, and that unwanted strain is minimized.

This personal approach can be inconvenient in that it requires higher maintenance and is usually less practical. One likes to take time when producing things and doesn't want to be pressured by financial concerns. For pragmatic purposes, a person may be incited to surrender control at times, even at the price of compromising the quality of the product or endeavor. However, since the evolutionary intent is to closely nurture personal creativity, it is likely that the person will prefer to operate on a smaller scale and compromise larger public involvement. Yet the lesson still remains to keep personal attachment in check because overprotection can hinder the development of creative processes.

In negative scenarios, when supportive conditions for personal creative development are lacking or disturbed, a chronic sense of insecurity may take over and lead to moodiness, inconsistent output, and a lack of productivity. The person may remain fragile and abandon personal projects and initiatives at the first sign of difficulty. While remaining attached to personal desires, a lack of endurance and potency may induce repeated failure. In this respect, one may be reduced to constantly depending on others and yet in a childlike way still attempt to control dynamics.

Under these influences, accessible areas of expression include social care, hospitality services, or food-related occupations. The ability to relate to children is pronounced because the person's own inner child is very much alive and validated. One may even recuperate lost or skipped phases in one's personal development by interacting with children and stimulating their creativity. Conversely, if the person's inner child is seriously wounded, he or she may feel threatened by children and compete with their neediness. In this case, one can expect narcissistic behavior.

The person can be drawn toward many areas of creative expression whether artistic or entrepreneurial in nature. But whatever one chooses to dedicate oneself to, it is usually something one is good at and enjoys doing. Rarely are things accomplished out of obligation; moreover, when one's heart is not invested, one can expect catastrophic failure.

These configurations point to a desire to promote family values and emphasize the need to establish a support system in life. For example, when managing others and making decisions, the person is usually more accessible and will consider employees' personal circumstances. In an impersonal and fast-paced world, the person with the Sun in these placements may seem at odds with common expectations and therefore be considered a rare bird for being more inclusive and patient, given that he or she doesn't succumb to the pressure to fit into the mainstream.

– *The relationship between one generation and the next, the relationship between the leader and the follower with mutual expectations to perform, inspire, and carry the torch. The relationship with the father, the description of his personality.*

The Sun in Cancer, in the fourth house, or in aspect to the Moon potentially describes a family atmosphere that is warm and supportive of the child's expression and ambitions. The parents may be dedicated to their children and provide personal attention and nurturing, usually being very generous toward the children. Yet the familial support system may be a harsh contrast to the more judgmental and rigorous outside world. The person may not always be taken seriously when asserting personal ideas or objectives in a public setting. Within the family, the mother may be glorified and put on a pedestal as a symbol of love and protection. The father may be kind, accessible, and childlike. He may be very maternal and participate in domestic activities. He may, in certain cases, lack the potency of leadership and possibly end up dominated and manipulated by the child because of his indulgent and accessible character.

In different circumstances, the family atmosphere may emanate weakness to the point of ineffectiveness. One or both parents may be too self-absorbed and fail to really address the child's needs, sometimes through an emotionally overbearing approach. Lacking a reliable support system, the child may become withdrawn; instead of developing, his or her vital energy may be consumed in surviving and consequently all creative potential may remain unrealized. The father may be inconsistent and lack credibility when attempting to assert his authority and expectations. In some circumstances, the father may compete with the child for attention and nurturing, and consequently deny the child support. The sum of these circumstances generates severe emotional displacement in the child that can result in emotional immaturity and a core feeling of insecurity.

Evolutionary Lesson

The Sun in these positions describes an evolutionary lesson to define and nurture one's core creative nature. Gradually, the person discovers what he or she is about and gains confidence in identifying with a defined sense of purpose. While the tendency is to keep one's field of action rather intimate and informal, once creative capacities are asserted one's influence can significantly affect other people and touch their emotional core.

The Sun in Leo ♌ or in the 5ᵗʰ House

– *The creative impulse emerging from one's love for life.*

– *Character and personality, leadership qualities, the ability to initiate and promote goals, the capacity to take the forefront.*

– *Self-actualization, creative qualities and insights, the need to have an impact and leave a legacy.*

– *Caring, generosity, one's personal investment in life and the living, issues of respect.*

With the Sun in Leo or in the fifth house, a person's love for life manifests in making sure that the flame of life continues to burn through ongoing creativity and that there is a next generation in place for the torch to pass on to. Creativity is peaking as one feels ripe to assume a role in enhancing and feeding existence, striving in such a way to overcome the ultimate dread of times ending and or extinction.

The person's sense of self is potent and so is one's personal engagement with life. There is an evolutionary need to give meaning to one's personal existence by fulfilling one's creative potential. The person wants to live for important things and influence the course of events. The ego recognizes the power of its impact and aspires to actively participate in the Creation; thus the ability to give something back to life is recognized as one now assumes some responsibility for the unfolding of existence.

The concept of carrying the torch of life is prominent; taking the role of the flame keeper, a person is under an evolutionary imperative to promote development and avoid extinction. Consequently, in the course of life, he or she needs to leave some form of a legacy for the sake of continuity; there is a strong pressure to create something of inspiring value for the next generation. Sometimes it is through having children and caring for them that one leaves a legacy.

These circumstances generate considerable expectations for success, even heroism, from parents, superiors, or the younger generation. Consequently, a fear of meaninglessness, mediocrity, and failure may haunt one. In some cases, the person finds his or her purpose in life rather quickly, but in other cases, the outlet for creative expression may not be immediately obvious leading to a feeling of frustration. Sometimes in the need for meaning and achievement, the person may follow parental expectations and take over the parents' business or continue their profession; while this is not necessarily a negative outcome, one must assess if it is a truly authentic choice.

Life is usually taken seriously under these influences. Every step and decision is given significance and meaning, and similarly personal attention is focused on details and nuances. A strong presence and involvement with creative projects generates a meaningful emotional association with things; every element of one's path is given weight. Likewise, the person expects the same amount of acknowledgment, consideration, and respect from others. Indifference and insolence are perceived as a vice. However, this highly personalized approach is high maintenance and can easily become excessive. Unimportant details and occurrences may be dramatized and unnecessarily complicate development—it is easy to lose perspective.

While a need for respect engenders a more serious approach, the need to celebrate existence encourages a playful approach. One needs to feel alive through strong emotions of joy, intensity, and passion. Personality and uniqueness often make one stand out from others, even when being discreet. Although the Leo archetype influence is usually extroverted, it is not unusual for some people to keep a low public profile as a way to reduce external expectations. In either case, one usually possesses a strong sense of purpose with defined principles.

For some, the very fact of existing may be a form of celebration because each day and each creation represents a victory over death. Therefore, one may be naturally inclined to approach life festively through fun and sensual pleasures such as fine wine, an abundance of food, sexual enjoyment, hobbies, and play. Nevertheless, failing to find's one path and meaning in life can lead to the opposite extreme of depression that often results from emotionally exaggerating negative emotions.

While striving to take charge of one's destiny, the individual fervently focuses on projects that make him or her feel passionate and determined. The cause is important, sometimes collectively so, and all efforts are directed toward manifesting the desired outcome. Other people may be inspired by such a creative approach and want to associate or contribute to the person's cause or endeavor; consequently, they come to accept his or her authority in the matter. Generosity and gratitude is usually expressed when other people partake in one's vision and projects; however, the fear of losing the initial purpose through too many external interventions may cause an uncompromising need to maintain authority.

Positively, the person develops distinctive leadership qualities and manages to bring people together in order to contribute toward important developments and causes. Naturally, success and wisdom make one an inspiring figure who sometimes even draws adoration. However, shining brightly also commonly attracts jealousy and with it sabotage attempts by others; this is something one has to intelligently address to avoid getting carried away in unnecessary power struggles.

When leadership positions are mismanaged, an overly dominant and inflexible approach may induce an abuse of authority; expecting absolute loyalty for one's generosity, the individual may become a benevolent dictator who tolerates no contradiction when bossing people around without considering their personalities. In further extremes, one may even exhibit ungratefulness and take another's effort for granted, literally generating a slave-master dynamic. Eventually, this attitude is bound to stimulate rebellion, antagonism, and defeat.

Similarly, being protective of personal creations, the person may refrain from releasing them when needed. He or she may see every creation as an extension of the self and not allow other people to use or manage the end product the way that circumstances require. This form of excessive control is bound to obstruct creative development.

One must understand that once created, projects and products have a life of their own and must pass hands and be subjected to different influences. One can inspire, but not dictate, the future of these creations.

Under these influences, there is an obvious appeal for artistic expression; the ability to move people is accentuated whether through stage performances, music composition, or the fine arts. Creativity can also manifest through becoming an entrepreneur and initiating projects. Otherwise, chosen professions may include any area of expertise in the fields of science or medicine.

With a wealth of inner resources and a predominantly emotional approach to life, the person knows that personal investment is the way to fulfillment. Caring about life can also manifest in promoting others' well-being, whether human or animal life. Love, generosity, and compassion may come naturally and motivate one to help, empower, and encourage others. In this regard, protecting human rights and respecting life may be prevailing principles that govern one's life.

> *– The relationship between one generation and the next, the relationship between the leader and the follower with mutual expectations to perform, inspire, and carry the torch. The relationship with the father, the description of his personality.*

With the Sun in Leo or in the fifth house, the family atmosphere may encourage achievement and creativity. The parents themselves may hold important career positions whether self-made entrepreneurial ventures or involvement in larger societal structures. The child may feel special and wanted, receiving considerable attention and resources in order to promote his or her personal development. However, it is common for the parents to unconsciously stimulate competition between siblings when assessing which child is the most promising. The child with these configurations may stand on either side of the fence, either becoming the "favorite" or the one "losing" the competition. Being perceived as "the chosen one" may provide privileges; however, it is a dynamic that can easily turn sour when expectations accumulate and end up becoming overwhelming. Moreover, this special treatment is likely to induce jealousy or even feelings of guilt among siblings. When this approach is better managed, the parents generously give each child the best care and individual attention, emphasizing his or her unique skills. The father is often a prominent figure with a strong presence. The child may feel close to the father and admire him.

In extreme cases, the pressure for success may generate a very unhealthy family dynamic. The parents, especially the father, may be highly controlling and unable to see the child for who he or she is. This dictator-like attitude stimulates a love-hate relationship toward the father; on the one hand, admiration is cultivated because of his prominent presence; on the other hand, anger accumulates because of his abusive character. The child may feel trapped in emotional blackmail when made to feel guilty or inadequate for not responding to family expectations. At some point, he or she may choose to rebel and detach from the father's grip. The father may be self-absorbed and even selfish, seeing his family and children as personal slaves. This attitude commonly manifests in being highly demanding of others while lenient with oneself.

In other circumstances, the family may be relatively liberal and generate a playful atmosphere. Exposing the child to different life experiences, instigating fun, and encouraging creative outlets, the parents may offer opportunities for growth while providing a solid support system. The father may be a playful individual, usually childish and self indulging to some degree, but accessible to the child.

Evolutionary Lesson

The Sun in these positions describes an evolutionary lesson to refrain from taking life for granted and to do what is in one's power to sustain and promote its development. Through inspired creativity, the person is in a giving mode and receives from others when he or she is moved and supported.

The Sun in Virgo ♍, in the 6th House, or in Aspect to Mercury ☿

— The creative impulse emerging from one's love for life.

— Character and personality, leadership qualities, the ability to initiate and promote goals, the capacity to take the forefront.

— Self-actualization, creative qualities and insights, the need to have an impact and leave a legacy.

— Caring, generosity, one's personal investment in life and the living, issues of respect.

With the Sun in Virgo, in the sixth house, or in aspect to Mercury, a person's love for life manifests in a continual effort to improve function and avoid waste so that the flow of life may be directed in the best known way. Accordingly, caring for life manifests in constantly analyzing existing dynamics to detect and implement better ways to use available resources and attain excellence.

On a personal level, there is an evolutionary need to increase the productivity and efficiency of one's creative expression and make the best of one's existing potential. The individual is usually blessed with fine talents, skills, and insights acquired through dedication and attention to details. Personal capabilities facilitate self-sufficiency and provide control over the unfolding of one's destiny. Navigation skills and goals are further refined and more precisely defined.

Under these influences, there is a strong focus on developing strategies to improve the quality and effect of one's efforts; the desire for optimal results requires a more thoughtful approach. The person is now well aware of environmental considerations and the best way to accomplish an end result; therefore, personal will-power increases in being "more on target." Confidence is gained that with enough effort, focus, and determination, any objective can be achieved. When materializing goals, the Sun in these positions describes an ability to operate in a fairly independent and self-driven way. Yielding to obstacles or waiting for things to happen is not so much on one's agenda; instead, one strives to work hard, produce high quality output, and materialize creative goals.

Through trial and error, one realizes that resources, time, and energy are not endless and must be used wisely. Thus when initiating new projects, more thought is given to efficiency and preservation. When making choices, the fear of waste makes one more cautious in order to avoid an unnecessary investment of time and resources. The motivating mantra is to create more in a shorter period of time while meeting standards of excellence. The emphasis on quality is strong because effectiveness depends on it. Thus there is a pronounced tendency to analyze everything in order to identify errors and redefine the best way to proceed. This approach induces a highly critical attitude both toward oneself and those taking part in shared endeavors.

Positively expressed, the person is recognized for his or her qualifications and possibly even for being an expert in his or her field. Proceeding with care, caution, and dedication, the ability to surpass common standards can put one in a position of high professional demand. An awareness of details usually generates a refined sense of taste and a high level of sophistication in many fields; often the individual is cultivated and appreciates art, food, design, or advanced technology. A healthy combination of practicality and aesthetic consciousness may bring praise, success, and admiration from the environment. The person's personality is usually powerful and strong spirited, albeit, more comfort is found in discreet manners and conduct. One may feel uncomfortable with attention that is projected toward oneself, preferring to divert it to the actual work done. Concerns about appropriateness dim flamboyant or other excessively extroverted behavior.

Negatively expressed, the person may become too attached to the details and lose perspective. Overanalyzing environmental dynamics and one's personal position can lead to stagnation. A fear of failure and wrongdoing can generate a feeling of never being ready to actualize one's creative potential; sometimes, when excessive, this approach can stimulate panic attacks. Debilitated by excessive self-consciousness, the person may fluctuate between rigidity and a lack of confidence. High standards are sought without compromise, but a continual feeling of never measuring up can block one from even trying to fulfill one's potential; in this case, the person may settle for security in a job that does not really match personal qualifications. Opting for practicality at the price of passion, one may end up leading a functional lifestyle denuded of personal meaning.

In other ways, conservatism and perfectionism can excessively accentuate the fear of uncertainty and the need for control. When proceeding with projects, the person may lack flexibility and want to control the way everything unfolds. Refusing to let go of personal preferences when necessary and trying to reach one's goal at all costs can prove detrimental and become exhausting. Efficiency requires improvisation and flexibility, something one may not always feel comfortable with.

The need to produce effectively also relies on understanding that other people depend on one's service for their own creativity. For example, an artist relies on the manufactured quality of his or her tools, a journalist on the effectiveness of distribution, and so on. Interdependence of services pressures the person with these configurations to perform highly for fear that personal shortcomings may have a domino effect on the rest of the service chain; if the electrician does not perform adequately, many other services that rely on receiving electricity are bound to suffer. Consequently, the sense of duty and responsibility increases and so does the criticism toward other people's functionality when it is perceived as inadequate. When extreme, the pressure can lead to obsession and induce workaholic behavior; it can become a never ending effort to beat a previous performance at the expense of self-care and stability.

High standards do not mingle well with vulnerabilities. The person may verbally humiliate those who do not perform effectively or those who lack style and refined manners. Criticism is important because it fosters improvement, but for it to be effective, it must come from positive intentions—humiliation naturally drowns the creative impulse.

Under these influences, natural creative inclinations and interests might include a profession within the wide variety of technological fields from mechanical inventiveness to infrastructure. The medical field or anything related to hygiene maintenance can also stimulate one's creativity and skillfulness. In different ways, one's aesthetic sensitivity and manual skills can lead one to artistic fields such as design, landscaping, and crafts.

A lot of care and dedication may be invested in developing an infrastructure and fostering efficiency. The person may be passionate about finding ways to combat any form of waste, decline, or chaos and consequently spend time restoring neglected environments or tools. One may adhere to other important causes including protecting the environment through recycling, caring for endangered species, or developing nonpolluting technology; one may live by the principle that the planet Earth is a valuable resource we cannot afford to waste.

— The relationship between one generation and the next, the relationship between the leader and the follower with mutual expectations to perform, inspire, and carry the torch. The relationship with the father, the description of his personality.

With the Sun in Virgo, in the sixth house, or in aspect to Mercury, the family atmosphere may emanate high standards and sophistication. The parents may be refined and cultivated, expecting the child to attain practical and intellectually esteemed goals in life. The parents may emphasize order and regulation, inciting the child to act and proceed with care, reliability, and good will, often at the cost of spontaneity. The child may be supported materially and intellectually and coached to carry on objectives and creativity. Faux pas are usually quickly recognized and attract corrective remarks. The father may be a refined figure that invests considerable effort in his profession, enjoying the subtleties of life. Possibly very particular, and thus not so easy going, he may be easily disappointed and not able to let go of his expectations for the child. Positively, his wisdom, experience, and craftsmanship may greatly inspire the child.

In a different way, the family atmosphere may emanate nervousness when each member presents a better strategy for dealing with life and challenges in general, and critically undermines each other's ideas. The child may feel easily invalidated, sometimes through plain criticism or sarcasm. While practical needs and efforts are addressed, the family environment may lack emotional support.

In a more extreme way, the child may grow up in a dysfunctional family where, for example, the parents are unemployed or have emotional hang-ups. Crises may dominate the family atmosphere and force the parents to constantly reassess their ways. As a result, the child may cease to rely on the parents and become self-sufficient in order to independently find answers for his or her problems—learning from the parents what *not* to do! The child's evolutionary impulse is to better regulate his or her life and transcend the state of being in a chronic crisis. Thus he or she may become the sane and a high-functioning person in the family, taking better charge of life. The father may be a somewhat self-righteous person who does not really do well in life. Nervous and impatient, he may often be inaccessible.

Evolutionary Lesson

The Sun in these positions reflects an evolutionary lesson to integrate one's creative expression into the environment and therefore test its effectiveness when other people use it. When creating something, the person is naturally pressured to produce a high quality product that can serve others in their creative process. When mastered, these configurations can bring excellence and grace.

The Sun in Libra ♎, in the 7ᵗʰ House, or in Aspect to Venus ♀

— The creative impulse emerging from one's love for life.

— Character and personality, leadership qualities, the ability to initiate and promote goals, the capacity to take the forefront.

— Self-actualization, creative qualities and insights, the need to have an impact and leave a legacy.

— Caring, generosity, one's personal investment in life and the living, issues of respect.

With the Sun in Libra, in the seventh house, or in aspect to Venus, a person's love for life manifests in striving to unite polarities and overcome duality so that life is experienced in its harmonious essence. Acknowledging the different ways creativity is expressed makes one aware that life takes many forms—each form fulfilling an essential role in the Creation without which other forms could not subsist.

There is an evolutionary need to develop a more expansive creative approach to life. The person may feel saturated with what he or she has done and yearn to add new dimensions of being and expressing to his or her life. A feeling of inner lack awakens one's interest in others in order to observe and learn new ways of creating and proceeding. The individual is often rich with insight, knowledge, and taste but goes through a self-doubting phase. The evolutionary purpose of these configurations is to grow and encompass a broader perspective by learning and exchanging concepts with others; consequently, there is a strong focus on social and relationship exchange.

One may be drawn to a variety of people who have different ways of expressing a strong personality and their creative nature. This attraction is not always conscious and formulated. The intensity of these relationships varies and can include brief encounters, friendships, and intimate bonds. In each case, one learns from observing what other people do and assimilates what is appreciated. Thus it is common for the person to develop a more neutral approach to different creative styles and leadership approaches ranging from, for example, a starving artist, to an educated scholar, to other cultural approaches altogether. Gaining wide exposure in such a manner provides inspiration, understanding, and a broader awareness.

When well balanced, the individual creative expression reflects a wealth of insight and a more sophisticated approach. Through the ability to introduce different elements into conventions, the person becomes highly creative and innovative. Libra reflects a need for balance; therefore, there is a natural draw to combine opposites, something that can ignite debate and controversy. Reaching a point of saturation, the person's personal approach to creativity and life goes through changing phases, moods, and experimentation.

Leadership qualities include neutrality whereby one may answer diverse needs and yet not really side with anyone specifically. This more impartial approach may upset people if they are looking for firm and definitive leadership. Often the individual inspires other people to find answers within themselves instead of providing them with a conclusive direction—the approach is a more open and reflective.

Commonly, the person may overidentify with other people's way of being. Often doubting oneself, others are easily glamorized sometimes to the point of losing oneself. The person may thoroughly identify with a partner, a leader, or another culture's way and lose touch with his or her own personal origins. Giving too much power to others can bring about abuse or dominance and submission themes. Sometimes, not knowing who he or she is anymore, personal desires and motivations become completely conditioned by someone else; it is an identity crisis that induces a loss of authenticity and true character.

Exposed to diverse ways and stimulated by a need to find a perfectly balanced approach, the person may end up overanalyzing and debating at the cost of his or her own productivity. Lost in theories about the best way to proceed, a simple decision may become a complex equation. When it is time to measure results, this high maintenance approach isn't very practical; the need for balance can leave one immobilized. Nonetheless, this reflective attitude stems from trying to do things the right way and not wanting to rush into decisions. Here the evolutionary lesson is to make a decision according to what is most appropriate in the present moment instead of trying to find the ultimate solution.

Generating a climate of optimism and creativity, the person may shine socially and possess natural talent in the social arena ranging from mediation, to public relations, to event coordination. Social skills may also manifest in promoting international exchange and other similar dynamics including guest hosting, diplomacy, or multicultural event management. The aspiration for balance and neutrality can also incite one to find a sense of purpose in the law profession, perhaps in the role of judge.

Strongly motivated and passionate about promoting tolerance and understanding among divided groups and populations, the person may easily become a freedom fighter who engages for the underdog regardless of who that underdog is. Generosity may be abundant for anyone who is in stressful situation or discriminated against, for the person naturally taps into other people's reality and understands them.

— *The relationship between one generation and the next, the relationship between the leader and the follower with mutual expectations to perform, inspire, and carry the torch. The relationship with the father, the description of his personality.*

The Sun in Libra, in the seventh house, or in aspect to Venus can describe a family atmosphere where the parents emphasize fairness and consideration. They may cultivate values of neutrality and incite the children to pay attention to the environment's needs. The parents may be highly cultivated, possibly intellectual, and politically aware, inspiring the child with ideals of social justice. This approach may at times emphasize larger needs rather than encourage or give special attention to the child him or herself. The father may be philosophically inclined and offer explanations and theories about everything; he may be kind and usually social, but also argumentative when offering alternative opinions to the ones presented.

In a different way, the family dynamics may revolve around the parents' own relationship; an unequal power distribution can create leader and follower roles. One or both of them may have low self-esteem and live with a sense of lack while always admiring what other people have or do. The child may grow up with a feeling that in order to be meaningful and have a purpose, he or she needs other people's approval; it can induce a pleasing attitude and dependency. The father may either be a passive figure who lacks character and individuality or an attractive person who is seldom present, often following friends or flirts. The child may adopt the counselor role within the family, striving to establish fairness and balance.

Similarly, the child may feel that role models at home are weak or uninspiring and be stimulated to search for answers elsewhere. The child may feel embarrassed by one or both parents, aware of more inspiring role models outside of the family. When this tendency is excessive, the sense of lack may never be satisfied with the grass always looking greener elsewhere. The child may eventually learn to accept his or her parents for who they are and be at peace with what is available.

Evolutionary Lesson

The Sun in these positions describes an evolutionary lesson to further develop personal creative capacities and one's involvement with life by stepping outside of oneself and reflecting upon life's diverse expression. The person does not take his or her instinctual expression as the definitive reference anymore, understanding there are other approaches that can be integrated in order to create more holistic results. At the risk of getting lost, one is on a quest for new answers and meaning in order to ultimately offer a better version of one's creativity.

The Sun in Scorpio ♏, in the 8th House, or in Aspect to Pluto ♇

— *The creative impulse emerging from one's love for life.*

— *Character and personality, leadership qualities, the ability to initiate and promote goals, the capacity to take the forefront.*

— *Self-actualization, creative qualities and insights, the need to have an impact and leave a legacy.*

— *Caring, generosity, one's personal investment in life and the living, issues of respect.*

With the Sun in Scorpio, in the eighth house, or in aspect to Pluto, a person's love for life manifests in the courage to confront any internal or external factor that hinders life's productive flow and development. Sharp psychological skills are developed to identify blockages so that change can be implemented for the light to shine brightly where there was darkness.

There is an evolutionary need to empower oneself through creative expression and self-actualization, and find a sense of personal meaning in life. The need for empowerment stems from an inner feeling of limitation; the person may feel that what he or she creates does not have the desired impact or that the passion to create is fundamentally lacking. Typically one experiences the highs and lows of success. When rejected, the decrease of potency generates a need for change and redefinition, and forces introspection in order to identify the root of the blockages.

The need to regain a sense of power and vitality compels the person to deconstruct all related dynamics and psychoanalyze his or her behavior (as well as others') so that a better way of proceeding can be found. The ultimate evolutionary purpose is to develop higher forms of creativity and self expression that more deeply and meaningfully touch people and life. When the transformation is successful, the person becomes a source of inspiration, serves as an agent of change, and incites others to evolve and deepen their existence.

The need for transformation often results from a crisis where rejection or failure is experienced. The person cannot take him or herself for granted and is pressured to question environmental conditions as well as personal approaches. The crisis varies in intensity but is a source of stress. Moreover, working on removing obstacles requires patience, insight, and perception. Sometimes the person blames the environment for personal failures and becomes angry that the imposed limitations are unjust. Negatively, this situation can generate resentment. One may go as far as behaving vindictively to release frustration. Yet even if the root of the problem is truly outside of oneself, problems can be solved through changing internal attitudes instead of getting carried away with anger. For example, when unjustly rejected, one can look inside to see why the need for approval is important.

Unresolved emotion may trigger unwanted results. For example, jealousy can cause power struggles and block the creative flow. In other ways, corruption and dishonest behavior can result in the loss of respect. In order to move beyond personal weakness, the person is pressured to look at his or her shadows and bring them to light. For example, when socially unpopular, one may suffer from low self-esteem and be forced to find ways to gain appeal. The crisis stimulates strong emotions, but if the person is willing to make the effort to change, he or she ultimately becomes more conscious and intelligent. Once success is attained, it is usually well deserved because there is a lot of psychological effort behind it. However, one must remember that success cannot be taken for granted nor can it be mismanaged; the person cannot afford to be naïve or deceitful as consequences soon follow.

Because there is a continual need to grow and increase the depth of one's creative expression and involvement with life, the person keeps redefining his or her way over and over again; identifying limitations and finding strategies to overcome them is an ongoing process. The person may feel there is more to life than current circumstances provide and consequently hunt for opportunities to develop oneself. A sense of hunger generates a magnetic attraction to elements that emanate intensity and strength. Eager for inspiration, there is a strong association with role models or opportunities that can take one to the next level.

The value system of the person determines what represents power and intensity. Some may crave more financial power while others seek deeper spiritual meaning. In either case, the hunger for more promotes transformation and deeper creative capabilities.

In productive ways, the individual constantly expands personal creative capacities and has a powerfully transformative effect on others as well. Having gone through crisis and failure, regenerative powers are developed and one learns to remain humble even when holding positions of influence. Challenging life experiences render one wise and deep, often putting one in a position of coaching others when they go through upheaval. Ultimately, having the power to generate metamorphoses, the person can bring light, life, and healing in places that were dark, dysfunctional, and destructive.

Moreover, as a result of the inner work that has been accomplished, a person's creative expression may go beyond what is currently established and stimulate collective change and growth. People holding on to obsolete ways may feel threatened when the person exposes their limitations and therefore may react in defiant ways. Yet if one remains centered, humble, and dedicated, inner strength and wisdom eventually dissolve power struggles. One may develop a very powerful and intense personality that becomes very magnetic.

Negatively, the person may end up possessed by his or her own hunger for more and seek immediate intensity fixes; this dynamic usually manifests in opportunism and a lack of loyalty at the first sign of a new fix. Such behavior commonly intensifies crises and dramas, ultimately leaving one empty and dissatisfied. When trying to regain power in a crisis, the person may resort to manipulating others through emotional blackmail.

With these configurations, one usually possesses a strong personality and sense of individuality. While attentive to external sources of inspiration, the connection to the inner self is highly developed because of ongoing introspection. Personal values, priorities, and principles are usually defined and consistent. When creating or associating with projects, there is a strong focus and complete emotional involvement; results usually reflect a high level of investment and dedication.

Natural areas of creativity and expression may include psychology as well as any other therapy-oriented modality. Having the insight to guide people from weakness to strength, the person can have a regenerative influence. Facing the shadows may also take one to the field of criminology. In a different way, one may actively exploit and develop resources.

Possessing a confrontational nature, the person may associate with causes and become an activist. Exposing limitations and aspiring for change, one may take a proactive role in many different arenas whether social, political, or environmental. Strongly identifying with abandoned beings, whether children or animals, it is not uncommon for the person with the Sun in these placements to take the role of an adoptive parent or mentor.

— *The relationship between one generation and the next, the relationship between the leader and the follower with mutual expectations to perform, inspire, and carry the torch. The relationship with the father, the description of his personality.*

The Sun in Scorpio, in the eighth house, or in aspect to Pluto can describe a family in which the experience of transformation and growth is strongly experienced. Parents may go through phases of success and then emotional crises that reflect the motion of evolution. For example, the family's income may increase over the years reflecting a sense of empowerment, and then the parents may breakup or go through phases of power struggles. Scenarios differ from case to case, but highs and lows are usually experienced in cycles. The father may be an individual with intensity; possibly a self-made person, he may go through upheaval and inspire the child through his regenerative powers. Or similarly, he may be an emotionally intense person who is strongly attached to his children and family. In the latter case, he may have high expectations for the child, sometimes overwhelmingly so. This emotional intensity is likely to generate a crisis when the child eventually seeks to change these dynamics and free him or herself from the father's emotional influence.

In other ways, the child feels a sense of limitation in the family atmosphere and seeks to outgrow and change what the parents embody. In searching for better ways of proceeding, the child may become confrontational with the parents and consistently expose them and their shadows. Specifically the child may perceive the father as an unreliable role model and reject him as such. For example, the father may either have a radically different value system or abuse his power. The father-child relationship may end up highly charged because the child seeks to change the father's ways. Positively, their relationship may be transformed and shift from antagonism to mutual acceptance.

In more extreme circumstances, the family atmosphere may be utterly dysfunctional. The father may abandon the child and family, creating a deep wound and sense of unworthiness in the child. From this vulnerable position, the child is pressured to grow and change his or her life circumstances. A mixture of different emotions may be projected on to the father from resentment to a need for care and attention. When becoming him or herself a parent, the child may repeat negative cycles of abandonment and loss if he or she is not careful. There is a need to transform the approach to parenthood and become a better parent. Sometimes the sense of abandonment may occur through the death of the father, rendering the child emotionally introspective and reflective of death and life cycles.

Evolutionary Lesson

The Sun in these positions describes an evolutionary lesson to symbolically die in order to transform one's creative expression and leadership capacity for the better. The ultimate purpose is to deepen one's life experience and approach so that more meaning is uncovered. Personal growth and evolution helps one have a stronger creative impact on life and find solutions for pain and limitations.

The Sun in Sagittarius ♐, in the 9th House, or in Aspect to Jupiter ♃

— The creative impulse emerging from one's love for life.

— Character and personality, leadership qualities, the ability to initiate and promote goals, the capacity to take the forefront.

— Self-actualization, creative qualities and insights, the need to have an impact and leave a legacy.

— Caring, generosity, one's personal investment in life and the living, issues of respect.

With the Sun in Sagittarius, in the ninth house, or in aspect to Jupiter, a person's love for life manifests in further researching the content of life's truth so that creativity is enhanced and life gains greater meaning and strength. Supporting naturalness and authenticity is a way to foster creative freedom so that new ground is gained.

There is an evolutionary need to realize the full potential of one's creativity and self-actualization process. Under these influences, a person feels the need to transcend established boundaries and work toward becoming more influential and potent through creative expression and production. Like the Scorpio Sun influence, the person feels that life must have more to offer than what is currently known; thus frustration is experienced when the present seems limited compared to what could be. Driven by the need for more—whether more meaning, success, influence, or opportunity. Intuiting that more is possible, the person speculates about a higher potential and is willing to risk immediate security for that sake—fear doesn't serve one's plans to conquer wider horizons.

Equipped with faith, optimism, and positive thinking, the person increases the odds of accessing a greater creative potential. Having the courage to dare often pays off because, indeed, life has more to offer beyond each horizon—evolution reflects the continual state of expansion. When expanding, the person may validate the truth of his or her perceived potential and materialize it. Coming back with the trophy of the conquest, he or she becomes a bearer of truth and testifies for it.

While striving to conceptualize a greater meaning for one's existence, one may explore spirituality in order to understand a larger framework for existence. The search starts through intuition, faith, and existential questions such as "What am I here to do?" "What is life about?" or "Why are we living?" One may become religiously or spiritually inspired and explore the vastness of philosophical realms. Spirituality may serve as an inspiration for one's creative expression—a higher meaning is associated with personal projects. However, it is not guaranteed that one's intuition is validated in actual reality; these higher meanings may remain an abstract and intangible speculation.

When proceeding in a healthy way, the person attains relatively significant success through personal endeavors; he or she may emanate passion and positivism often infusing people with that enthusiasm and freeing them from negative mindsets. With a strong personality, one becomes an "engine" of development and creates new opportunities for oneself and others. Through boosting creativity and opening doors, the quality of one's life increases accordingly. Sharing success with others allows one to expand personal influence beyond the current environment, for example, by establishing a successful international business or through disseminating ideas. In other cases, the person may not necessarily expand in a material sense but rather through freedom of spirit. Serving as a reliable authority with wisdom and experience, one may inspire others by being truthful, authentic, and courageous.

When failing to find one's personal sense of purpose, the desire for expansion, inspiration, and success can be projected on to an external figure. Admiring a teacher type or a powerful personality of sorts, one may vicariously live through him or her and associate the purpose of this external figure as one's own. Such compensating behavior cannot last for long without generating disappointment when expectations fail. Eventually, the person learns to earn their own sense of meaning.

In another way, mismanaging these influences, the person may force his or her intuition and faith upon reality in order to validate it at all costs. Blindly pushing massive projects forward without proper backing, this dynamic is prone to create crises through excesses or delusions. Optimism can become poisonous as it strips one of objectivity and clarity. Similarly when proceeding with projects, the person may neglect details and only focus on "the greater picture," while those details may actually be of great importance. Beyond exaggeration and a tendency to get carried away, one's attitude may end up verbally or physically imposing and forceful; becoming a conqueror in literal ways, one may bulldoze one's way forward from a place of self-righteousness. Instead of experiencing success, one's excessive affirmation of confidence usually results in crisis, dysfunction, and the creation of more limitations. While seeking creative freedom and expansion, ultimately the opposite may occur because so many resources are wasted in this process.

On a day to day basis, the person is usually casual and aspires to lead a more free-spirited lifestyle. One's approach to life is more direct and stripped of artifices. Needing authenticity and wanting to celebrate life in its original forms, there can be a strong affiliation with the natural world, open spaces, or the untamed and primal. In this regard, the person may promote ideals of democracy or respect for people and animals with the goal of respecting everyone's natural way of being.

When spiritually inclined, the individual often associates with a belief system in order to be motivated to create and feel a part of life.

These beliefs may be personal or part of a wider culture. When facing adversities and challenges, the spiritual or religious inclination provides a support system. One is not likely to allow external obstacles to easily break one's spirit.

Natural avenues of creativity and professional expression may include entrepreneurial ventures as well as sales and advertising. One may also be involved in academia as a scholar or in some other related role often focusing on religious, philosophical, or anthropological research. One may naturally become a teacher and challenge students with reflective questions. In other ways, the attraction to the natural world can also stimulate activities and creative endeavors related to the outdoors.

> — *The relationship between one generation and the next, the relationship between the leader and the follower with mutual expectations to perform, inspire, and carry the torch. The relationship with the father, the description of his personality.*

With the Sun in Sagittarius, in the ninth house, or in aspect to Jupiter, the family atmosphere may emanate positivism. The parents may encourage freedom of expression and creativity, doing their best to open doors and offer options. Whether through resources or inspiration, the child may feel special and have access to abundance. Having an expectation of grandeur or enjoyment, the parents may unconsciously pressure the child to bear only good news. A spiritual overtone may color the family dynamics and provide a greater sense of meaning for the child. A strong personality asserting defined opinions, the father may be a success story who makes the family proud. He may be adventurous, generous, and outgoing, but usually very subjective and argumentative as well.

In other cases, the family atmosphere focuses on leading a natural lifestyle where the doors of the house remain unlocked and a sense of freedom is emphasized through outdoor activities. Privacy and maintenance details may not be a priority, leaving the child to independently find his or her sense of purpose in life. The father may be an authentic personality, somewhat casual, and at times rather coarse. In extreme cases, he may be imposing and self righteous, pressuring the child to be strong and discouraging any expression of weakness or neediness.

In other scenarios, denial and neglect may be camouflaged under an outwardly positive attitude. The parents may impose their faith or belief system on the children, presenting their vision of things as full of wonder. This form of indoctrination generates an atmosphere of seeming happiness when in fact excesses, dysfunction, arguments, and fracas cause frequent chaos in the home. The father may be dogmatic, delusional in his sense of grandeur, righteous, and often bigoted. The child may either continue the same path and repeat the dysfunctional behavior or instead seek truthfulness and challenge the parents.

Evolutionary Lessons

The Sun in these positions describes an evolutionary lesson to get in touch with one's natural sense of self so that the product of personal creative output may be untainted and authentic. Truthfulness naturally inspires expansion and further development because it continually exposes one to new dimensions of existence. When successful, one may embody spiritual wisdom and naturally generate abundance and positivism through creative endeavors.

The Sun in Capricorn ♑, in the 10th House, or in aspect to Saturn ♄

— *The creative impulse emerging from one's love for life.*

— *Character and personality, leadership qualities, the ability to initiate and promote goals, the capacity to take the forefront.*

— *Self-actualization, creative qualities and insights, the need to have an impact and leave a legacy.*

— *Caring, generosity, one's personal investment in life and the living, issues of respect.*

With the Sun in Capricorn, in the tenth house, or in aspect to Saturn, a person's love for life manifests in establishing and following principles that align with the way life works even if such an effort may, at times, be at the cost of immediate gratification. Providing and living by reliable references is a way to protect the course of existence on both a personal and a collective level. Results are measured by the test of time, inspiring one to promote guidelines for oneself and future generations that serve as a solid foundation for creativity and life to thrive.

There is an evolutionary need to actively participate in existence and express one's creativity in a way that aligns with what is perceived as just and reliable. The person must perform highly, not only for personal gain, but also to serve as a guiding example. One's success may become a reference for others, just as elders' experiences served as a source of inspiration. Yet one's actions are not only evaluated according to productive results, but also according to an ethical point of view. Doing the right thing means adhering to the Truth, and this carries both practical and moral weight.

The reference point for performance standards varies according to one's value system and level of consciousness. The person may compliantly adopt what is culturally considered righteous or determine the basis of these standards for him or herself through personal soul searching and practical experience. To define an ethical code of behavior, the person may exclusively rely on an external authority or instead develop an inner authority, using critical thinking to discriminate right from wrong.

Generally, a more serious attitude is adopted because of a fear of possible consequences and misleading others through making mistakes. When lacking ethics and rigor, the person eventually attracts judgment and failure that makes him or her aware of misalignment. In extreme cases, one may even be prosecuted by the system to learn about the consequences of one's actions. There is a need to learn to do things the right way and express creativity constructively—learning from errors and aiming for better results is a part of the process. Patience and endurance are gradually acquired, helping one overcome obstacles and achieve ambitions and goals.

When well managed, leadership capacities may put one in a position of being a role model and an authority in one's field of expertise. Naturally ambitious, immediate gratification is set aside for a greater goal of creating things that have lasting value. A practical approach combined with higher inspiration helps one achieve meaningful goals. A person is taken seriously based on his or her record of wisdom and capacity. Accordingly over time, one may gain more status because of diligent and consistent efforts. The benefit of such an approach not only allows one to achieve more, making things happen for oneself and others, but also to establish standards that may outlive one's own time—a valuable legacy for future generations.

When mismanaging these influences, a person may fail to gain credibility and suffer from never being taken seriously. Sometimes lacking true merit, he or she may try to become an authority but fail to impress or bring valuable results. The reason for the dysfunction is sometimes rooted in not being mature enough to yield immediate gratification and align the ego with higher principles. This attitude is likely to deprive one of respect and attract negative judgment that dampens self-confidence.

In other circumstances, the person may fear not being taken seriously or being unable to provide adequate results and refrain from any form of public exposure. Creativity may be kept private, if at all expressed, in order to avoid potential failure or humiliation altogether—measuring oneself by very high standards, there is little interest in experimentation. One may feel that unless the best results are delivered, it is not worth doing things and wasting effort. This self-defeating approach is often rooted in wanting to skip developmental steps and become a masterful authority right away. There is no acceptance of intermediary stages of performance which gradually lead to higher levels of mastery. Often this approach results from earlier childhood memories of humiliation.

In other scenarios, the failure to be taken seriously may not necessarily result from the person's mismanagement but happen because of discrepancies between what the person perceives to be right versus other authority figures' references. The gap in value systems and perceptions of life may cause misunderstandings and prejudice. When challenging mainstream expectations, the person must be judged according to results and consequences instead of an authority's personal bias and taste. However, self-righteousness may prevent this more neutral and fair approach, rendering one vulnerable to narrow-mindedness. If one is right, it may take time before standards are modified to fit one's new approaches. This is why patience and endurance are important qualities to cultivate.

However, sometimes it is the person him or herself that acts in a self-righteous way. When enjoying success and respect, one may take one's status for granted and never doubt personal perceptions—this can lead to dogmatic behavior. In further extremes, one may become corrupt if using a leadership position to promote personal favorites instead of deserving individuals. The person can become tyrannical when refusing to tolerate vulnerabilities and projecting expectations for perfection on others. Eventually, consequences for this type of behavior follow with the person possibly experiencing a loss of privileges and public humiliation.

With the Sun in these positions, a person may naturally be drawn to express his or her creativity through architecture, design, or music. Success in these fields comes from understanding boundaries and the use of form and structure. Leadership and creativity may position one in any management role, regardless of the field. Politics can also be a natural platform for one's creative and leading capacities.

Responsibility and inner strength naturally attract people who yearn for guidance and need training. In this regard, the person may assume a parental or coaching role, sometimes working with a population in need of rehabilitation.

> — *The relationship between one generation and the next, the relationship between the leader and the follower with mutual expectations to perform, inspire, and carry the torch. The relationship with the father, the description of his personality.*

With the Sun in Capricorn, in the tenth house, or in aspect to Saturn, the family atmosphere may emphasize ambition and achievement. The child may be inspired to do something important and want to have an influential role—a respectable academic path is usually expected from the child in order to secure a successful and respectful professional life. This dynamic, however, can intensify a fear of failure and therefore prevent one from experimenting or playing. Already wanting to be an adult, or pressured to be so, the child may exhibit striking maturity and a capacity to handle responsibility, sometimes to the point of being disinterested in youthful activities.

The family may also emanate an atmosphere of nobility and importance where tradition and ancestors are given prominence. The father may be respected for his wisdom and guidance or else for his achievement and status. He may be a dependable figure who possesses high ethics, but sometimes lacks playfulness and casualness.

In more extreme scenarios, rigidity may be emphasized and amplify pressure to the point of overwhelming the child. Weakness is not tolerated and the parents may use every opportunity to preach their self-righteousness and rigor while not always fulfilling those standards themselves. The dynamics may rely on a regime of discipline, sometimes to the point of cruelty. The father may be an imposing, inaccessible, and intimidating figure, fast to punish what he perceives as wrong. This atmosphere conditions the child with a constant feeling of guilt and self-negation; traits that may take a long time to heal.

In other ways, these influences may reflect a household that is not fully functional or well regulated. The parents may be weak or unavailable, pressuring the child to assume responsibility from an early age; having a role to fulfill can inspire the child unless the pressure to do so is excessive. The father may be emotionally repressed, sometimes limited by a physical or mental handicap, and therefore not able to offer significant guidance.

Evolutionary Lesson

The Sun in these positions describes an evolutionary lesson to treat life rightly and transcend personal whims for the sake of understanding how to successfully manage creative power. In producing meaningful creations, caring is expressed through a willingness to dedicate effort and thoughtfulness toward preserving higher principles and ethical values.

The Sun in Aquarius ♒, in the 11ᵗʰ House, or in aspect to Uranus ♅

— *The creative impulse emerging from one's love for life.*

— *Character and personality, leadership qualities, the ability to initiate and promote goals, the capacity to take the forefront.*

— *Self-actualization, creative qualities and insights, the need to have an impact and leave a legacy.*

— *Caring, generosity, one's personal investment in life and the living, issues of respect.*

With the Sun in Aquarius, in the eleventh house, or in aspect to Uranus, a person's love for life manifests in bringing out the best of oneself when addressing life's quandaries so that one may be part of the solution instead of the problem. Intellectual creativity and a higher awareness are used to find new and more effective pathways for creativity to thrive on both an individual and a collective level. Helping to create a more advanced and enlightened civilization is a way to guarantee a higher quality of life and increase creative expression.

There is an evolutionary need for personal creativity and self-actualization to promote progress and development both personally and collectively. A person may realize a higher creative potential and elevate the standards of expression and production. A strong emphasis on the mind provides perspective and objectivity, allowing one to observe oneself and constantly refine one's creative expression; a combination of intelligence and inspiration promises great results.

The purpose of these influences is to take one's destiny and life forward instead of recycling what already exists. Consequently, a critical approach is adopted in order to discriminate what is worth developing versus what is obsolete. Typically, the individual is unimpressed by average results or poor character and leadership. Because there is a strong desire for emancipation, experimental approaches take priority over security needs. Aspiring for broader and more enlightening life conditions, one cannot afford to remain too emotionally attached to old standards when limitations are evident; better life conditions can be created!

There is a tendency to lose interest in people who are overly self-absorbed or lack self-awareness. Similarly, the person may attract indifference from others if he or she is overly infatuated with ideas or projects to a point of losing perspective; there is pressure to remain emotionally centered and neutral instead of getting carried away in drama that might derail important matters. The emphasis on the mind helps one maintain clarity and stay aligned with what is appropriate and can truly bring results.

These configurations also encourage group creativity manifesting through friendships, organizations, or communities; gathering different talents under the same umbrella augments the potential to attain a higher level of achievement. The person may also seek partners who share common aspirations and goals, in such a way boosting creativity and production. A stronger impact and greater depth can be attained through group work that relies on mutual inspiration and a common purpose.

When optimally expressed, the Sun in these positions describes a rich, refined, and sophisticated personality—someone with high values, talent, and infinite creative potential whose achievements often surpass common expectations. The person is highly cultivated either through being academically educated or simply through possessing a relatively wide awareness of life's mechanism and diversity. Bringing forth new ideas in any chosen field of expertise, one may become an engine of progress and innovation. Broad awareness, high standards, objective perspective, and inspiration encourage experimentation in hope of eventually finding new solutions to elevate life standards.

The person may also exhibit social leadership qualities and inspire communities with progressive ideals. On a smaller scale, this tendency can simply manifest in social popularity. One may possess natural social skills and consequently encourage social interactions that in turn lead to exchange and creativity.

When mismanaged, creative potential may remain unfulfilled because of an overly critical approach. The person may fear failing his or her own high standards and consequently prefer to analyze and talk about ideas rather than risk taking action. Concerns about making a fool out of oneself, or simply disappointing others, may keep one from the performing stage. Striving to appear cool and unshaken by pressure, the person can remain indifferent and numb passion as a result of being excessively self-conscious. When paralyzed by one's own critical mind, one can become sarcastic toward other people's performances, usually by preying on their flaws. This negative attitude is camouflaged with wit and humor, but inwardly it reflects a deep seated lack of self-confidence. Accordingly, the person may diminish others, reflecting his or her own insecurities.

Similarly while possessing distinguished talents, the person may become arrogant and emotionally inaccessible. High standards can induce an elitist attitude that breeds disdain toward others perceived as inferior. This elitism can manifest on different levels whether intellectually, socioeconomically, or spiritually; isolating oneself from commoners, one may lose the heart connection and care little for other people, preferring to focus only on brilliance. Escalating to further extremes, one may promote the ideals of superior genes, races, or breeds, usually in a self-inclusive way, and feed antagonism through racism, social discrimination, or other purity complexes. The severity of this approach varies from case to case.

Typically, the Sun in these positions encourages self-actualization through science or technology; the aspiration to find new solutions and the natural drive to further understand the complexity of existence draws the person to these fields. Computers and the high-tech industry may also be a part of this path.

Differently, it may be through social skills that one fulfills one's potential; networking, the media, diplomacy, or even politics may be natural avenues of creative expression. The person may also be involved in an organization with social or humanitarian goals. Alternative knowledge and new-age modalities may also be a source of interest and creativity such as astrology, energy healing, or other similar mediums. The person may see the future in these fields and be an agent of their development.

Combining the higher mind with a heart-centered focus, the individual may promote humanitarian ideals and raise the standards of life for underprivileged communities; this effort may also be geared toward raising the level of life for the whole, not only the deprived. In these circumstances, education is encouraged to free people from the tangles of obsolete perspectives and habits. Values of respect, dignity, and equality may also be strongly advocated.

– *The relationship between one generation and the next, the relationship between the leader and the follower with mutual expectations to perform, inspire, and carry the torch. The relationship with the father, the description of his personality.*

With the Sun in Aquarius, the eleventh house, or in aspect to Uranus, the family atmosphere may emphasize the cultivation of personality, culture, and creativity. From an early age, the child may be encouraged to expand his or her academic horizons in order to foster creative potential, for example, through learning a second language or joining an art class. The fear of wasting potential may, at times, overly pressure the child through these additional educational commitments. The family may reflect an atmosphere of civility and a relatively broad awareness, but block a more primal way of expression. The father may be an intellectual and a seeker who is refined but wary of exhibiting weakness. He may be witty, sarcastic, and rational; while admired by the child for his qualities and talent, he may be a hard critic to please.

In other scenarios, the family may be very progressive and aware of new trends. The awareness of new cultural and social developments may amplify consumerism as each new gadget or designer outfit has to be purchased. The family may be relatively liberal and encourage the children to choose their own path of self-actualization; albeit underneath the coolness, cynicism and sarcasm, the parents may keep the children self-conscious. The father, possibly living beyond his means, may seek success, and be socially involved but potentially snobbish and exclusive.

These configurations can also describe a family atmosphere that doesn't meet the child's standards. Parents may idealize other people's popularity and success, and seek to be included in social dynamics at the cost of their own personality. The child may compare the parents to other families and perceive them as less sophisticated—this perception breeds disdain and a fear of embarrassment. The child may have little respect for the father, possibly because of a conflict of values, and express indifference or even verbal abuse. There may be a desire to do and be exactly the opposite of what the family and the father represent because their values and behavior are perceived as limited and uninspiring. In other cases, the child may be a snob and feel shame toward the father because in the child's eyes he is not considered smart enough. Whether the sense of alienation is justified or not, criticism can escalate to the point where the child cuts the father out of his or her life and disengages from any interaction with him.

The Sun in these positions can indicate that the person is raised in a family where the connections extend beyond biological ties. The child may have stepsiblings or stepparents because the parents remarried or because the child was adopted. People born with these signatures may also adopt children or be involved in circumstances where they raise stepchildren and face the rewards and the challenges therein.

Evolutionary Lesson

The Sun in these positions describes an evolutionary lesson to find a personal way to contribute to the development of civilization, in simple or elaborate ways. Using intelligence as a creative tool, one is inspired to bring the best out of oneself and get in touch with one's refined essence in order foster progress whether through personal or joint endeavors. Education, development, and innovation are a means to manifest this goal through one's chosen field of expression.

The Sun in Pisces ♓, in the 12th House, or in Aspect to Neptune ♆

— *The creative impulse emerging from one's love for life.*

— *Character and personality, leadership qualities, the ability to initiate and promote goals, the capacity to take the forefront.*

— *Self-actualization, creative qualities and insights, the need to have an impact and leave a legacy.*

— *Caring, generosity, one's personal investment in life and the living, issues of respect.*

With the Sun in Pisces, in the twelfth house, or in aspect to Neptune, a person's love for life manifests through dedicating one's creativity and vitality toward serving goals that benefit individuals or the masses. Accordingly, caring for life involves adapting to what life brings and finding ways to make the best of every situation. Creativity is fueled by higher inspiration when personal goals are rooted in compassion and the Truth.

There is an evolutionary need to harmonize one's personal meaning and creative self-actualization with a larger collective meaning; one's personal output becomes aligned with public needs or spiritual purposes. This dynamic can take various forms: one may feel that one's participation in life must serve a meaningful cause or one's personal creativity may be inspired by spiritual ideals.

These configurations reflect a paradox as they require both active expression (creativity) and passive flow (adaptation to larger dynamics). The person may overdo one or the other until the right balance between these extremes is mastered. For example, when coming on strong with personal ambitions, one may face public snubbing; conversely, when remaining passive, creativity may stall and one's potential end up wasted. The person may feel confused about when to be proactive and when to let go. The answer lies in being sensitive to what each moment requires instead of following a preplanned formula for handling life—improvisation is a creative effort in itself.

Humility is an important quality to develop because in order to align one's egocentric expression with higher principles, the person must develop values of service and see him or herself as an instrument through which a higher purpose manifests. The need for control or an attachment to personal preferences must be adjusted to adapt to what is required—it is not necessarily about what one wants but instead about what is needed. Often, the individual feels he or she has no control over the unfolding of his or her creative self-actualization—development can occur in unexpected ways and in unexpected times, and this dynamic keeps the person humble as he or she cannot fully control the direction of events. However, humility must not induce self-neglect or self-effacement, for without proper self-care one's self-esteem and potency may dwindle and impede the creative process. One may end up sacrificing personal needs to serve everyone else's cause and end up drained. Being taken advantage of, or in extreme cases even being victimized, is not what the evolutionary lesson is about.

Being inspired to create something that has significant meaning for the whole may, at times, end up confusing. High ideals are hard to materialize, and the person may end up never feeling satisfied with what he or she actually does, perceiving the result as narrow when compared to the grandeur of what could potentially be. Trapped in the search for greater meaning, one may end up not doing much at all. Failing to manifest a destiny as the years go by, a fear of losing one's calling may emerge. One must understand that destiny cannot be controlled through personal projections. The individual must start his or her creative journey with an open heart and a sincere desire to promote good; from there, one thing will lead to another.

One may start with simple goals and slowly invite opportunities to have a greater influence. What initially matters is having the right motive and producing sincere work. Expecting sensation, grandeur, and public acclaim right away is a recipe for disappointment. Intention matters first; the rest follows, beyond one's ability to control the outcome.

Positively expressed, these influences reflect a highly developed and inspired personality that adapts its vision and achievements to what life brings and what is necessary—hearing the calling where its skills are needed. Support through life circumstances allows one to develop in meaningful and often unpredictable ways; the person may synchronistically meet the right person at the right time to promote projects. Like riding on a wave, one may successfully proceed forward yet often without a clear perception of the destination—one's path often unfolds in unexpected ways to one's own amazement. When tremendously successful, highly valuable services are offered to people and existence as a whole, sometimes in the form of becoming famous and publicly recognized. The person may be elevated to the status of a leader or an icon and raise public identification for his or her contribution. Glamour may result from these circumstances, but the key is to remain unattached to it and stay focused on the purpose.

When mismanaged, or if the underlying motivation of service is lost in the process, the person may become too attached to the prospect of extraordinary meaning, fame, or easy success. This dynamic may reflect past life memories of glory and heroism; consequently, there may be an unconscious need to recreate it. This expectation is likely to fail in materializing anything inspirational because true content is lacking. Resources and time are likely to be wasted on self-indulgent projects that fail to pick up.

Similarly, one may believe that he or she is spiritually inspired to lead the way or save people and become consumed by delusions. Messianic complexes stimulated by self-adulation may be camouflaged as noble causes, but false modesty is bound to eventually transpire and lead to crisis and failure.

Even when coming with a sincere intention to help, overly naive goals generate disillusionment and failure. One may expect easy success or take on projects that end up being too large and return to square one when they fail to materialize. The person eventually realizes that life is a complex organism that requires more effort and proper management.

In other ways, mismanagement may result from an overly passive approach to life that results from a lack of passion and involvement. The reasons for this overly detached approach may originate from low self-esteem and self-defeating attitudes, or in other cases from simple laziness. Consequently, years may pass by with one's creative potential unattended to.

Lacking a conscious desire to participate in life, the person becomes unproductive. He or she may perceive the world as a hostile or uninspiring place and give up on it. Having personal ideals crushed by rampant greed or corruption can make one cynical and apathetic. Beginning from a place of naiveté and blind idealism, the opposite extreme is now experienced—but making the world a better place is a work in process and patience is required for that process.

In extreme cases, this approach leads to parasitic behavior when the person uses or abuses other people's resources because he or she has failed to generate his or her own. One can exhibit acute selfishness, sometimes to the point of becoming completely narcissistic and lacking any compassion for others. Wanting easy success and lacking the skills or the desire to work, the person self-indulgently manipulates his or her way as an opportunist.

These configurations may reflect finding a sense of purpose and meaning through associating with the natural world, for example, through geology, zoology, or in the development of natural resources. Similarly, there may be a particular focus on oceanic activities such as fishing, sailing, or oceanography. In other ways, one may gain popularity through artistic venues, sometimes through show business ventures. The world of entertainment reflects the potential to tap into mass appeal. Professions related to children, from pediatric medicine to school teaching or special education, also resonate with these influences.

The Sun in these placements may describe a naturally altruistic approach to life and self-dedication to various causes. An innate desire to save life and restore existential harmony can motivate one to volunteer and partake in different charity causes. One may also inspire others spiritually and serve as a counselor for people seeking guidance and direction in a confusing world.

— *The relationship between one generation and the next, the relationship between the leader and the follower with mutual expectations to perform, inspire, and carry the torch. The relationship with the father, the description of his personality.*

The Sun in Pisces, in the twelfth house, or in aspect to Neptune can describe a family atmosphere where the parents are relatively permissive and supportive. A focus on having an easy going attitude, trust, and faith can stimulate creativity and freedom of inspiration; albeit, the child may sometimes be overly sheltered from difficulty to the point of keeping him or her relatively naïve and unable to cope with stress. With all best intentions, the parents may fail to adequately prepare the child to experience challenges. The father may be easy-going, artistically inclined, sometimes idealized, and generous, although often not physically accessible. He may shy away from intimate involvement, immerse himself in external activities, and have a harder time providing personal attention. This potential situation reflects a reality where everything appears smooth on the surface, but underneath it all, true support and encouragement are lacking. With an easy-going attitude, the child is expected to figure things out alone, and while this approach provides a sense of freedom, it lacks a proper backbone.

In further extremes, the child's qualities and talents may not be recognized by the parents and remain uncultivated. Parents who are too busy, overwhelmed by existential challenges, or simply dimly aware may fail to provide personal attention. The child may grow up with a self-effacing attitude, trying not to burden already complicated circumstances, and consequently overlook his or her own creative potential. The father may be impersonal, seldom present, or even completely absent. He may be a weak figure, perhaps taken advantage of by others, and fail to inspire the child in meaningful ways. In extreme cases, the child may realize that he or she has a different biological father than the one who is known. These circumstances create an identity crisis and sometimes disorientation because role models are lacking. Evolutionarily speaking, the challenge is for the child to find his or her inspiration from within and take advantage of a lack of heavy parental conditioning.

As an adult with these signatures, one may face a loss of control with regard to children and conception. This can manifest in either excessive fertility or infertility. In the first scenario, having many children, sometimes more than one can handle, results from an absence of boundaries. When the opposite applies and there are obstacles to conceiving, the person again feels that he or she has no control over the situation, as if being in the hands of fate. In some cases, persistence and treatment help overcome fertility problems; in other cases, adoption may be an option—transcending the biological aspect of parenting also relates to these influences. It may also be that the person is fertile but consciously chooses not to have children. The tendency to be less emotionally attached on a personal level can stimulate this decision.

The person may also experience a loss of control when children end up having behavioral problems or learning disabilities. When faced with these circumstances, the parents realize the importance of boundaries and consistency.

Evolutionary Lesson

The Sun in these positions describes an evolutionary lesson to realize that larger life forces conduct the direction and flow of one's personal creativity. The person is inspired to create and bring the best out of him or herself while learning to let go of controlling the end result of personal efforts—what matters is one's dedication to service and sincerity. These circumstances require the person to improvise and adapt to what life brings. Once at peace with such a process, inspiration abounds.

The Sun in Synthesis

Using the same strategy found in the "The Moon in Synthesis" section, examples of the Sun in different signs and houses are analyzed to provide a better grasp of how to combine the different energies at play in a birth chart.

Example One: The Sun in Taurus in the 11th House

- *Unifying factors:* The Taurus and eleventh house (Aquarius) archetypes are both resourceful, individualistic, and creative. Together they work toward solidity and quality—they both have a sensible side.

- *Contradictions:* Taurus seeks tangibility and is focused on matter and form, whereas Aquarius is cerebral and seeks to move beyond the limitations of form and matter. Moreover, Taurus is self-sufficient and personal, whereas Aquarius strives to apply things on a larger scale by stimulating teamwork and community dynamics.

- *Excesses:* There may be an excess of pragmatism or an inclination to only produce for exclusive needs (either for oneself or small groups)—there can be a tendency toward exclusivity.

- *The sign and house integration:* The eleventh house represents *the area or context* of progress, the development of civilization, social interaction, and intellectual creativity. Through this house, the person experiences the need to move forward in life. Thus there is an incentive to upgrade life conditions and include elements or people who facilitate this direction. Additionally, the eleventh house describes social contexts, friendships, and teamwork for the sake of combining resources and insights in order to achieve greater goals. It also emphasizes the need to objectively reflect on our lives so that we can gain greater perspective, awareness, and knowledge of the facts.

The sign of Taurus describes *the way* a person approaches the context of the eleventh house; it defines *how and where* progress and the upgrading process unfolds. With a Taurus Sun influencing the eleventh house, the person's resources and talents are upgraded and renewed (eleventh house). Progress is instigated by achieving a higher level of production. Fostering sophistication, talent, and creativity, this combination can describe the capacity to generate wealth and lead a more upscale lifestyle. A refined sense of taste elevates the quality of one's life in general. In a different way, these influences may describe a more communal approach (eleventh house) toward using resources (Taurus). Creativity may be focused toward developing new financial models with the goal of establishing a more egalitarian distribution of goods.

This configuration brings a need to objectify and reflect upon (eleventh house) one's use of resources in order to better utilize what is available. In this regard, social exchange and community dynamics can provide insight and inspiration.

Combining talent with progressive development, the person may be an artist (Sun in Taurus) who uses advanced technology (eleventh house) as his or her creative medium of expression and becomes a graphic designer or an avantgarde artist. Advanced technology may also be used to upgrade production in other fields such as agriculture, construction, or any other Taurus-related creative expression.

The Evolutionary Purposes and Dynamics of a Taurus Sun in the 11th House

- *The creative impulse emerging from one's love for life.*

- *Character and personality, leadership qualities, the ability to initiate and promote goals, the capacity to take the forefront.*

- *Self-actualization, creative qualities and insights, the need to have an impact and leave a legacy.*

- *Caring, generosity, one's personal investment in life and the living, issues of respect.*

With the Sun in Taurus in the eleventh house, there is an evolutionary need to upgrade the quality and means of creativity and to self-actualize in a way that inspires progress and innovation; self-actualization must eventually blend progressive ideas with resources. There is a need to stimulate creativity on a more communal level and promote a rewarding exchange of resources among the people involved. Additionally, there is an evolutionary need to intellectually reflect on the use of available resources—whether talents, material assets, or insights—in order to eventually upgrade their use leading to further refinement, abundance, and excellence.

Consequently, this configuration enhances the use of resources, productivity, and quality on both a personal and a collective level. The person learns to balance isolation and social interaction, needing both time to get in touch with oneself (Taurus) and time for creative exchange with others (eleventh house).

Positively expressed, the person may have a potent and sophisticated personality, and possess outstanding artistic, intellectual, and or social talents. Inner wealth combined with perspective and intelligence generates an ability to be innovative and impress the environment whether through art, research studies, or community dynamics. Having a vision and yet staying grounded, one may achieve important goals in practical ways that benefit both oneself and society as a whole. One's focus may be directed toward enhancing economic development, creating jobs, offering loans and investment opportunities to stimulate development, or providing a platform to encourage artistic creativity.

Negatively expressed, the person may use his or her resources and intelligence only for personal immediate comfort (Taurus) thus creating a dynamic of exclusivity and socioeconomic (Taurus) elitism (eleventh house). On a personal level, cooperation may be rejected because one is unwilling to share, yet help may be sought when resources dwindle because one's taste for sophistication may cause one to live beyond available means. The person may get accustomed to expensive habits and privileges but refrain from "getting dirty" and working in order to be able to afford them.

 — *The relationship with one's parents—especially the father, the relationship between the leader and the follower with mutual expectations to perform, inspire, and carry the torch.*

The family environment may offer a supportive platform for the child's development and creativity either through financial means or creative inspiration. There are likely expectations for the child to perform highly. The father may be a talented and successful figure yet not easily approachable because of a tendency for solitude and a disinterest in mundane affairs. The challenge for the parent-child rapport is to provide both tangible developmental support and higher inspiration. Lacking the latter, the child may lose respect for his or her father and feel that he is not a stimulating role model.

Conclusions

The inherently high level of creative potential that exists in this configuration must be supported by values of solidarity and humility in order to be channeled productively and manifest its potential to foster social well-being. Adopting an approach that is too exclusive is, at some point, likely to cause a decrease of creative inspiration, possibly causing the well of creativity to run dry. When well managed, this configuration may describe inspired genius that is used for collective development.

Example Two: The Sun in Virgo in the 1st House

- *Unifying factors*: The Virgo and first house (Aries) archetypes are both active and independent. The doers of the zodiac, they are focused on using time wisely and aiming for optimal results.

- *Contradictions*: Virgo is practical, analytical, and emotionally reserved in order to remain appropriate within the environment while the first house (Aries) reflects an emotionally charged, impulsive, and reactive mode.

- *Excesses*: There may be an excessive use of force and control that results in coming on too strong.

- *Sign and house integration*: The first house represents the *area and context of* individuation. Through this house, the person learns to separate from external influence and control in order to take charge of his or her destiny. A proactive and defensive approach is adopted to assure that objectives are carried out in spite of possible obstacles.

The sign of Virgo describes *how* the need to take charge of one's destiny through the Sun is accomplished and the *way* one proceeds in taking action. With the Sun in Virgo in the first house, the person has a goal-oriented personality and therefore has a great deal of energy to burn. A combination of organizational skills (Virgo) and a desire to make things happen can stimulate many successful projects and endeavors (first house). The person may be a "busy bee," constantly active and involved in launching and managing projects. This combination also describes the potential for self-actualization through competitive sports or physical training because Virgo regulates the use of the body and the first house carries the stamina and conquering drive. In any case, the person is likely to be busy, restless, creative, fast, precise, self-motivated, and highly independent when handling personal projects. There is a considerable need for control because one wants to guarantee quick results and a high level of functionality. While sharp and effective, the person may lose his or her temper when faced with other people's incompetence.

The Evolutionary Purposes and Dynamics of a Virgo Sun in the 1st House

> *— The creative impulse emerging from one's love for life.*

> *— Character and personality, leadership qualities, the ability to initiate and promote goals, the capacity to take the forefront.*

> *— Self-actualization, creative qualities and insights, the need to have an impact and leave a legacy.*

> *— Caring, generosity, one's personal investment in life and the living, issues of respect.*

With the Sun in Virgo in the first house, the evolutionary intent is to launch new creative projects that are highly functional and efficiently managed. The person learns to develop unique ways of proceeding with his or her projects and requires tremendous independence to focus on all the details required for the task. There may be a need to do everything on one's own in order to make sure that everything is perfectly handled and that high efficiency levels are guaranteed.

The purpose is to optimize efficiency, soundness, and precision (Virgo) in one's endeavors (first house) minimizing the odds of failure or sabotage. Refined physical and organizational skills may help one proceed with excellence and successfully overcome potential resistance and obstacles. The person is likely to be immensely creative and physically potent.

Positively expressed, the person emanates strength on both physical and psychological levels. A hard worker—creative, perceptive, and fast to act—one may accomplish projects of high quality and answer needs for people rendering life more functional. Seldom giving up, one may develop practical strategies (Virgo) to overcome obstacles and reach desired objectives (first house) accumulating a string of valuable accomplishments during one's life. The job is likely to be done on time and with care and thought. Through art or sports, the person may reach climaxes of inspiration through a detail-oriented focus (Virgo). Management and technical skills may also be in high demand as one's predisposition for fast and effective action may help resolve crises and restore order.

Negatively expressed, the person may be utterly stubborn and inflexible. Emotionally charged and defensive about his or her particular way (Virgo) of doing things (first house), the person may perceive threat in any external intervention and consequently generate power struggles. Excessive need for control (Virgo) may render one obsessive and nervous (Virgo). Personal failures or other people's wrongdoing may trigger harsh criticism. Moreover, obsessive tendencies and a reluctance to let go may affect one's health when overtaxing one's system and losing the initial potency.

> *– The relationship with one's parents—especially the father, the*
> *relationship between the leader and the follower with mutual expectations*
> *to perform, inspire, and carry the torch.*

With the Sun in Virgo in the first house, the family atmosphere may reflect strong working values. The parents, busy providing and producing, may reflect an ideal of productivity. Possibly critical, they can make the child self-conscious about the result of his or her endeavors. The father may be a physically sound figure but somewhat pushy in his approach. Reliable but possibly temperamental, he may come on too strong at times. The challenge for the parent-child dynamic is to share mutual goals and undertake things together so that encouragement and constructive criticism is provided.

Conclusions

Channeling physical strength through an analytical approach with the aim of producing practical results is not an easy task. Yet when the person focuses on living in a healthy way and taking care of maintenance, production can significantly increase. The person may succeed in both creating meaningful products and living well. To attain such a goal, one must understand that at times it is necessary to stop the action, reflect, and use the mind to regulate proper creative output.

Chapter Seven

The Moon and the Sun
in Synthesis

Together the Moon and the Sun represent one's sense of identity and personal orientation in life. These two energies reflect how we connect with existence and find our personal place and role within the greater scheme of life. Moon and Sun dynamics largely describe egocentric processes because together they represent the emotional center through which all of life's experiences are processed and assimilated into one's system. Through these channels, existence becomes personal instead of remaining an abstract collective experience, allowing us to relate to and make our individual existence unique.

The Moon represents the way we perceive and intimately experience life; accordingly, it describes what we choose to emotionally attach to, consciously or unconsciously. This subjective perspective conditions what we end up doing with our lives and how we go about it—the Sun. Our sense of creative purpose (Sun) derives from our personal perception, needs, and experience of life (Moon).

In this chapter, all the possible sign placement combinations of the Moon and the Sun are listed with a brief and concise description of each influence. You can interchange the sign placement with the corresponding house placement. For example, the themes of the Moon in Aries and the Sun in Libra can also apply to a first house Moon and a seventh house Sun.

In order to maintain focus and simplicity, the Moon and Sun descriptions are narrowed to just a few key phrases. For a deeper and more thorough understanding of these placements, please refer back to Chapters Five and Six. It is also important to realize that only Moon and Sun placements are addressed in this chapter—in the final analysis, the whole chart must be considered as mitigating factors may weaken or strengthen some of the dynamics described below.

Basic Moon and Sun keywords

- *Moon: Emotional association with life elements, personal experience of life, personal needs serving the growth process, the management of emotions, the support system and security.*

- *Sun: Life force, creative expression, active participation, the need to leave a legacy, one's personal sense of purpose.*

Moon in Aries Combinations

Moon in Aries, Sun in Aries

Orientation: Seeking to validate personal causes by asserting emotional charge in a passionate and involved fashion, while possessing a strong sense of purpose that is cyclically renewed and oriented toward unrestrained creativity and promoting causes considered important.

Outcome: A passionate, creative, and stimulating personality that is inclined to develop new projects and engage in activism while cyclically changing life directions because of the ongoing need to conquer new ground and the tendency to react defensively.

Famous figure: Marlon Brando

Moon in Aries, Sun in Taurus

Orientation: Seeking to validate personal causes by asserting emotional charge in a passionate and involved fashion, while possessing a wealth of inner and or material resources to self-sufficiently create for stable results.

Outcome: A resourceful and talented personality that is territorial, single-minded, and self-motivated with the objective of surviving the odds.

Famous figure: Salvador Dali

Moon in Aries, Sun in Gemini

Orientation: Seeking to validate personal causes by asserting emotional charge in a passionate and involved fashion, while motivated to create through coordinating diverse sources of interest on an intellectual, technological, and or cultural level.

Outcome: A colorful personality that is restless, mobile, astute, quick to change, and driven to experience life's diversity.

Famous figure: Angelina Jolie

Moon in Aries, Sun in Cancer

Orientation: Seeking to validate personal causes by asserting emotional charge in a passionate and involved fashion, while striving to establish supportive conditions for creative expression and development.

Outcome: A highly protective, reactive, and warm personality that addresses needs and objectives in a dedicated manner.

Famous figure: Muhammad Yunus

Moon in Aries, Sun in Leo

Orientation: Seeking to validate personal causes by asserting emotional charge in a passionate and involved fashion, while feeling poised to personally participate in and influence life through various forms of creativity.

Outcome: A highly creative personality that is strong-spirited, willful, and emotionally dramatic.

Famous figure: Andy Warhol

Moon in Aries, Sun in Virgo

Orientation: Seeking to validate personal causes by asserting emotional charge in a passionate and involved fashion, while motivated to organize and optimize one's creative productivity through conscious reflection and refinement.

Outcome: A resourceful, vibrant, and dynamic personality that takes calculated risks to advance and prevail.

Famous figure: Salma Hayek

Moon in Aries, Sun in Libra

Orientation: Seeking to validate personal causes by asserting emotional charge in a passionate and involved fashion, while adopting a broader and more balanced perspective through one's creative endeavors.

Outcome: An idealistic personality that is thought provoking and inwardly torn when striving to create something that transcends small-mindedness without losing larger appeal.

Famous figure: Divine

Moon in Aries, Sun in Scorpio

Orientation: Seeking to validate personal causes by asserting emotional charge in a passionate and involved fashion, while striving to powerfully impact others through one's creative efforts with the aim of fostering important changes both inwardly and outwardly.

Outcome: A reactive, confrontational, and courageous personality that adopts a radical approach to maximize impact.

Famous figure: Bill Gates

Moon in Aries, Sun in Sagittarius

Orientation: Seeking to validate personal causes by asserting emotional charge in a passionate and involved fashion, while having faith that a larger life potential can be accessed and creatively accomplished.

Outcome: An adventurous, ideological, enthusiastic, and argumentative personality that creates and pursues opportunities on different levels with zeal.

Famous figure: Tyra Banks

Moon in Aries, Sun in Capricorn

Orientation: Seeking to validate personal causes by asserting emotional charge in a passionate and involved fashion, while focused on creating something of serious, inspiring, and reliable value.

Outcome: A tenacious, firm, and artistic personality that is determined to overcome obstacles for causes considered important.

Famous figure: Mother Meera

Moon in Aries, Sun in Aquarius

Orientation: Seeking to validate personal causes by asserting emotional charge in a passionate and involved fashion, while using perspective and intelligence to inspire the creation of things that surpass and eventually upgrade current standards.

Outcome: A highly ingenious, witty, and free-spirited personality that is capable of wonders but fast to disengage.

Famous figure: Francis Bacon

Moon in Aries, Sun in Pisces

Orientation: Seeking to validate personal causes by asserting emotional charge in a passionate and involved fashion, while called to make personal sacrifices for the sake of actualizing a destiny that addresses larger needs and possibly inspires the collective.

Outcome: A highly romantic and idealistic personality that is sensitive to feelings of discrimination while possessing a touch of boldness, wildness, and naiveté.

Famous figure: Galilei Galilee

Moon in Taurus Combinations

Moon in Taurus, Sun in Aries

Orientation: Seeking security in self-sufficiency and stability, emotionally processing and growing through using the senses, expressing talent, and managing resources, while possessing a strong sense of purpose that is cyclically renewed and oriented toward unrestrained creativity and promoting causes considered important.

Outcome: An artistic, instinctive, and highly autonomous personality that seeks to develop the self through new ventures but is reluctant to change unless absolutely convinced.

Famous figure: Elton John

Moon in Taurus, Sun in Taurus

Orientation: Seeking security in self-sufficiency and stability, emotionally processing and growing through using the senses, expressing talent, and managing resources, while possessing a wealth of inner and or material resources to self-sufficiently create for stable results.

Outcome: A loner, robust, and highly sensual personality that is rich with inner and or material resources yet hesitant to communicate and include others in its intimate world.

Famous figure: Karl Marx

Moon in Taurus, Sun in Gemini

Orientation: Seeking security in self-sufficiency and stability, emotionally processing and growing through using the senses, expressing talent, and managing resources, while motivated to create through coordinating diverse sources of interest on an intellectual, technological, and or cultural level.

Outcome: A resourceful and poetic personality that possesses a rich inner world and a wealth of cultural knowledge and insights.

Famous figure: Bob Dylan

Moon in Taurus, Sun in Cancer

Orientation: Seeking security in self-sufficiency and stability, emotionally processing and growing through using the senses, expressing talent, and managing resources, while striving to establish supportive conditions for creative expression and development.

Outcome: A nourishing, intimate, and self-accepting personality that remains loyal to its natural self and is driven by a compelling need for security and sense of well-being.

Famous figure: Frida Khalo

Moon in Taurus, Sun in Leo

Orientation: Seeking security in self-sufficiency and stability, emotionally processing and growing through using the senses, expressing talent, and managing resources, while feeling poised to personally participate in and influence life through various forms of creativity.

Outcome: An abounding, artistic, creative, and sensual personality that focuses on building and establishing a legacy of lasting value.

Famous figure: Bill Clinton

Moon in Taurus, Sun in Virgo

Orientation: Seeking security in self-sufficiency and stability, emotionally processing and growing through using the senses, expressing talent, and managing resources, while motivated to organize and optimize one's creative productivity through conscious reflection and refinement.

Outcome: A skillful, tasteful, and practical personality that is aware of details and needs that must be addressed.

Famous figure: Yogi Bhajan

Moon in Taurus, Sun in Libra

Orientation: Seeking security in self-sufficiency and stability, emotionally processing and growing through using the senses, expressing talent, and managing resources, while adopting a broader and more balanced perspective through one's creative endeavors.

Outcome: A sensitive, appreciative, and patient personality that learns to communicate and exchange in noninvasive ways.

Famous figure: Ammachi

Moon in Taurus, Sun in Scorpio

Orientation: Seeking security in self-sufficiency and stability, emotionally processing and growing through using the senses, expressing talent, and managing resources, while striving to powerfully impact others through one's creative efforts with the aim of fostering important changes both inwardly and outwardly.

Outcome: A potent, resistant, sexual, and possessive personality that seeks abundance and power through effectively exchanging and managing resources.

Famous figure: Michael Crichton

Moon in Taurus, Sun in Sagittarius

Orientation: Seeking security in self-sufficiency and stability, emotionally processing and growing through using the senses, expressing talent, and managing resources, while having faith that a larger life potential can be accessed and creatively accomplished.

Outcome: An authentic, independent, strongly convinced, and resourceful personality that rejects external pressure and limitations in order to thrive and prosper his or her own way.

Famous figure: Baruch Spinoza

Moon in Taurus, Sun in Capricorn

Orientation: Seeking security in self-sufficiency and stability, emotionally processing and growing through using the senses, expressing talent, and managing resources, while focusing on creating something that is of serious, inspiring, and reliable value.

Outcome: An artistic, self-made, resolute personality that focuses on building and designing reliable foundations for life.

Famous figure: Conrad Hilton

Moon in Taurus, Sun in Aquarius

Orientation: Seeking security in self-sufficiency and stability, emotionally processing and growing through using the senses, expressing talent, and managing resources, while using perspective and intelligence to inspire the creation of things that surpass and eventually upgrade current standards.

Outcome: A talented, maverick, and self-deductive personality with good taste that seeks to improve the quality of life through a more refined use of resources.

Famous figure: Jimmy Hoffa

Moon in Taurus, Sun in Pisces

Orientation: Seeking security in self-sufficiency and stability, emotionally processing and growing through using the senses, expressing talent, and managing resources, while called to make personal sacrifices for the sake of actualizing a destiny that addresses larger needs and possibly inspires the collective.

Outcome: An artistic, tranquil, and natural personality that strives to capture and embody universal beauty and peace.

Famous figure: Edgar Cayce

Moon in Gemini Combinations

Moon in Gemini, Sun in Aries

Orientation: Seeking to logically understand emotions and life's multiplicity from internal and external sources in order to effectively process and safely navigate life experiences, while possessing a strong sense of purpose that is cyclically renewed and oriented toward unrestrained creativity and promoting causes considered important.

Outcome: A curious and restless personality that is fascinated by life experiences and simultaneously able to create and coordinate on different dimensions.

Famous figure: Bette Davis

Moon in Gemini, Sun in Taurus

Orientation: Seeking to logically understand emotions and life's multiplicity from internal and external sources in order to effectively process and safely navigate life experiences, while possessing a wealth of inner and or material resources to self-sufficiently create for stable results.

Outcome: A cultivated, informed, trendy, and gifted personality that considers diverse options and dimensions while eventually opting to solely focus on what is personally considered valuable.

Famous figure: Sigmund Freud

Moon in Gemini, Sun in Gemini

Orientation: Seeking to logically understand emotions and life's multiplicity from internal and external sources in order to effectively process and safely navigate life experiences, while motivated to create through coordinating diverse sources of interest on an intellectual, technological, and or cultural level.

Outcome: A cultured, perceptive, and impatient personality that is ever seeking to update an understanding of the multidimensional aspect of life on both profane and complex levels.

Famous figure: Heidi Klum

Moon in Gemini, Sun in Cancer

Orientation: Seeking to logically understand emotions and life's multiplicity from internal and external sources in order to effectively process and safely navigate life experiences, while striving to establish supportive conditions for creative expression and development.

Outcome: A sheltered and psychologically perceptive personality that is exposed to diversity and yet strives to experience life's wealth at its own pace.

Famous figure: Franz Kafka

Moon in Gemini, Sun in Leo

Orientation: Seeking to logically understand emotions and life's multiplicity from internal and external sources in order to effectively process and safely navigate life experiences, while feeling poised to personally participate in and influence life through various forms of creativity.

Outcome: A colorful, sociable, far-sighted, and modern personality that creates a relatively wide support system to progress and take advantage of what life offers.

Famous figure: Barack Obama

Moon in Gemini, Sun in Virgo

Orientation: Seeking to logically understand emotions and life's multiplicity from internal and external sources in order to effectively process and safely navigate life experiences, while motivated to organize and optimize one's creative productivity through conscious reflection and refinement.

Outcome: A refined, cerebral, somewhat nervous, and busy type of personality that is witty and accomplished in many fields—a connoisseur.

Famous figure: Claudia Schiffer

Moon in Gemini, Sun in Libra

Orientation: Seeking to logically understand emotions and life's multiplicity from internal and external sources in order to effectively process and safely navigate life experiences, while adopting a broader and more balanced perspective through one's creative endeavors.

Outcome: A diplomatic, idealistic, and understanding personality that is stimulated by difference and seeks constant trade and exchange to enrich the self and make the world a more accessible and welcoming place.

Famous figure: David Ben-Gurion

Moon in Gemini, Sun in Scorpio

Orientation: Seeking to logically understand emotions and life's multiplicity from internal and external sources in order to effectively process and safely navigate life experiences, while striving to powerfully impact others through one's creative efforts with the aim of fostering important changes both inwardly and outwardly.

Outcome: A sharply perceptive and clever personality that longs to fulfill many desires by exploring all the corners of life from the shadowy to the bright in order to incessantly promote growth.

Famous figure: Bernard Kouchner

Moon in Gemini, Sun in Sagittarius

Orientation: Seeking to logically understand emotions and life's multiplicity from internal and external sources in order to effectively process and safely navigate life experiences, while having faith that a larger life potential can be accessed and creatively accomplished.

Outcome: A talkative, outgoing, and philosophically seeking personality that moves multidirectionally through cross-cultural and general life experiences.

Famous figure: Edith Piaf

Moon in Gemini, Sun in Capricorn

Orientation: Seeking to logically understand emotions and life's multiplicity from internal and external sources in order to effectively process and safely navigate life experiences, while focusing on creating something of serious, inspiring, and reliable value.

Outcome: A controlled, educated, and urban personality that is ambitious and inclined to participate in social or political dynamics.

Famous figure: Louis Pasteur

Moon in Gemini, Sun in Aquarius

Orientation: Seeking to logically understand emotions and life's multiplicity from internal and external sources in order to effectively process and safely navigate life experiences, while using perspective and intelligence to inspire the creation of things that surpass and eventually upgrade current standards.

Outcome: A fast-paced, progressive, and cerebral personality that is involved in multilevel exchange and development while seldom feeling a sense of permanent belonging.

Famous figure: Roy Gillett

Moon in Gemini, Sun in Pisces

Orientation: Seeking to logically understand emotions and life's multiplicity from internal and external sources in order to effectively process and safely navigate life experiences, while called to make personal sacrifices for the sake of actualizing a destiny that addresses larger needs and possibly inspires the collective.

Outcome: An adaptive, dispersed, imaginative personality that goes in and out of the regularity of time in ways that puzzle and captivate the environment.

Famous figure: Maryse Bastie

Moon in Cancer Combinations

Moon in Cancer, Sun in Aries

Orientation: Seeking to establish a reliable support system in order to address and process the array of emotional needs necessary for a gradual and healthy development, while possessing a strong sense of purpose that is cyclically renewed and oriented toward unrestrained creativity and promoting causes considered important.

Outcome: A protective, emotive, accessible, and straightforward personality that is driven by the immediacy of needs and yet capable of initiating creative efforts to secure a sense of well-being.

Famous figure: Kofi Annan

Moon in Cancer, Sun in Taurus

Orientation: Seeking to establish a reliable support system in order to address and process the array of emotional needs necessary for a gradual and healthy development, while possessing a wealth of inner and or material resources to self-sufficiently create for stable results.

Outcome: A nurturing, cautious, and calm-seeking personality that strives to have all its needs addressed in order to create and proceed with life at its own pace.

Famous figure: Aaron Spelling

Moon in Cancer, Sun in Gemini

Orientation: Seeking to establish a reliable support system in order to address and process the array of emotional needs necessary for a gradual and healthy development, while motivated to create through coordinating diverse sources of interest on an intellectual, technological, and or cultural level.

Outcome: A convivial, connected, and permissive personality that strives to personalize environmental conditions in order to create a supportive and interesting life.

Famous figure: Igor Stravinsky

Moon in Cancer, Sun in Cancer

Orientation: Seeking to establish a reliable support system in order to address and process the array of emotional needs necessary for a gradual and healthy development, while striving to establish supportive conditions for creative expression and development.

Outcome: A sensitive, personable, and authentic personality that is drawn into the unpredictable nature of emotional processing and seeks to strengthen inner foundations in order to live well.

Famous figure: Charlotte Gainsbourg

Moon in Cancer, Sun in Leo

Orientation: Seeking to establish a reliable support system in order to address and process the array of emotional needs necessary for a gradual and healthy development, while feeling poised to personally participate in and influence life through various forms of creativity.

Outcome: A warm, playful, familial, and self-indulgent personality that is focused on fostering prosperity and securing favorable conditions for its lineage to thrive.

Famous figure: Hugo Chavez

Moon in Cancer, Sun in Virgo

Orientation: Seeking to establish a reliable support system in order to address and process the array of emotional needs necessary for a gradual and healthy development, while motivated to organize and optimize one's creative productivity through conscious reflection and refinement.

Outcome: A caring, intimate, prudent, and attentive personality that is very particular about taste and the way to handle things while focused on establishing optimal conditions to develop and heal.

Famous figure: Julio Iglesias

Moon in Cancer, Sun in Libra

Orientation: Seeking to establish a reliable support system in order to address and process the array of emotional needs necessary for a gradual and healthy development, while adopting a broader and more balanced perspective through one's creative endeavors.

Outcome: A considerate, accessible, charismatic, and socially involved personality that strives to foster a reliable support system in order to promote rights and well-being for all involved.

Famous figure: Pedro Almodovar

Moon in Cancer, Sun in Scorpio

Orientation: Seeking to establish a reliable support system in order to address and process the array of emotional needs necessary for a gradual and healthy development, while striving to powerfully impact others through one's creative efforts with the aim of fostering important changes both inwardly and outwardly.

Outcome: A protective, intimate, and giving personality that is strongly attached and emotionally intense yet discriminating when deciding whom or what to include in its personal sphere in order to foster both growth and security.

Famous figure: Teddy Roosevelt

Moon in Cancer, Sun in Sagittarius

Orientation: Seeking to establish a reliable support system in order to address and process the array of emotional needs necessary for a gradual and healthy development, while having faith that a larger life potential can be accessed and creatively accomplished.

Outcome: A natural, inherently subjective, and pleasurable personality that is engaged in generating a positive environment that supports freedom of being, positive life conditions, and a feeling of belonging through philosophical associations.

Famous figure: Giacomo Puccini

Moon in Cancer, Sun in Capricorn

Orientation: Seeking to establish a reliable support system in order to address and process the array of emotional needs necessary for a gradual and healthy development, while focusing on creating something of serious, inspiring, and reliable value.

Outcome: A parental, moderate, and considerate personality that focuses on working through weaknesses to gain credibility and establish a safe and reliable path of development.

Famous figure: Ramana Maharishi

Moon in Cancer, Sun in Aquarius

Orientation: Seeking to establish a reliable support system in order to address and process the array of emotional needs necessary for a gradual and healthy development, while using perspective and intelligence to inspire the creation of things that surpass and eventually upgrade current standards.

Outcome: A liberal, emotionally intelligent, and socially conscious personality that is interested in taking part in interactive communal exchanges so that everyone's welfare and well-being is enhanced.

Famous figure: Simone Weil

Moon in Cancer, Sun in Pisces

Orientation: Seeking to establish a reliable support system in order to address and process the array of emotional needs necessary for a gradual and healthy development, while called to make personal sacrifices for the sake of actualizing a destiny that addresses larger needs and possibly inspires the collective.

Outcome: A sensitive, informal, and innocent personality that strives to find a sense of safety and reliability when dealing with the vastness of the world, sometimes at the price of mood swings.

Famous figure: Kurt Cobain

Moon in Leo Combinations

Moon in Leo, Sun in Aries

Orientation: Seeking to bring needs and personal qualities to the forefront so they can be better addressed and play a more meaningful and influential role in life, while possessing a strong sense of purpose that is cyclically renewed and oriented toward unrestrained creativity and promoting causes considered important.

Outcome: A passionate, creative, and expressive personality that is subject to emotional extremes and immersed in its personal vision and objectives in life.

Famous figure: Andrew Lloyd Webber

Moon in Leo, Sun in Taurus

Orientation: Seeking to bring needs and personal qualities to the forefront so they can be better addressed and play a more meaningful and influential role in life, while possessing a wealth of inner and or material resources to self-sufficiently create for stable results.

Outcome: An artistic, prosperous, and territorial personality that seeks to maintain control over its means and ways of action so that from its perspective solidity and value can be guaranteed.

Famous figure: Elizabeth II, Queen of England

Moon in Leo, Sun in Gemini

Orientation: Seeking to bring needs and personal qualities to the forefront so they can be better addressed and play a more meaningful and influential role in life, while motivated to create through coordinating diverse sources of interest on an intellectual, technological, and or cultural level.

Outcome: A warm, sociable, and animated personality that is capable of fostering development through multiple outlets.

Famous figure: Jacques Yves Cousteau

Moon in Leo, Sun in Cancer

Orientation: Seeking to bring needs and personal qualities to the forefront so they can be better addressed and play a more meaningful and influential role in life, while striving to establish supportive conditions for creative expression and development.

Outcome: An emotional, nurturing, familial, and permissive personality that seeks to solidify and take good care of anything within the compound of its personal realm.

Famous figure: Tom Hanks

Moon in Leo, Sun in Leo

Orientation: Seeking to bring needs and personal qualities to the forefront so they can be better addressed and play a more meaningful and influential role in life, while feeling poised to personally participate in and influence life through various forms of creativity.

Outcome: An inspired, strongly present, and emotive personality that is convinced of its need to fulfill a meaningful destiny so that a better future can be created.

Famous figure: Tem Tarriktar

Moon in Leo, Sun in Virgo

Orientation: Seeking to bring needs and personal qualities to the forefront so they can be better addressed and play a more meaningful and influential role in life, while motivated to organize and optimize one's creative productivity through conscious reflection and refinement.

Outcome: A talented, civil, refined, and focused personality that seeks control of means and the environment to assure a safe and productive outcome for invested efforts.

Famous figure: Princess Rania of Jordan

Moon in Leo, Sun in Libra

Orientation: Seeking to bring needs and personal qualities to the forefront so they can be better addressed and play a more meaningful and influential role in life, while adopting a broader and more balanced perspective through one's creative endeavors.

Outcome: A hospitable, supportive, and graceful personality that perceives diverse ways to manifest creative potential in oneself and others.

Famous figure: Mohandas Gandhi

Moon in Leo, Sun in Scorpio

Orientation: Seeking to bring needs and personal qualities to the forefront so they can be better addressed and play a more meaningful and influential role in life, while striving to powerfully impact others through one's creative efforts with the aim of fostering important changes both inwardly and outwardly.

Outcome: A creative, potent, and dramatic personality that is very attached to whatever it is involved with to make sure that it will have a transformative impact on the self and others.

Famous figure: Julia Roberts

Moon in Leo, Sun in Sagittarius

Orientation: Seeking to bring needs and personal qualities to the forefront so they can be better addressed and play a more meaningful and influential role in life, while having faith that a larger life potential can be accessed and creatively accomplished.

Outcome: A prolific, inspired, and expressive personality that proceeds with high expectations for making the best out of life.

Famous figure: Winston Churchill

Moon in Leo, Sun in Capricorn

Orientation: Seeking to bring needs and personal qualities to the forefront so they can be better addressed and play a more meaningful and influential role in life, while focusing on creating something of serious, inspiring, and reliable value.

Outcome: A serious, dignified, and ambitious personality that possesses leadership qualities and aspires to model noble values through prominence.

Famous figure: Paramahansa Yogananda

Moon in Leo, Sun in Aquarius

Orientation: Seeking to bring needs and personal qualities to the forefront so they can be better addressed and play a more meaningful and influential role in life, while using perspective and intelligence to inspire the creation of things that surpass and eventually upgrade current standards.

Outcome: A sophisticated, sometimes posh, and ingenious personality that aims to inspire and offer ways of promoting higher standards to benefit life.

Famous figure: James Joyce

Moon in Leo, Sun in Pisces

Orientation: Seeking to bring needs and personal qualities to the forefront so they can be better addressed and play a more meaningful and influential role in life, while called to make personal sacrifices for the sake of actualizing a destiny that addresses larger needs and possibly inspires the collective.

Outcome: An artistic, fanciful, dramatic, and altruistic personality that strives to have its personal qualities touch and benefit a larger whole while expecting gratitude for it.

Famous figure: Kemal Attaturk

Moon in Virgo Combinations

Moon in Virgo, Sun in Aries

Orientation: Seeking security in the optimal function of one's personal life through properly caring for needs and overcoming weaknesses, while possessing a strong sense of purpose that is cyclically renewed and oriented toward unrestrained creativity and promoting causes considered important.

Outcome: A focused, proficient, and vigorous personality that is highly physical and determined to accurately achieve what it wants.

Famous figure: Akira Kurosawa

Moon in Virgo, Sun in Taurus

Orientation: Seeking security in the optimal function of one's personal life through properly caring for needs and overcoming weaknesses, while possessing a wealth of inner and or material resources to self-sufficiently create for stable results.

Outcome: A resourceful, artistic, elegant, and practical personality that yearns for beauty and peace while aiming to create a secure, productive, and comfortable life.

Famous figure: Hirohito, Emperor of Japan

Moon in Virgo, Sun in Gemini

Orientation: Seeking security in optimal function of one's personal life through properly caring for needs and overcoming weaknesses, while motivated to create through coordinating diverse sources of interest on an intellectual, technological, and or cultural level.

Outcome: An urbane, witty, dexterous, and knowledgeable personality that possesses a good sense of orientation in life and is inspired to share insights about ways to manage existence.

Famous figure: John F. Kennedy

Moon in Virgo, Sun in Cancer

Orientation: Seeking security in the optimal function of one's personal life through properly caring for needs and overcoming weaknesses, while striving to establish supportive conditions for creative expression and development.

Outcome: A sensitive, concerned, and caring personality that is focused on creating an environment that addresses needs and objectives in the way it deems most effective.

Famous figure: Dalai Lama

Moon in Virgo, Sun in Leo

Orientation: Seeking security in the optimal function of one's personal life through properly caring for needs and overcoming weaknesses, while feeling poised to personally participate in and influence life through various forms of creativity.

Outcome: An autonomous, productive, and creative personality that is highly capable and seeks full control of its destiny and purpose.

Famous figure: Madonna

Moon in Virgo, Sun in Virgo

Orientation: Seeking security in the optimal function of one's personal life through properly caring for needs and overcoming weaknesses, while motivated to organize and optimize one's creative productivity through conscious reflection and refinement.

Outcome: A perceptive, polished, rather sarcastic, and conscientious personality that constantly refines itself and the use of resources to achieve excellence and a high level of productivity.

Famous figure: Lance Armstrong

Moon Virgo, Sun in Libra

Orientation: Seeking security in the optimal function of one's personal life through properly caring for needs and overcoming weaknesses, while adopting a broader and more balanced perspective through one's creative endeavors.

Outcome: A civil, service-oriented, and thoughtful personality that is prepared to make personal sacrifices to create what is closest to perfection.

Famous figure: Deepak Chopra

Moon in Virgo, Sun in Scorpio

Orientation: Seeking security in the optimal function of one's personal life through properly caring for needs and overcoming weaknesses, while striving to powerfully impact others through one's creative efforts with the aim of fostering important changes both inwardly and outwardly.

Outcome: A discerning, critical, and competent personality that is highly conscious of any dysfunction or limitation needing to be addressed for therapeutic or growth purposes.

Famous figure: Jodie Foster

Moon in Virgo, Sun in Sagittarius

Orientation: Seeking security in the optimal function of one's personal life through properly caring for needs and overcoming weaknesses, while having faith that a larger life potential can be accessed and creatively accomplished.

Outcome: A strong-spirited, argumentative, and resourceful personality that uses effective strategies to conquer new ground.

Famous figure: Maria Callas

Moon in Virgo, Sun in Capricorn

Orientation: Seeking security in the optimal function of one's personal life through properly caring for needs and overcoming weaknesses, while focusing on creating something of serious, inspiring, and reliable value.

Outcome: A dutiful, consistent, and self-demanding personality that seeks a reliable reference of order to direct and heal the self and others.

Famous figure: David Lynch

Moon in Virgo, Sun in Aquarius

Orientation: Seeking security in the optimal function of one's personal life through properly caring for needs and overcoming weaknesses, while using perspective and intelligence to inspire the creation of things that surpass and eventually upgrade current standards.

Outcome: A sophisticated, cerebral, rather sarcastic, and inventive personality that offer solutions for civilization to outgrow its predicaments.

Famous figure: Gertrude Stein

Moon in Virgo, Sun in Pisces

Orientation: Seeking security in the optimal function of one's personal life through properly caring for needs and overcoming weaknesses, while called to make personal sacrifices for the sake of actualizing a destiny that addresses larger needs and possibly inspires the collective.

Outcome: An idealistic, self-sacrificing, and highly-talented personality that aims to transcend weaknesses and obstacles in order to access what is most pure and complete.

Famous figure: Rudolph Steiner

Moon in Libra Combinations

Moon in Libra, Sun in Aries

Orientation: Seeking to comprehensively address needs and opening to diverse approaches so that life can be handled in a more balanced and appropriate way, while possessing a strong sense of purpose that is cyclically renewed and oriented toward unrestrained creativity and promoting causes considered important.

Outcome: A benevolent, argumentative, and controversial personality that is inclined to periodically redefine its sense of identity in the search for justice and balance.

Famous figure: Maya Angelou

Moon in Libra, Sun in Taurus

Orientation: Seeking to comprehensively address needs and opening to diverse approaches so that life can be handled in a more balanced and appropriate way, while possessing a wealth of inner and or material resources to self-sufficiently create for stable results.

Outcome: A gentle, tolerant, and sensuous personality that attempts to find value and worth in everything and everyone to support an ideal of harmony, even if against the odds.

Famous figure: William Shakespeare

Moon in Libra, Sun in Gemini

Orientation: Seeking to comprehensively address needs and opening to diverse approaches so that life can be handled in a more balanced and appropriate way, while motivated to create through coordinating diverse sources of interest on an intellectual, technological, and or cultural level.

Outcome: An open-minded, welcoming, and widely exposed personality with remarkable networking skills that attempts to uncover the link between life's diverse components despite their apparent divergence.

Famous figure: Josephine Baker

Moon in Libra, Sun in Cancer

Orientation: Seeking to comprehensively address needs and opening to diverse approaches so that life can be handled in a more balanced and appropriate way, while striving to establish supportive conditions for creative expression and development.

Outcome: A personable, giving, and cautiously curious personality that attempts to expand in inclusive ways while refraining from compromising on security needs.

Famous figure: Nikola Telsa

Moon in Libra, Sun in Leo

Orientation: Seeking to comprehensively address needs and opening to diverse approaches so that life can be handled in a more balanced and appropriate way, while feeling poised to personally participate in and influence life through various forms of creativity.

Outcome: A supportive, hopeful, and complex personality determined to creatively actualize goals that serve justice and balance.

Famous figure: Fidel Castro

Moon in Libra, Sun in Virgo

Orientation: Seeking to comprehensively address needs and opening to diverse approaches so that life can be handled in a more balanced and appropriate way, while motivated to organize and optimize one's creative productivity through conscious reflection and refinement.

Outcome: A courteous, elegant, and cultivated personality that uses social skills to advance goals deemed valuable.

Famous figure: Agatha Christie

Moon in Libra, Sun in Libra

Orientation: Seeking to comprehensively address needs and opening to diverse approaches so that life can be handled in a more balanced and appropriate way, while adopting a broader and more balanced perspective through one's creative endeavors.

Outcome: A social, sometimes controversial, and open-minded personality that opts to approach life in a relatively neutral way in order to promote fair and authentic chances of development for all, eventually including oneself.

Famous figure: Bruce Springsteen

Moon in Libra, Sun in Scorpio

Orientation: Seeking to comprehensively address needs and opening to diverse approaches so that life can be handled in a more balanced and appropriate way, while striving to powerfully impact others through one's creative efforts wanting to foster important changes both inwardly and outwardly.

Outcome: A psychologically perceptive, conscious, and adaptable personality that seeks different means and approaches that can lead to an ever more fulfilling life.

Famous figure: Ofra Haza

Moon in Libra, Sun in Sagittarius:

Orientation: Seeking to comprehensively address needs and opening to diverse approaches so that life can be handled in a more balanced and appropriate way, while having faith that a larger life potential can be accessed and creatively accomplished.

Outcome: A knowledgeable, talkative, and spirited personality that indulges in theoretical pursuits seeking to access more of life's potential through exposure to cultural and or social diversity.

Famous figure: Noam Chomsky

Moon in Libra, Sun in Capricorn:

Orientation: Seeking to comprehensively address needs and opening to diverse approaches so that life can be handled in a more balanced and appropriate way, while focusing on creating something of serious, inspiring, and reliable value.

Outcome: An attentive, thoughtful, and righteous personality that seeks fairness and reliability in people and systems in order to be guided and guide well when proceeding with life.

Famous figure: Christiane Amanpour

Moon in Libra, Sun in Aquarius:

Orientation: Seeking to comprehensively address needs and opening to diverse approaches so that life can be handled in a more balanced and appropriate way, while using perspective and intelligence to inspire the creation of things that surpass and eventually upgrade current standards.

Outcome: A liberal, social, and visionary personality that is stimulated by interactive dynamics yet often struggles to find a comfortable position in a world perceived as lacking.

Famous figure: Jerry Springer

Moon in Libra, Sun in Pisces:

Orientation: Seeking to comprehensively address needs and opening to diverse approaches so that life can be handled in a more balanced and appropriate way, while called to make personal sacrifices for the sake of actualizing a destiny that addresses larger needs and possibly inspires the collective.

Outcome: A smooth, accommodating, and sometimes enchanting personality that is reluctant to discriminate in order to preserve an all-inclusive ideal of diversity and oneness.

Famous figure: Michael Caine

Moon in Scorpio Combinations

Moon in Scorpio, Sun in Aries

Orientation: Seeking to establish a trusting intimacy in order to safely process the intensity of recurrent life changes and facilitate one's own emotional growth, while possessing a strong sense of purpose that is cyclically renewed and oriented toward unrestrained creativity and promoting causes considered important.

Outcome: A highly sensitive, sharp, and determined personality that is prepared to face necessary challenges to create both internal and external changes.

Famous figure: Harry Houdini

Moon in Scorpio, Sun in Taurus

Orientation: Seeking to establish a trusting intimacy in order to safely process the intensity of recurrent life changes and facilitate one's own emotional growth, while possessing a wealth of inner and or material resources to self-sufficiently create for stable results.

Outcome: A concentrated, sexual, and creative personality that is invested in increasing its worth and power, sometimes through unavoidable upheaval.

Famous figure: Bono Vox

Moon in Scorpio, Sun in Gemini

Orientation: Seeking to establish a trusting intimacy in order to safely process the intensity of recurrent life changes and facilitate one's own emotional growth, while motivated to create through coordinating diverse sources of interest on an intellectual, technological, and or cultural level.

Outcome: A clever, enquiring, and watchful personality that seeks strong stimulation and learning experiences, while eager to expose inaccuracies and deceit when encountered.

Famous figure: Morrissey

Moon in Scorpio, Sun in Cancer

Orientation: Seeking to establish a trusting intimacy in order to safely process the intensity of recurrent life changes and facilitate one's own emotional growth, while striving to establish supportive conditions for creative expression and development.

Outcome: An intimate, cautious, and protective personality that yearns to create a healthy attachment to trusted people in order to become stronger in union and address shifting needs with proper care.

Famous figure: Nelson Mandela

Moon in Scorpio, Sun in Leo

Orientation: Seeking to establish a trusting intimacy in order to safely process the intensity of recurrent life changes and facilitate one's own emotional growth, while feeling poised to personally participate in and influence life through various forms of creativity.

Outcome: A potent, dramatic, and generous personality that is focused on increasing the odds for a better future in places affected by internal or external pain and damage.

Famous figure: Alfred Hitchcock

Moon in Scorpio, Sun in Virgo

Orientation: Seeking to establish a trusting intimacy in order to safely process the intensity of recurrent life changes and facilitate one's own emotional growth, while motivated to organize and optimize one's creative productivity through conscious reflection and refinement.

Outcome: A discerning, bright, and apprehensive personality that is conscious of problems and dysfunction yet resourceful enough to effectively address them.

Famous figure: Maria Montessori

Moon in Scorpio, Sun in Libra

Orientation: Seeking to establish a trusting intimacy in order to safely process the intensity of recurrent life changes and facilitate one's own emotional growth, while adopting a broader and more balanced perspective through one's creative endeavors.

Outcome: A psychologically perceptive, understanding, and liberal personality that understands that compromise can serve growth and prosperity.

Famous figure: Jimmy Carter

Moon in Scorpio, Sun in Scorpio

Orientation: Seeking to establish a trusting intimacy in order to safely process the intensity of recurrent life changes and facilitate one's own emotional growth, while striving to powerfully impact others through one's creative efforts with the aim of fostering important changes both internally and externally.

Outcome: A potent, immersed, and guarded personality that is exposed to emotional intensity resulting from recurrent self-transformational processes that serve the longing for fulfillment and love.

Famous figure: Bjork

Moon in Scorpio, Sun in Sagittarius

Orientation: Seeking to establish a trusting intimacy in order to safely process the intensity of recurrent life changes and facilitate one's own emotional growth, while having faith that a larger life potential can be accessed and creatively accomplished.

Outcome: A truth-seeking, penetrating, and direct personality that is stimulated by the concealed and uncharted potential of life, sometimes becoming overwhelming in its fervent approach.

Famous figure: Uri Geller

Moon in Scorpio, Sun in Capricorn

Orientation: Seeking to establish a trusting intimacy in order to safely process the intensity of recurrent life changes and facilitate one's own emotional growth, while focusing on creating something of serious, inspiring, and reliable value.

Outcome: A wise, ambitious, watchful, and politically conscious personality that fluctuates between conformity and defiance when wanting to foster personal or collective development.

Famous figure: Michel De Nostradamus

Moon in Scorpio, Sun in Aquarius

Orientation: Seeking to establish a trusting intimacy in order to safely process the intensity of recurrent life changes and facilitate one's own emotional growth, while using perspective and intelligence to inspire the creation of things that surpass and eventually upgrade current standards.

Outcome: A reflective, thought-provoking, intricate, and inventive personality that is motivated by a need for ingenuity and love but also prepared for disappointment.

Famous figure: Jules Verne

Moon in Scorpio, Sun in Pisces

Orientation: Seeking to establish a trusting intimacy in order to safely process the intensity of recurrent life changes and facilitate one's own emotional growth, while called to make personal sacrifices for the sake of actualizing a destiny that addresses larger needs and possibly inspires the collective.

Outcome: An ambiguous, receptive, and longing personality that oscillates between having a distrusting and audacious attitude, to experiencing the intensity of delight when venturing in the vast ocean of life.

Famous figure: David Livingstone

Moon in Sagittarius Combinations

Moon in Sagittarius, Sun in Aries

Orientation: Seeking the freedom to address emotional needs and live as authentically as possible relative to a chosen philosophy or viewpoint of life resonating with one's current state of being, while possessing a strong sense of purpose that is cyclically renewed and oriented toward unrestrained creativity and promoting causes considered important.

Outcome: A natural, animated, and uncompromising personality that aims to transcend the constraints of time and space, or any other distraction, to experience the vast array of creative possibilities at large.

Famous figure: Vincent Van Gogh

Moon in Sagittarius, Sun in Taurus

Orientation: Seeking the freedom to address emotional needs and live as authentically as possible relative to a chosen philosophy or viewpoint of life resonating with one's current state of being, while possessing a wealth of inner and or material resources to self-sufficiently create for stable results.

Outcome: An autonomous, resourceful, headstrong, and pleasure-loving personality that is capable of important achievements when inspired, and inclined to be at its best when in natural environments.

Famous figure: Jiddu Krishnamurti

Moon in Sagittarius, Sun in Gemini

Orientation: Seeking the freedom to address emotional needs and live as authentically as possible relative to a chosen philosophy or viewpoint of life resonating with one's current state of being, while motivated to create through coordinating diverse sources of interest on an intellectual, technological, and or cultural level.

Outcome: An expressive, busy-minded, and nomadic personality that seeks authentic and insightful experiences that it will eventually need to share and discuss.

Famous figure: Donald Trump

Moon in Sagittarius, Sun in Cancer

Orientation: Seeking the freedom to address emotional needs and live as authentically as possible relative to a chosen philosophy or viewpoint of life resonating with one's current state of being, while striving to establish supportive conditions for creative expression and development.

Outcome: A sincere, natural, and highly subjective personality that attempts to create supportive conditions to keep its spirit free and belief system undisturbed.

Famous figure: Michael Phelps

Moon in Sagittarius, Sun in Leo

Orientation: Seeking the freedom to address emotional needs and live as authentically as possible relative to a chosen philosophy or viewpoint of life resonating with one's current state of being, while feeling poised to personally participate in and influence life through various forms of creativity.

Outcome: A creative, dramatic, and generous personality that is subject to getting carried away when enthused by greatness and high expectations for manifesting a special destiny

Famous figure: Neil Armstrong

Moon in Sagittarius, Sun in Virgo

Orientation: Seeking the freedom to address emotional needs and live as authentically as possible relative to a chosen philosophy or viewpoint of life resonating with one's current state of being, while motivated to organize and optimize one's creative productivity through conscious reflection and refinement.

Outcome: A self-directed, tenacious, and robust personality that seeks extensive control over its life development in the hope of turning personal visions into reality.

Famous figure: Liz Greene

Moon in Sagittarius, Sun in Libra

Orientation: Seeking the freedom to address emotional needs and live as authentically as possible relative to a chosen philosophy or viewpoint of life resonating with one's current state of being, while motivated to organize and optimize one's creative productivity through conscious reflection and refinement.

Outcome: An inquisitive, contemplative, and outgoing personality that attempts to find a coherent way to address life's cultural and social multiplicity, sometimes in controversial ways.

Famous figure: Frederich Nietzsche

Moon in Sagittarius, Sun in Scorpio

Orientation: Seeking the freedom to address emotional needs and live as authentically as possible relative to a chosen philosophy or viewpoint of life resonating with one's current state of being, while striving to powerfully impact others through one's creative efforts with the aim of fostering important changes both inwardly and outwardly.

Outcome: An intense, confrontational, keen, and creative personality that attempts to expose and manifest the perceived truth or unfulfilled potential in ways that have an impact.

Famous figure: Pablo Picasso

Moon in Sagittarius, Sun in Sagittarius

Orientation: Seeking the freedom to address emotional needs and live as authentically as possible relative to a chosen philosophy or viewpoint of life resonating with one's current state of being, while having faith that a larger life potential can be accessed and creatively accomplished.

Outcome: An authentic, convinced, and resourceful personality that comes on strong, enthused by the promise of a better tomorrow.

Famous figure: Ludwig van Beethoven

Moon in Sagittarius, Sun in Capricorn

Orientation: Seeking the freedom to address emotional needs and live as authentically as possible relative to a chosen philosophy or viewpoint of life resonating with one's current state of being, while focusing on creating something of serious, inspiring, and reliable value.

Outcome: A knowledgeable, self-assured, opinionated, and steadfast personality that possesses leadership qualities and is inspired to train and direct people in the perceived reliable and righteous way.

Famous figure: Kahlil Gibran

Moon in Sagittarius, Sun in Aquarius

Orientation: Seeking the freedom to address emotional needs and live as authentically as possible relative to a chosen philosophy or viewpoint of life resonating with one's current state of being, while using perspective and intelligence to inspire the creation of things that surpass and eventually upgrade current standards.

Outcome: A busy-minded, inventive, nonconforming, and immoderate personality that fluctuates between being socially inclusive and utterly disengaged when incorporating distinctive ideas and schemes within life dynamics.

Famous figure: Wolfgang Mozart

Moon in Sagittarius, Sun in Pisces

Orientation: Seeking the freedom to address emotional needs and live as authentically as possible relative to a chosen philosophy or viewpoint of life resonating with one's current state of being, while called to make personal sacrifices for the sake of actualizing a destiny that addresses larger needs and possibly inspires the collective.

Outcome: A rather bold, untamed, and optimistic personality that disregards the boundaries of time and space to access the vastness of yet unconfirmed life potential at his or her own risk.

Famous figure: Albert Einstein

Moon in Capricorn Combinations

Moon in Capricorn, Sun in Aries

Orientation: Seeking strength and wisdom to address emotional needs and maturation processes the perceived right way in the hope of securing a healthy development, while possessing a strong sense of purpose that is cyclically renewed and oriented toward unrestrained creativity and promoting causes considered important.

Outcome: A firm, commanding, courageous, and ambitious personality that perseveres against defiance and obstacles to achieve objectives perceived as worthwhile.

Famous figure: Al Gore

Moon in Capricorn, Sun in Taurus

Orientation: Seeking strength and wisdom to address emotional needs and maturation processes the perceived right way in the hope of securing a healthy development, while possessing a wealth of inner and or material resources to self-sufficiently create for stable results.

Outcome: An artistic, resilient, and self-contained personality that aims to build and establish things of lasting value in the physical realm.

Famous figure: David Byrne

Moon in Capricorn, Sun in Gemini

Orientation: Seeking strength and wisdom to address emotional needs and maturation processes the perceived right way in the hope of securing a healthy development, while motivated to create through coordinating diverse sources of interest on an intellectual, technological, and or cultural level.

Outcome: A socially aware, educated, and sensible personality that is prepared to quickly ascend to positions of influence to in turn facilitate enterprise development through meaningful cooperation.

Famous figure: Johnny Depp

Moon in Capricorn, Sun in Cancer

Orientation: Seeking strength and wisdom to address emotional needs and maturation processes the perceived right way in the hope of securing a healthy development, while striving to establish supportive conditions for creative expression and development.

Outcome: A protective, patient, and relatively conservative personality that is inspired by ancestral heritage and strives to find the appropriate rhythm of maturation to guarantee that life unfolds safely and productively.

Famous Figure: Carly Simon

Moon in Capricorn, Sun in Leo

Orientation: Seeking strength and wisdom to address emotional needs and maturation processes the perceived right way in the hope of securing a healthy development, while feeling poised to personally participate in and influence life through various forms of creativity.

Outcome: A ceremonial, consistent, and commendable personality that seeks to carry forward the legacy of elders with dignity and distinction.

Famous figure: Napoleon I Bonaparte

Moon in Capricorn, Sun in Virgo

Orientation: Seeking strength and wisdom to address emotional needs and maturation processes in the perceived right way in the hope of securing a healthy development, while motivated to organize and optimize one's creative productivity through conscious reflection and refinement.

Outcome: A self-controlled, determined, and cautious personality that relies on a perceived ideal of order when using acquired wealth—whether material resources, skills, or knowledge—to create what is closest to perfection and guarantee safety.

Famous figure: Brian de Palma

Moon in Capricorn, Sun in Libra

Orientation: Seeking strength and wisdom to address emotional needs and maturation processes the perceived right way in the hope of securing a healthy development, while adopting a broader and more balanced perspective through one's creative endeavors.

Outcome: A mature, dependable, and mentoring personality that relies on perceived ideals of justice and fairness to establish a foundation that serves as a reference for guiding people from diverse backgrounds.

Famous figure: Susan Sarandon

Moon in Capricorn, Sun in Scorpio

Orientation: Seeking strength and wisdom to address emotional needs and maturation processes the perceived right way in the hope of securing a healthy development, while striving to powerfully impact others through one's creative efforts with the aim of fostering important changes both inwardly and outwardly.

Outcome: A reserved, cautious, and highly capable personality that does not easily reveal its emotional sensitivity, demonstrating patience and acuity in the hope of guaranteeing effective impact and change.

Famous figure: Robert Kennedy

Moon in Capricorn, Sun in Sagittarius

Orientation: Seeking strength and wisdom to address emotional needs and maturation processes the perceived right way in the hope of securing a healthy development, while having faith that a larger life potential can be accessed and creatively accomplished.

Outcome: A pious, experienced, robust, and commanding personality that is dedicated to diffusing acquired knowledge and wisdom in an effort to educate and promote perceived righteousness.

Famous figure: Rachida Dati

Moon in Capricorn, Sun in Capricorn

Orientation: Seeking strength and wisdom to address emotional needs and maturation processes the perceived right way in the hope of a securing a healthy development, while focusing on creating something of serious, inspiring, and reliable value.

Outcome: A gifted, committed, dependable, and melancholic personality that yearns to gain credibility for its efforts and achievements with the aim of inspiring people to do the perceived right thing.

Famous figure: Clara Barton

Moon in Capricorn, Sun in Aquarius

Orientation: Seeking strength and wisdom to address emotional needs and maturation processes the perceived right way in the hope of securing healthy development, while using perspective and intelligence to inspire the creation of things that surpass and eventually upgrade current standards.

Outcome: A serious, academic, and self-demanding personality that transcends emotionality while eager to resolve and overcome existing debilities for the sake of successfully developing and managing larger scale systems.

Famous figure: Abraham Lincoln

Moon in Capricorn, Sun in Pisces

Orientation: Seeking strength and wisdom to address emotional needs and maturation processes the perceived right way in the hope of securing a healthy development, while called to make personal sacrifices for the sake of actualizing a destiny that addresses larger needs and possibly inspires the collective.

Outcome: A poetic, introverted, and dutiful personality that is disposed to make extensive sacrifices for the sake of an ultimate sense of guidance that would restore collective well-being.

Famous figure: Percival Lowell

Moon in Aquarius Combinations

Moon in Aquarius, Sun in Aries

Orientation: Seeking to clarify emotions and upgrade processing mechanisms in order to resolve impediments, reduce pain, and induce progress, while possessing a strong sense of purpose that is cyclically renewed and oriented toward unrestrained creativity and promoting causes considered important.

Outcome: A thought-provoking, daring, impatient, and unpredictable personality that is willing to experiment and assume challenges in order to turn ideas into action.

Famous figure: Dane Rudhyar

Moon in Aquarius, Sun in Taurus

Orientation: Seeking to clarify emotions and upgrade processing mechanisms in order to resolve impediments, reduce pain, and induce progress, while possessing a wealth of inner and or material resources to self-sufficiently create for stable results.

Outcome: A self-deducing, gifted, and individualistic personality that wants to create and establish things on foundations of high quality and worth.

Famous figure: Vladimir Lenin

Moon in Aquarius, Sun in Gemini

Orientation: Seeking to clarify emotions and upgrade processing mechanisms in order to resolve impediments, reduce pain, and induce progress, while motivated to create through coordinating diverse sources of interest on an intellectual, technological, and or cultural level.

Outcome: A witty, highly aware, and well-informed personality that progresses faster than average on many fronts, sometimes to the extent of losing presence in the process.

Famous figure: Jean Paul Sartre

Moon in Aquarius, Sun in Cancer

Orientation: Seeking to clarify emotions and upgrade processing mechanisms in order to resolve impediments, reduce pain, and induce progress, while striving to establish supportive conditions for creative expression and development.

Outcome: A particular, conceptually tolerant, and perceptive personality that invests in identifying and developing the most advanced ways to intimately address emotional, communal, and or educational issues.

Famous figure: Diana Princess of Wales

Moon in Aquarius, Sun in Leo

Orientation: Seeking to clarify emotions and upgrade processing mechanisms in order to resolve impediments, reduce pain, and induce progress, while feeling poised to personally participate in and influence life through various forms of creativity.

Outcome: A noble, proud, and gifted personality that uses personal creativity and will to promote a better future with higher standards.

Famous figure: Kate Bush

Moon in Aquarius, Sun in Virgo

Orientation: Seeking to clarify emotions and upgrade processing mechanisms in order to resolve impediments, reduce pain, and induce progress while motivated to organize and optimize one's creative productivity through conscious reflection and refinement.

Outcome: A brilliant, sharp, elitist, and environmentally sensitive personality that is eager to replace obsolete ways of addressing predicaments to maintain a highly functional environment with as little disturbance possible.

Famous figure: David Copperfield

Moon in Aquarius, Sun in Libra

Orientation: Seeking to clarify emotions and upgrade processing mechanisms in order to resolve impediments, reduce pain, and induce progress, while adopting a broader and more balanced perspective through one's creative endeavors.

Outcome: A provocative, socially conscious, sociable, and enquiring personality that ponders progressive concepts to bring people or even humanity to a more peaceful and functional level, often motivated by long-lasting internal dissatisfaction.

Famous figure: John Lennon

Moon in Aquarius, Sun in Scorpio

Orientation: Seeking to clarify emotions and upgrade processing mechanisms in order to resolve impediments, reduce pain, and induce progress, while striving to powerfully impact others through one's creative efforts with the aim of fostering important changes both inwardly and outwardly.

Outcome: An intelligent, conscious, radical, and confrontational personality that is willing to delve into taboos so that better solutions can be found for intimate and social ills.

Famous figure: Voltaire

Moon in Aquarius, Sun in Sagittarius

Orientation: Seeking to clarify emotions and upgrade processing mechanisms in order to resolve impediments, reduce pain, and induce progress, while having faith that a larger life potential can be accessed and creatively accomplished.

Outcome: An eccentric, inventive, and bold personality that constantly explores life's multiple and unpredictable ways of development.

Famous figure: Woody Allen

Moon in Aquarius, Sun in Capricorn

Orientation: Seeking to clarify emotions and upgrade processing mechanisms in order to resolve impediments, reduce pain, and induce progress, while focusing on creating something of serious, inspiring, and reliable value.

Outcome: A mature, erudite, aloof, and sensible personality that is capable of achieving a high degree of expertise in its field, while striving to assemble highly capable individuals who can develop useful strategies for guiding and promoting progress within systems.

Famous figure: Helena Rubinstein

Moon in Aquarius, Sun in Aquarius

Orientation: Seeking to clarify emotions and upgrade processing mechanisms in order to resolve impediments, reduce pain, and induce progress, while using perspective and intelligence to inspire the creation of things that surpass and eventually upgrade current standards.

Outcome: A reflective, mature, impassive, and visionary personality that remains poised under straining circumstances and is eager to explore and understand life's complexity through social interactions or solitary inquiries.

Famous figure: Charles Darwin

Moon in Aquarius, Sun in Pisces

Orientation: Seeking to clarify emotions and upgrade processing mechanisms in order to resolve impediments, reduce pain, and induce progress, while called to make personal sacrifices for the sake of actualizing a destiny that addresses larger needs and possibly inspires the collective.

Outcome: A visionary, rather eccentric, and community-inclined personality whose capacity to detach from the trivialities of the present can render it brilliant or idiotic, exceptionally social or utterly disengaged, compliant or fiercely dissident.

Famous figure: Baron Meyer Amschel de Rothschild

Moon in Pisces Combinations

Moon in Pisces, Sun in Aries

Orientation: Seeking a sense of wholeness through personally identifying with every living aspect of life, often at the expense of setting personal emotional needs aside, while possessing a strong sense of purpose that is cyclically renewed and oriented toward unrestrained creativity and promoting causes considered important.

Outcome: A transparent, spontaneous, romantic, and touchy personality that is engaged to defend victims, oneself included, and blessed with profuse inspiration to launch new creations.

Famous figure: Cesar Chavez

Moon in Pisces, Sun in Taurus

Orientation: Seeking a sense of wholeness through personally identifying with every living aspect of life, often at the expense of setting personal emotional needs aside, while possessing a wealth of inner and or material resources to self-sufficiently create for stable results.

Outcome: An appreciative, passive, and talented personality that seeks to manifest beauty and harmony in tangible ways through the use of the senses.

Famous figure: Leonardo da Vinci

Moon in Pisces, Sun in Gemini

Orientation: Seeking a sense of wholeness through personally identifying with every living aspect of life, often at the expense of setting personal emotional needs aside, while motivated to create through coordinating diverse sources of interest on an intellectual, technological, and or cultural level.

Outcome: An adaptable, flowing, open, and ambiguous personality that is capable of processing multiple and diverse sources of input, sometimes at the price of emotional confusion and unpredictability.

Famous figure: Harvey Milk

Moon in Pisces, Sun in Cancer

Orientation: Seeking a sense of wholeness through personally identifying with every living aspect of life, often at the expense of setting personal emotional needs aside, while striving to establish supportive conditions for creative expression and development.

Outcome: A sensitive, compassionate, and child-like personality that may be overwhelmed by a wide array of emotions and strives to establish a safe haven for those in need of support, oneself included.

Famous figure: Herman Hesse

Moon in Pisces, Sun in Leo

Orientation: Seeking a sense of wholeness through personally identifying with every living aspect of life, often at the expense of setting personal emotional needs aside, while feeling poised to personally participate in and influence life through various forms of creativity.

Outcome: A generous, inspired, and melodramatic personality that aims to leave a legacy of significant value while adjusting personal attitudes to remain humble.

Famous figure: Coco Chanel

Moon in Pisces, Sun in Virgo

Orientation: Seeking a sense of wholeness through personally identifying with every living aspect of life, often at the expense of setting personal emotional needs aside, while motivated to organize and optimize one's creative productivity through conscious reflection and refinement.

Outcome: A devoted, absorbed, and often self-denying personality that fluctuates between idealism and practicality in the attempt to materialize something complete and pure.

Famous figure: Leonard Cohen

Moon in Pisces, Sun in Libra

Orientation: Seeking a sense of wholeness through personally identifying with every living aspect of life, often at the expense of setting personal emotional needs aside, while adopting a broader and more balanced perspective through one's creative endeavors.

Outcome: An idealistic, sympathetic, and accommodating personality that is inclined to sacrifice personal needs for the sake of a broader sense of peace and acceptance.

Famous figure: Alfred Dreyfuss

Moon in Pisces, Sun in Scorpio

Orientation: Seeking a sense of wholeness through personally identifying with every living aspect of life, often at the expense of setting personal emotional needs aside, while striving to powerfully impact others through one's creative efforts with the aim of fostering important changes both inwardly and outwardly.

Outcome: A mystifying, perceptive, and intricate personality that strives to transcend emotional limitations in order to touch and heal the core essence of pain.

Famous figure: Marie Curie

Moon in Pisces, Sun in Sagittarius

Orientation: Seeking a sense of wholeness through personally identifying with every living aspect of life, often at the expense of setting personal emotional needs aside, while having faith that a larger life potential can be accessed and creatively accomplished.

Outcome: A free-spirited, hopeful, and adventurous personality that seeks to transcend existing boundaries in search for a greater truth and or life potential while risking loss and excess if need be.

Famous figure: Bill. G. Wilson (AA founder)

Moon in Pisces, Sun in Capricorn

Orientation: Seeking a sense of wholeness through personally identifying with every living aspect of life, often at the expense of setting personal emotional needs aside, while focusing on creating something of serious, inspiring, and reliable value.

Outcome: A poetic, melancholic, and dedicated personality that searches for the right path and virtue to eventually embody them and guide others.

Famous figure: Joan of Arc

Moon in Pisces, Sun in Aquarius

Orientation: Seeking a sense of wholeness through personally identifying with every living aspect of life, often at the expense of setting personal emotional needs aside, while using perspective and intelligence to inspire the creation of things that surpass and eventually upgrade current standards.

Outcome: A far-sighted, daring, and unpredictable personality that adopts an impersonal approach to life in order to understand collective dynamics and address larger scale projects in new ways, often at the expense of personal intimacy.

Famous figure: Ken Wilber

Moon in Pisces, Sun in Pisces

Orientation: Seeking a sense of wholeness through personally identifying with every living aspect of life, often at the expense of setting personal emotional needs aside, while called to make personal sacrifices for the sake of actualizing a destiny that addresses larger needs and possibly inspires the collective.

Outcome: A youthful, flowing, and unfettered personality that is transported by the streams of life to an unforeseen destiny where simplicity and intensity often collide.

Famous figure: Linda Tucker

Chapter Eight

The Evolutionary Levels of
Consciousness

When analyzing a birth chart, one of the most important things to understand and consider is that the person's evolutionary level of consciousness greatly influences how the chart's energy is used. A birth chart represents themes and energies symbolically reflecting the individual's entire reality, yet there is no way to know from the chart alone to what extent these energies and themes have been applied in actual reality. For example, if we find an astrological signature that describes unresolved anger, it is not possible to know in advance if the person remains consumed by that anger and has had violent outbursts throughout his or her life, or with higher awareness has eventually found other ways to address these strong emotions.

A chart describes evolutionary themes and the potential development associated with those themes, but in order to assess how far and in what manner a person is likely to access the described potential, it is essential to identify the person's evolutionary level of consciousness. One's current level of consciousness indicates where one's soul is at on its evolutionary journey; from this perspective, one gains a better understanding of how chart challenges may be addressed and how deep the person is likely to go with the chart themes. *The more conscious a person is, the deeper he or she can go when addressing the themes of the birth chart.*

In the first chapter, we discussed the concept that all souls embark on an evolutionary journey. We all originate from the same source and begin from the same starting point, and we all aim for the same ultimate goal of self-realization (whether we are conscious of it or not). Yet in the course of this journey, we each have our own pace and direction. Time and space create gaps between each living being.

Understanding the evolutionary levels of consciousness adds a completely new dimension to chart analysis. While a chart itself describes the different themes a person focuses on during his or her life, the evolutionary level of consciousness describes *to what depth* these themes are addressed!

One's evolutionary level reflects how much work of consciousness a person has done in past lives and in such a way refers to *the maturity level of the soul,* regardless of how old a person happens to be in this life. For example, some young children may be highly evolved souls while their elders have a relatively dim awareness.

The level of one's consciousness is measured according to how much of the Truth a person has realized and accordingly the capacity of his or her vessel of consciousness—in simple terms it describes how conscious a person is. The more of the Truth a person has assimilated, the more he or she is aligned with divine principles and the better he or she can eventually navigate through life. It doesn't mean that more evolved people are guaranteed a smooth sail through life, but instead that they will likely be able to access their core issues at a deeper level.

Existing gaps in consciousness reinforce the validity of reincarnation: if a young child possesses advanced wisdom while his or her parents are dimly evolved, clearly this wisdom was not acquired through his or her upbringing—it is the fruit of previous lifetimes of learning. A soul arrives in this incarnation already conditioned by past life experiences.

It is very important to realize that *the evolutionary level of consciousness is not described in a person's chart in any way*: it can only be assessed when making contact with the individual. Two people born at the same exact time and place, and thus possessing the same birth chart, will manifest the potential of that chart on different levels or more accurately to a different depth relative to their personal evolutionary level of consciousness. This dynamic also applies to twins, who would share the same chart if they were born at the same exact time. Twins are two different souls, and each one is at a potentially different level of the evolutionary ladder.

People with the same exact chart face the same themes and possibly similar life circumstances; however, their response to the circumstances will vary according to their level of consciousness. When their response is different, sooner or later their life paths are likely to diverge. Let's take, for example, a chart that describes the capacity to generate wealth. A lesser evolved person might become strongly attached and even obsessed with making money, never feeling satisfied despite an overflowing bank account; whereas a more consciously evolved person might generate a good income without being overly attached to possessions and possibly take the initiative to redistribute the wealth to those less privileged. The chart themes and general life circumstances may be the same but the approach and outcomes different; as a result, different life circumstances are eventually created.

The way to identify a person's level of consciousness is through assessing the nature of *his or her values and choices in life*. Sometimes the level of evolution is very easy to detect right away; in other cases, it can be a little confusing. Studying the different evolutionary levels of consciousness, as described in this chapter, provides one with clues and factors to consider when identifying the level of a soul's maturity and awareness.

The concept of levels of consciousness fully relies on the consideration of free will. A person is confronted with life circumstances and evolutionary lessons that are the fruit of previous experiences—they cannot be changed. However, one's response to these circumstances completely depends on one's free will which in turn depends on one's personal value system. People learn lessons at a slower or faster pace and change the circumstances of their lives accordingly. While evolution is not a matter of choice, the pace and extent of one's evolution is a matter of personal responsibility and depends on free will.

Concepts related to the levels of the soul's consciousness are discussed in Dane Rudhyar's book *Astrology of Transformation* and Jeffrey Wolf Green's books *Pluto, Volume I: The Evolutionary Journey of the Soul* and *Pluto, Volume II: The Soul's Evolution Through Relationships*. These concepts have been researched and validated, and add tremendous value to chart analysis.

It is important to understand that while the levels of consciousness define the soul's degree of maturity and depth, it does not mean that a more evolved person should feel arrogantly superior to a lesser evolved one. These levels reflect a general idea of the soul's age and maturity level; thus while some souls are younger and others older, we all fulfill a unique role and are equally important in the greater scheme of Creation.

There are three main evolutionary levels of consciousness, each one comprising three stages.

- Level One: Consensus Consciousness
  - First Stage Consensus
  - Second Stage Consensus
  - Third Stage Consensus

- Level Two: Individuated Consciousness
  - First Stage Individuated
  - Second Stage Individuated
  - Third Stage Individuated

- Level Three: Spiritual Consciousness
  - First Stage Spiritual
  - Second Stage Spiritual
  - Third Stage Spiritual

A fourth level of evolution, sometimes called *biological consciousness* or *the dimly evolved* level, is also considered in available literature on the subject. This level of consciousness describes souls operating on a strictly biologically impulsive response such as hunger and thirst, immediate well-being and security, or procreative sexual instincts. These souls are newly evolving into human consciousness and may, for example, include what society considers to be mentally disabled people, though not exclusively. I personally assess this soul group as belonging to the very early stages of the Consensus level. Importantly, I would refrain from categorizing every mentally challenged person into this soul group, for each case must be assessed on its own. Some mentally challenged individuals may suffer mental handicaps but actually possess a formulated awareness of life and Truth.

Level One: Consensus Consciousness

Phase: *Infancy*
Mode: *Survival and productive function*
Consciousness: *Tribal, herd, security, foundation*
Demographic: *Estimated 70 to 75% of the world population*

The Consensus evolutionary level of consciousness includes younger souls that are in the process of integrating into the general mechanism of life. Consequently, the approach to life is predominantly based on survival and security needs. Individuals in this developmental phase are more conservative and adhere to values defined by the society they happen to belong to, hence the term "consensus" which refers to general agreement.

In this level, the need to belong is paramount. One's identity becomes an extension of society's because of the driving concept that "union makes us stronger"; it is the herd mentality, and the bigger the herd, the better the chances of survival against external threats. Society offers guidelines for survival, most of them usually derived from the wisdom of religious scriptures when applied to the masses. This is not only true in religious societies but also secular ones; for example, biblical concepts—such as forbidding killing or stealing—pervade most cultures whether secular or religious. This wisdom is based on a human interpretation of the universal and natural laws by which life operates.

The codes of conduct and guidelines that a society relies on have survived the test of time, and even if they are not perfect, they are good enough and set minimum standards that allow survival, function, and a basic sense of well-being. Thus in this level of consciousness, people accept society's laws and customs as matters of fact and integrate them into their value system and mode of operation. Since consciousness in this phase is relatively young, there is a need to be guided and have a framework of reference in a life so full of hazards. Social laws and norms offer a solid base, even if they are not final.

The need to follow society's norms reflects a very *deep fear of chaos*. In these earlier stages of being, the soul is inwardly disoriented and urgently needs structure and a sense of order. If ejected from the community, it is not only the danger of facing survival challenges alone that looms, but also the threat of facing existential chaos. Despite its flaws, society offers a support system and a protective womb; outside of it, severe dangers of deprivation, illness, madness, and eventual death are more significantly ominous. Society's norms provide a sense of order that keeps people from losing themselves in chaos; the Consensus reality provides a sense of gravity that serves as a foundation for basic health, sanity, and productivity. Just like a child needs parents, souls in this stage rely on society's rules, values, and codes to feel secure: authority is primarily external.

Society conditions us to specific ways of living beginning with parents asserting their values, followed by school education, and then by random environmental influences. For example, Western society conditions everyone that getting married, having children, and living in the suburbs is the measure of fulfillment. Thus there are guidelines and values people follow that in turn provide a sense of order and direction. Whether someone in the Consensus level gets married and lives in the suburbs is not guaranteed, but he or she is driven by these values and feels satisfied upon accomplishing the goal, or disappointed if not. While everyone is conditioned by the society they live in, at least to some extent, those within the Consensus level do not question that conditioning: they accept it faithfully (usually unconsciously), live by it, and pass it on. With survival and order as priorities, doubt is seldom affordable.

Social conditioning defines larger existential concepts such as ideas about heaven and hell, as well as small details such as, for example, men wearing ties and women high heels when wishing to be elegant in the context of Western society. People assimilate what to do with themselves: how to stay healthy, prosper, feel satisfied, raise children, address sexuality, or choose a profession. All answers come from what one's culture and society inspires and dictates. The closer one manages to adhere to the goals and values set by the community, the greater the sense of achievement. For a Consensus indigenous in Papua New Guinea, owning many pigs is the definition of success, whereas for a Consensus American it might mean becoming a popular entertainer.

While society's laws and norms are not perfect and need to evolve and change over time, it is very difficult to introduce change because a false move can dangerously destabilize the foundations everyone relies on. Experimentation is not welcome, and changes have to be absolutely necessary in order to be eventually implemented; thus there is resistance and even a degree of rigidity within Consensus structures, but from this point of view necessarily so. For example, it took a long time before women were allowed to become pilots in the air force or even vote. The norm used to be that only men were perceived as capable of fulfilling these roles because women were not "biologically designed" for such activities. Women had to pass the test of credibility and time, proving their capability and transcending the notion that they were not "sensible enough" for these and similar other tasks.

In the Consensus stages of consciousness, men's and women's roles are very deeply engrained according to the interpretation of their biological function; hence from this traditional point of view, women are usually expected to remain more passive—because their biological role is associated with nursing babies—whereas men are traditionally expected to exhibit strength and suppress vulnerabilities in order to fit the more active principle. Yet with time, a greater understanding of each gender's nature and capacity eventually instigates reform. Consensus norms are upgrading as women's and men's roles expand within society.

Within the Consensus mentality, there is a great fear of attracting negative attention such as being shamed or embarrassed, or facing the threat of losing esteem and being excluded by peers. Thus considerable effort is invested on appearances while weakness and dysfunction tend to be hidden or repressed. It is very important to first of all be considered "normal" and then successful according to local values; taboos and most forms of experimentation—whether in lifestyle, art, or management—are not encouraged, and in some cases, severe repercussions ensue if one deviates from society's norms.

This dynamic can easily incite prejudice and misconceptions when facing something different. Because the main goal is security and survival, staying on the safe path is usually the preferred option. For example, in the Western society the majority of people within the Consensus level believe that astrology is not valid. This assumption is not the result of personal research on the matter but rather comes from either relying on narrow interpretations of the Bible that portray astrology as blasphemous, or on scientists who do yet not have the tools to comprehend its mechanism. People might read the newspaper horoscopes for entertainment, but dare not associate with it publicly. If a person in the Consensus level happens to have genuine interest in astrology, he or she is likely to hide it for fear of ridicule.

By adhering to society's codes of conducts and values, a person gradually learns about life. Following traditions that have passed the test of time provides a sense of safety and protection from chaos that is essential for survival. Gradually maturing within the spectrum of the community, a person eventually gains status, privileges, and more creative freedom.

Consensus level of consciousness keywords
Foundations for existence, reliance on tested, traditional values and external authority, conformity, desire for normalcy, fear of chaos, desire for security, ambition for status, fear of shame, a tendency for denial and repression, stability as a central driving force.

The Three Consensus Stages of Consciousness

First Stage Consensus
The first Consensus stage of consciousness refers to a very primal level of awareness that is essentially collective and founded on the most basic survival needs. In this stage, a person is a complete extension of the group he or she belongs to—whether family, clan, tribe, religious stream, or society—and has little sense of individual consciousness. People do not address each other according to who they actually are as individuals but instead according to their collective identity. For example, one may be addressed as a Jehovah Witness, a member of the Johnson family, or as someone living in a particular part of the country. Thus decisions and choices are made according to these more general associations. For example, a person may not get a job because he or she belongs to a particular clan that is not respected. There is little if any individual ambition and free will. Marriages may be arranged and matches made according to one's roots and belonging or family interest instead of personal traits or mutual attraction. Members of one church are not likely to marry members of another church and so on. One's profession and name is usually decided by one's lineage;

boys might carry the father's first name and are commonly incited to continue whatever he was doing.

Just as tribal identity is given immense importance so is gender association. Definitions and roles for males and females are usually rigidly defined without any room for compromise. Details about each of these roles vary from culture to culture, but in most cases, females are conditioned to fulfill submissive domestic roles often without access to a formal education while males are favored and conditioned to control the household.

These rules make things simple and provide a basic sense of order. Without a sense of individuality, people obey and follow the motion of the tribe or society they are part of. This approach supports the survival of the collective and provides a minimum standard of function, resource use, and health.

Without a developed sense of self and little ambition, the person in the first stage Consensus usually (but not exclusively) has a blue-collar job. Consequently, in the majority of cases, the person belongs to the lower class of society and populates the villages, small towns, or less privileged neighborhoods of the cities. Emotional and psychological needs are completely ignored for the emphasis is primarily on fulfilling external function and meeting external pressure.

Families may have many children and each child must justify his or her existence through a defined function. Thus personal attention is not usually affordable beyond the fact that it is not really sought. Because of the emphasis on function rather than individual need, it is not uncommon to rigorously reprimand a child if there is any sign of disobedience or weakness. There is little awareness of the reasons why a problem may occur or the ways to improve things. Rules are clear and so are the methods of implementation. The individual is not important—it is the greater sense of order that matters.

Religion can play a central role in the lives of first stage Consensus people, often becoming the core of their lives, because their sense of order is based on it. For example, in some Asian cultures, young children are sent away to become monks as a way to get shelter and an education for them. Religious commands may be strongly embedded in one's consciousness and often followed blindly and faithfully.

Naiveté and innocence are common in this stage of evolution because questions are not asked. The established order or life circumstances are taken for granted and trust is easily given to existing authority figures as one tends to adapt to what is imposed. Naiveté results from relative ignorance of larger existing options. In some cases, the strong sense of tribal identification may induce rivalry between different groups. Members of certain groups are liked or disliked according to their clan association rather than on the basis of their personal character.

In opposite scenarios, a lack of individual identity and attention to emotional needs can manifest in the absence of boundaries instead of rigid rules. When lacking reliable role models and structure, the person in this stage may lose him or herself through different forms of mismanagement, excess, and dysfunction such as alcoholism, rampant sexual abuse, teenage pregnancy, poor education, poverty, or mental illness. Because the person has not yet established his or her inner authority, poor and overly simplistic judgment may result when addressing existence. Without belonging to a reliable structure that provides order, the person may easily fail when confronted by life's complexity and generate rather chaotic life situations as a result. In this case, the need to improve function and restore order will drive the person to eventually search for an authority figure—for example, by joining a church.

Since individual free will is barely existent in this stage of consciousness, change usually occurs because of external circumstances instead of personal choice. The need for regularity incites one to adapt to whatever one has even if it is not very pleasant. The lack of focus on individual needs renders the person highly tolerant of pain. Thus changes are implemented only when it is absolutely necessary or inevitable. Consequently, this dynamic can lead to dramatic crises because only a crisis stimulates change. For example, it may not be until crops are destroyed by floods that a person seeks to change professions or until a spouse becomes mentally ill that one seeks a divorce. Because circumstances are not choice based, life is experienced in a more fatalistic way.

Nonetheless, regardless of how monotonous or dramatic life ends up being under these conditions, lessons are gradually learned. Learning to manage the basic things in life such as work, food, health, and community helps one gain consciousness and better understand life. Slowly, the person realizes there is room for improvement as more appropriate choices are made.

Second Stage Consensus

In the second Consensus stage of consciousness, the primary development is oriented toward the gradual emergence of individual and personal consciousness. The person is still conditioned by social standards but starts to recognize more of his or her individual needs. A stronger sense of self is developed as the ego matures to better define what one is about. More attention and care is provided for personal needs, and as this happens the person learns to differentiate him or herself from others. Thus ambition naturally develops as one gains a better understanding of personal likes and dislikes. With ambition comes an awareness of choice and the capacity to make independent decisions instead of blindly following external motions. There is an emerging desire to find a better place within the herd thus a wider spectrum of opportunities and options opens up.

A person is likely to want to improve personal life conditions, starting with getting a better and more remunerating job. Accordingly, receiving a proper formal education and refining personal skills is emphasized. This stage of consciousness stimulates a stronger movement from rural to urban environments (but not exclusively so). With more effort invested in self-development and the creation of better life conditions, the person also becomes more aware of popular trends and fashion. The level of consumption increases because one is in touch with what one wants and learns how to get it. Examples reflecting newly acquired standards include committing to a life-long mortgage payment to own a better house, becoming aware and attending trendier cultural events such as seeing the new Hollywood movie, or taking an occasional vacation trip to the coast. Generally speaking, this state of evolution populates (but not exclusively) the lower-middle to middle class.

One's identity is now more predominantly focused on the intimacy of one's own family and less on the larger community or tribe. The family size is likely reduced, and girls usually have easier access to a more thorough education. However, gender differences still remain strongly defined with a tendency in Western society for women to get nursing, school teaching, or secretarial training and for men to associate with their favorite sports team and become more conscious of their social and professional status. Religious community life often remains a central part of the lifestyle with holidays faithfully celebrated. The individual in this stage is more aware of the potential for personal success and feels more confident that he or she will be able to achieve and enjoy what society emphasizes as valuable.

Ambition engenders competitiveness and comparisons with other families that can lead to jealousy and gossip. Competition stimulates self-improvement and eventual results. In this stage of consciousness, the person may increase his or her socioeconomic status and upgrade lifestyle conditions. A sense of achievement and superiority may arise when observing people in the first Consensus stage with their simpler lifestyle or mentality.

Compared to the first Consensus stage, people in the second Consensus stage have more autonomy, opportunities, and navigation skills when proceeding with life. As the sense of self and personal needs are better defined, problems are addressed more attentively, albeit still conservatively. The ego grounds itself more firmly and one's personal sense of destiny begins to forge its way forward.

Third Stage Consensus

The third Consensus stage of consciousness includes people who are fully integrated into society and naturally understand its mechanism. As a result, they operate faster, feel more at ease with the challenges, and perform at a higher level. While strongly identified with society's norms and values, they now play a greater role in dictating the pace and flavor of the culture because they represent the most prolific portion of it.

Individuals in this stage of consciousness usually (but not exclusively) represent the middle to upper class and generally have easier access to resources, higher education, and opportunities. Some of them are role models who represent success; they are what society looks up to. For example, this group may include wealthy business people who live in luxury and generate envy or admiration, or dedicated doctors who provide a sense of care or security through their expertise and parental presence. We can also find higher status individuals and those fulfilling prominent professional functions such as professors, prominent politicians, CEOs, a good portion of celebrities, and prominent religious leaders. In this stage, people tend to gravitate toward more cultivated and sophisticated environments such as the bigger cities where stimulation and choices abound and life is lived at a faster pace. Consequently, people are generally more sophisticated, cultivated, exposed to diversity, and worldly.

Religion may still play a central role in the lives of the majority of this group; however, a stronger secular current is forming because they are more open to modernity and diversity. Opinions and views tend to be a little more lax because people are more exposed to a variety of options and witness different lifestyles and cultural norms. Thus rules and regulations are not taken as much for granted; however, even though the person may be more intellectually open minded, there is still a tendency to lead a rather conservative lifestyle. For example, one may be tolerant of cultural diversity but rather distraught if one's child chooses to marry someone from another race.

Symbols of success hold prime importance and may include living in a fashionable neighborhood, studying in a more exclusive school, aspiring to accumulate wealth, having a strong interest in beauty and fashion, meeting the standards of a Western lifestyle, developing the intellect, holding a position of responsibility, or living in stability. Of course, these standards vary from culture to culture.

Higher standards and sophistication often stem from the capacity to generate a higher income, naturally allowing better access to refinement and quality as the person develops a more delicate taste for things. Often there is a desire to show off the results of success and achievement because appearances are important in this stage of consciousness. Living a more cultivated lifestyle is a mixture of natural development as well as a need for egocentric prominence.

While gender role definitions become more flexible, there can still be an underlying expectation to conform to society's standards. Emancipation can manifest in women who are able to enjoy more liberties, for example, by holding more prominent leadership positions. Yet traditional dress codes still remain firmly respected for both genders with ties for men and high heels for women (in Western society). Gender bias may also show in the choice of hobbies each gender chooses.

Leadership potential is higher in this stage of consciousness; however, it is subject to management tests. Some people will hold their position with responsibility and perform highly, but the potential for corruption exists. As a person gains power and leads larger groups, he or she may misuse authority privileges to benefit personal agendas. For example, if a white man leads a community, he may be less inclined to promote females or other minorities' rights. Personal biases, consciously or unconsciously, lead to the abuse of power. Positively, a person honorably fulfills leadership positions and provides services and inspiration for the whole such as a doctor or an educator who is dedicated to providing the best care.

The ego reaches a climax in this stage because personal qualities and efforts are individually recognized. Some people in this stage feel on top of the world as they hold positions of authority and influence, benefiting from the system they operate through. They are more confident in their judgments, sometimes because they are scientists who can prove what they assert, or in other cases simply because their success is proof enough to them that they must have it right.

However, it is important to realize that this stage of consciousness not only comprises leaders and wealthy people, but also people who are simply more cultivated, educated, and versed in socially respected fields whether oriented toward business, politics, science, technology, academic development, culture, or social trends. The reference for one's level of consciousness is measured by one's value system rather than the volume of the bank account. Notwithstanding, people in this stage of consciousness are likely to benefit from having more material stability and gaining more authority in their field.

While living up to the formula for success and consequently benefiting by living more comfortably, the person in this stage of consciousness is prone to sink into the illusion of perfection. Having done everything by the book—such as marrying a beautiful spouse, living in a beautiful house, providing a respectful education for their children, managing a more remunerating and respectful profession, and more frequently travelling the world—one may be surprised to realize that one is not sheltered from pain and crises. The dream of success usually shows its cracks sooner or later when, for example, a promising child turns into a drug addict or an admired husband is exposed in a corruption scandal. Additionally, the pressure of maintaining the façade of success and perfection may lead to superficiality. The person may start to ask deeper existential questions when, for example, health starts to fail and prestigious doctors find no cures, or when wealth is lost and once inviting doors are shut one by one.

Confronted with accumulating limitations and dysfunctions, the person gradually realizes that society does not have all answers to life's challenges. Yet since all the rules were faithfully followed, one may be disillusioned at first as everything seemed to be "under control" and the expectation was to gracefully sail forward in all glory. Gradually, one dares to doubt consensus conventions and starts searching for answers outside the compound of society's proposed values. An important leap in one's evolution of consciousness is being prepared when these questions arise.

Level Two: Individuated Consciousness

Phase: *Adolescence*
Mode: *Creativity and progress*
Consciousness: *Inner authority, experimental, authentic, free spirited*
Demographic: *Estimated 20 to 25% of the world population*

The Individuated evolutionary level of consciousness includes people who are in the process of developing their own inner authority and reaching conclusions about life based on personal experience instead of established convention or tradition. When deciding what is right or wrong, there is a need for proof instead of relying on society's moral codes. Therefore, people in this stage set forth on a personal journey through existence to find out these answers on their own and dare to challenge concepts that are taken for granted by society and the Consensus, exploring a vaster life potential on both a personal and a collective level.

Mainstream cultural, religious, and social conventions cease to be the main reference for living life, urging individuals within this level of consciousness to consider life's potential beyond what has been established so far. The shift from Consensus to Individuated consciousness is usually motivated by an acute sense of limitation that is experienced when following society's established order—there is a sense of not really living one's life authentically. Often a crisis stimulates the shift when Consensus reality fails to provide adequate answers for one's dilemmas; the person is then stimulated to seek alternative and less conventional solutions.

The need for security ceases to be the main priority; instead, the need for authenticity and finding one's personal truth becomes the driving force. The person is willing to risk venturing into the unknown to find more meaning because he or she is now aware that the price of security may compromise his or her personal truth. Rather than meet external expectations, there is an urge to set the spirit free and get in touch with what one is naturally inspired to do. Accordingly, the person ceases to be concerned by the fear of shame or ridicule because he or she realizes that society and culture can be limited or plain wrong in their judgment. Mainstream opinion and expectations lose their weight as the person is now mature enough to develop an internal authority.

One realizes that doubting accepted norms is a valid thing to do since these norms are not absolute and perfect. A sense of guilt for going against tradition fades as it becomes clear that deviating from society's expectations does not necessarily mean going against the natural order of life. One comes to understand that mainstream society represents only a fragment of life's potential, not its entirety; consequently, it is legitimate to venture outside of it. For example, the person in this level does not dismiss astrology just because a priest or a scientist claims it is not valid; he or she needs to personally explore the modality before reaching a conclusion. Thus these people dare to walk on a more solitary path, inspired and directed by their own convictions; as a result they are bound to explore societal taboos.

A stronger character is forged because one becomes significantly more independent in resisting pressure from the Consensus to conform. A greater sense of alienation requires strength of spirit because the person cannot easily find support in others who may not understand what he or she is going through. Moreover, following one's own truth and exploring taboos may add stress to one's life. For example, the person may be a Jew who falls in love with a Muslim and decides not to let religious origins disturb the relationship, despite the disapproval of the respective communities. People are more open to cultural diversity in this level of consciousness, therefore, religious diversity may actually be perceived as an enriching experience rather than a threatening one. However, antagonism and possible persecution may be experienced when families disapprove of such a choice. Despite external pressure, the couple's inner conviction to be true to themselves and their souls keeps them going; their point of reference is their personal experience instead of external expectations.

In the desire for more authenticity and truthfulness, the person becomes more honest with him or herself consequently diminishing the tendency for emotional repression, denial, or hypocrisy. In this same vein, one is less willing to compromise personal convictions, inciting one to choose a lifestyle and a profession that is more deeply fulfilling and in alignment with one's true nature. Through this level of consciousness, focus is oriented toward developing the ego to a fuller extent in order to find out in more meaningful ways what one is about. Consequently, greater creative potential is accessed when liberating oneself from external judgment. It is not uncommon for people in this level of consciousness to choose a career in the arts, alterative modalities, or freelance professions. When choosing a profession, financial security and social status cease to be the main incentive— what matters is the need for personal meaning and fulfillment.

The person develops greater psychological depth when seeking answers and becoming more introspective. Crises and problems are more likely to be addressed holistically rather than symptomatically. For example, when going through a divorce, the person is more inclined to seek a higher understanding of the dynamics that were involved and the deeper reasons why the circumstances occurred in order to break negative patterns, rather than simplistically moving on to the next relationship without learning from the experience. Additionally gender roles are less defined because the person tends to perceive him or herself as a human being first before a specific gender. Moreover, the person may connect with both female and male energies within his or her sense of being. For example, men may express their sensitive and emotional nature while women get in touch with their creative side that extends beyond the biological role of being mothers.

As the individual increasingly becomes more in touch with him or herself and gains a wider perspective of life, a desire emerges to change the way things are handled within mainstream society. Consequently, strong activist movements develop within this level of consciousness with the aim of promoting change, progress, and development in the established order. Activism may be oriented toward social or political causes.

Activists expose and protest the dysfunction or corruption in the way society is managed. Those involved may include reporters, humanitarian advocates, conspiracy theorists, intellectuals, or revolutionaries who raise controversy and doubt about matters that tend to be taken for granted by the mainstream. Causes of interest may include human rights, animal rights, homosexual rights, gender equality, political reforms, or cultural freedom, among others.

Similarly, confronted with society's limited solutions and conventions, a growing interest emerges in alternative modalities such as alternative healing methods, astrology, or meditation. When facing life's quandaries, the person may embrace these modalities wanting to approach life's challenges more holistically. Expanding horizons beyond personal cultural origins, one may also be inspired to bridge Eastern and Western philosophies, sometimes to the point of integrating a whole new spiritual orientation into one's lifestyle.

Because of the more independent and experimental approach, boundaries are less defined in the Individuated level of consciousness. Positively, when liberated from the pressure to conform, one becomes more confident and open to a whole new dimension of experience and insight. Life gains more meaning as one lives more authentically and creatively. Gaining more expertise, the individual can offer completely unique perspectives on solving existing problems.

Negatively, experimentation may lead to excesses and extremes that result in repeated failure and dysfunction. Possessing a more rebellious attitude and having less of a support system, a person may end up wasting resources through all kinds of dead-end fated choices. While letting go of the old sense of order, new solutions are not readily available causing one to experience varying degrees of chaos. Mismanagement may lead to drug abuse, financial failure, a lack of consistency, cultish brainwashing, or fragmentation. Notwithstanding, lessons are eventually learned through the crises and solidification eventually occurs in the course of time (sometimes over many incarnations). Despite the possible difficulty, a sense of internal freedom glows as one's inner authority is forged.

People in the Individuated level of consciousness are often perceived as eccentric or extreme by those in the Consensus state. In more rigid societies, Individuated people can endure persecution for choosing differently. Even though they may intimidate the Consensus by their more daring approach, there is often a certain amount of fascination with them and their less predictable lifestyle. It is also common to take them and their efforts less seriously because many of them are on the fringe of mainstream society and thus not established in the respected system.

While many efforts, theories, and perspectives generated through the Individuated level may not always produce tangible results, some do end up seeding very important changes for the Consensus. Through this evolutionary level, the person accesses his or her own genius and brings forth concepts that may later reveal themselves to be transformative and meaningful. For example at first, before women's rights were established in the Consensus reality, feminist movements were only part of the Individuated state. With time and continual effort, laws began to change and the concept of gender equality filtered through from the Individuated to the Consensus reality. Suddenly, it became acceptable for women to vote! Nonetheless, since the Consensus state only integrates something that is thoroughly tested, it takes a relatively long time for concepts developed through the Individuated level to permeate the Consensus reality. Yet regardless of the time it takes, discoveries and concepts that are validated are eventually adapted to the established order of mainstream society.

Despite the natural need to separate from Consensus values, people in the Individuated level keep referring to them. The Consensus level of consciousness remains the foundation of society's order, obviously influencing Individuated people as well. Hence while branching out, experimenting, and leading alternative lifestyles, the role of people in the Individuated level is to eventually emancipate Consensus mainstream values.

Individuated level of consciousness keywords

Internal authority, freedom from shame, question and doubt, experimental approach and openness, investigating taboos, increased creativity, redefinition of boundaries, decreased focus on security needs, more holistic values, feeling of alienation and aloneness, risk and courage to be more authentic.

The Three Individuated Stages of Consciousness

First Stage Individuated

In the first Individuated stage of consciousness, the person takes his or her first steps in venturing beyond the womb of society's order. This transition generates a deep sense of liberation as the newly opened door exposes a whole new dimension to existence. Previously, these new opportunities were either looked at from afar or totally ignored altogether. Now more confident to venture beyond social expectations, the person is willing to be different even at the risk of ridicule or shame.

However, this passage often manifests in the motion of going back and forth between Consensus values and the newly acquired Individuated values that are more holistic and experimental. For example, the person may still hold a job that provides security, such as working as an accountant, but participate in alternative modalities and openly express different points of view that confront conventional wisdom. In this stage of consciousness, the person seeks new ways of thinking and adopts new values. It may seem as if these values always sounded true, but one now takes the step to really live by and defend them. As these new concepts become better assimilated, one's lifestyle adapts and changes accordingly.

The feeling of liberation experienced in this stage manifests in different ways. Previously adhering to Consensus values, a person may have carried feelings of guilt or anxieties that can now be relinquished. For example, one may more confidently let go of the guilt of not making a lot of money or of being unmarried. The opportunity to free oneself from expectations and prejudices is seized, and one embarks on a life that is more in harmony with one's true nature. The person is ripe to navigate life strongly relying on internal judgment instead of considering what other people think.

The sense of liberation may engender new career and lifestyle choices. For example, the person may move from a financially rewarding but lackluster career to a vocation in humanitarian work, leaving security behind to relocate to a more precarious environment because the cause is important. The sense of purpose allows the soul to thrive despite facing uncertainty. Another example may involve a person wanting to openly express homosexual tendencies in a society where such an orientation is shamed, and possibly having to leave a marriage and free him or herself from the fear of prejudice. This is not to say that every homosexual or humanitarian worker is invariably in the Individuated state, but the greater aspiration for authenticity and the courage to defy public opinion is representative of this level of consciousness.

As described in the above examples, often people in this evolutionary stage lead the earlier part of their lives conforming to Consensus values and norms, and then at some point experience an awakening of consciousness that inspires them to free their spirit and change their lives accordingly. The awakening often follows a crisis that causes one to doubt the way that life was led up to that point; the crisis may be a divorce, a health crisis, or a loss. The crisis makes one realize that previous values are not reliable anymore and that compromises can no longer be tolerated.

Commonly, the person in this evolutionary stage begins to get involved in various alternative thinking movements. Venturing into new territory and gaining new perspectives can, however, at times be disorienting; the person opens up to a wealth of new insights but may lack the experience to be able to discriminate between them. Thus one may end up naively following these alternative movements and get carried away. Whether attending New Age oriented studies or gatherings of political activists, one may gullibly accept controversial perspectives. In extreme cases, this inclination derails into cultish associations and the blind following of charismatic leaders.

In most cases, however, the progression to the first Individuated stage is rather liberating, and while the newness does involve a certain amount of naiveté and scattering, the person eventually develops a perspective that helps him or her discriminate what is reliable from what is not. It may be that one becomes disillusioned with a certain movement before realizing that not all alternative approaches are valid.

Venturing into the Individuated stage, the person more readily explores social taboos: experiences may range from sexual experimentation to controversial relationship choices and lifestyles. The individual may also join activist movements and aspire to create social change.

Compared to the third Consensus stage, the socioeconomic status in this stage may decrease. The reasons for this decrease are obvious given that the person releases the hold on security needs and opens up to a life that is more on the fringe of society. However, people in the first Individuated stage may remain strong active forces inside society because they offer progressive ideas to the Consensus without being too radical. Their experimental approach is usually not extremely radical and may therefore be more accessible to traditional people. For example, the person may be a newspaper reporter who fully participates in mainstream society and yet offers more progressive or controversial perspectives to his or her readers, raising doubt where people had taken things for granted. Initially, these more progressive ideas may face resistance, but eventually they filter through.

Through the first Individuated stage, the person takes his or her first steps into a new dimension of being where a greater sense of creative freedom is accessible. This transition generates tremendous excitement because the person gets in touch with a deeper sense of self and gains more existential meaning. Confusion may arise because this is a relatively new orientation and the open field has no clearly defined pathway. Ultimately, more individual freedom means more personal responsibility.

Second Stage Individuated

The second Individuated stage of consciousness reflects a more radical approach to self-exploration and experimentation. In this phase, the departure from mainstream values is at the point of no return; the sense of alienation is more extreme and very obvious, usually from the very start of the person's life. As a child, one may already feel considerably at odds with parental expectations and their life orientation. Emotional support may be available but acute mentality gaps are often too wide to bridge. The person often feels completely misunderstood by his or her environment and is forced upon him or herself.

As a child, one may not necessarily be unruly and reactively rebel against authority, but rather feel as if living on a foreign planet where one cannot agree and associate with the presented values and lifestyle. Consequently, one usually grows up without role models to associate with and instead relies on inner authority when discriminating right from wrong. Such an inner knowing reflects a strong personality from the very start.

Conventional authorities usually criticize the actions and choices of such a person because the experimental approach does not always produce results. Because of the lack of identification with social norms, the person may not hold a job for long, preferring instead to immerse him or herself in art or take a spiritual journey to unknown destinations. Constant pressure from conventional people can take its toll and generate low self-esteem, self-doubt, and even guilt. Yet when trying at times to come back to a path of regularity and security, the person may end up failing miserably with low self-esteem only getting worse. One realizes that there is no way back and that the only solution is to go forward despite the absence of a clear destination. Remaining loyal to one's true self and values is the only reference one can rely on. In a way, the second Individuated stage serves as a test of personality and spirit whereby a person who lacks any consistent sense of security learns about the value of living truthfully.

The person may become angry at the system for being unjust, narrow, and corrupt. Anger may be particularly directed toward religious and political institutions that impose dogma and assume absolute authority in deciding what is considered righteous. Generally, every emotion is experienced viscerally—from passion, to anger, to excitement, and loneliness. The person may also become self-righteous, accusing everyone of being completely stupid and believing that he or she has all answers.

Unable to fully integrate into the mainstream, the individual usually lives on the fringe of society. Examples may include a starving artist who creates magnificent pieces of art from meager means, or an idealistic activist who boycotts consumption in a world considered "wasteful and immoral," or a transsexual who burns all bridges for the sake of his or her internal truth. Extreme behavior and lifestyle choices are more common in this stage because boundaries are pulverized; any barrier that prevents one from getting to the bottom of one's authentic core is removed. The expression is not necessarily completely extreme, such as going through a sex change surgery, but generally it is characterized by an uncompromising and daring attitude.

Often in this stage of consciousness, the person's life is oriented toward *defying fear*. The urge to transcend judgments or preconceived beliefs incites one to test "danger zones" because the person must find out for him or herself what is truthful from what is not. Since society's morals have lost their credibility in one's eyes, one more readily ventures into what is considered forbidden and taboo. Living more on the edge, the person dissolves sexual, racial, guilt, and traditional barriers. Experimenting with different lifestyles, one may choose to have open relationships, join a community founded on communist ideals in a society based on consumerism, or become a rock artist who plays in music festivals.

However, experiencing freedom of spirit can seriously compromise survival needs. Ejecting oneself from the system, the person has a smaller pool to receive resources from. While like-minded groups are created and can serve as a support system, the individual is often reduced to living with modest means, sometimes from hand to mouth. In more privileged situations, one may receive financial support from one's family who usually perceives the person as a "problem child."

It is very important to realize that this stage of consciousness does not invariably include all rebellious teenagers or antisocial drug addicts. One must first assess what their value system is founded on and identify if it is more evolved than the mainstream Consensus stage. For example, a racist, antisocial skinhead spending his time drinking and mistreating his girlfriend would better fit the second or even first Consensus stage with such limited awareness. Similarly, a brainwashed Al-Qaeda suicide bomber, stripped of a personal sense of identity and blindly following his community leader, would fit the first Consensus stage. Conversely, a person using Ayahuasca for transcendental purposes, or a poet spending his days writing instead of making "more practical use" of his academic degree, would be more fitting to this stage. One must assess the level of consciousness behind the actions— simply being rebellious is not enough of an indication.

Individuals in the second Individuated stage may gain public recognition and become recognized in what they do, affecting culture through their more radical approach to life. Yet success is more commonly defined by the freedom of spirit— they tend to stay on the fringe of society and create subcultures; the chasm between them and mainstream society serves as a test of value. Because of the sense of alienation and isolation, group and community cells are formed. The group replaces the larger framework of mainstream society, or sometimes one's own family, and serves as an alternative structure and frame of reference. Over time, self-confidence and self-acceptance are better grounded allowing one to attain a sense of balance and proceed with the next evolutionary leap.

Third Stage Individuated

The third Individuated stage of consciousness reflects the maturity to stay fully loyal to one's individuality and chosen values while also participating in and influencing mainstream society. In this phase, the person more easily finds the balance between holding on to one's internal truth and adapting when necessary. There is a greater understanding of the need to participate in society in order to proactively stimulate social change. Thus one reengages into the mainstream but on one's own terms rather than adhering to conventional values and expectations.

For example, many professional astrologers fit this category as they are fully confident of the truthfulness of their practice and are able to provide a service to society through their unique path—they benefit from relative success without compromising their core values. The person in this stage of consciousness confidently asserts progressive perspectives of life yet with a greater understanding that change cannot be instantaneous. The more solid sense of identity and inner balance provides one with a better chance of affecting and inspiring progress in various fields.

The value system and approach is more resolutely holistic, multicultural, interfaith oriented, emotionally conscious, gender equal, and truth oriented. The wisdom acquired through the journey of self-discovery, unbiased by prejudice or the fear of shame, is not only personally experienced but can also now be delivered and serve to inspire others.

Some people in this stage stand out and create historical changes because of their innovative influence; however, the greater majority simply consists of individuals who are loyal to conscious values, secure in their individuality, free spirited, and who live an authentic lifestyle in a way that allows them to comfortably participate in society. It is not uncommon for the person to become an authority in an alternative, artistic, or activist field and help infiltrate new perspectives into the mainstream that eventually raise the collective vibration.

In the Individuated stages of consciousness, there are three main ideological orientations processed along the evolutionary journey: *social, creative, and spiritual.* These three prominent streams become more firmly established in the third Individuated stage.

Those who have developed more toward a *social* orientation primarily express their individuality through activism and political involvement and strive to foster higher standards of justice to improve human rights. Among them are reporters, humanitarian workers, social leaders, and activists who want to expose society's limitations so that changes can be implemented.

Those who have developed more toward a *creative* orientation include people who express their individuality through different dimensions of art, exploration, and invention. They are motivated to combine materials and ideas in new ways and create results that affect people on deeper levels, usually confronting existing conditioning through their creations. Among them are artists in all available mediums such as independent film makers or avant-garde designers. Also included in this stream are philosophers, adventurers, inventors, and pioneering researchers in technological and scientific fields who may revolutionize thinking patterns.

Those who have developed more toward a *spiritual* orientation comprise individuals who study and practice alternative modalities and seek to understand the higher and collective meaning of our existence in order to better address existential challenges. Commonly, many of them synthesize philosophical and spiritual systems from different sources—Eastern philosophies, native cultures, esoteric interpretations of religious scriptures, or personally inspired insights—in order to expand their perspective on the nature of existence. They seek to live more consciously in health and harmony in order to tap into a higher living experience. Among them are established alternative practitioners, practicing astrologers, yoga instructors, body workers, or martial arts teachers.

These orientations can intermingle for the person may be artistically oriented and simultaneously participate in activist movements. The lines between these streams can easily be blurred.

Level Three: Spiritual Consciousness

Phase: *Maturity*
Mode: *Alignment to the Truth, service, humility*
Consciousness: *Righteousness, Truth, compassion, transpersonal*
Demographic: *Estimated about 5% of world population*

The Spiritual evolutionary level of consciousness reflects a commitment to live according to the higher Truth and surrender attachments to personal wishful thinking and projections about what life should be. Since human beings did not create life, they cannot fully conceptualize its mechanism, but the obvious observation that life does not operate at random unveils there is intelligence behind it. This intelligence consists of divine principles and laws that embody the Truth of life—the basis from which life operates on all dimensions. What defines the Spiritual level of consciousness is the primary choice to study and live according to the Truth to the best of one's knowledge without any compromise. The purpose of this effort is to attain a consistent sense of well-being undisturbed by life's tidal ebbs and flows—the freedom of inner peace relies on harmonizing with life.

A person in this evolutionary level realizes that life is not about personal wants but rather about what is right; hence his or her consciousness shifts from being motivated by personal development and freedom of spirit to alignment with divine principles—*always and on a daily basis.* Ironically, living in alignment with the Truth eventually leads to personal development and freedom of the highest kind.

One may attain this level of awareness when realizing that it is not possible to control all of life's development and circumstances; therefore, surrendering personal projections and attachments is understood to be the path of true meaning. This realization prompts a search for larger life meanings. Existential crises and the overall experience of pain urges one to no longer compromise on finding out the fundamental Truth behind it all. Until this point, spirituality may have been a subject of study and even practice, but now one is mature enough to make it the central part of one's existence and being.

When the person realizes that personal attachments are usually a mere product of one's limited vision, a more neutral approach is adopted. Consequently, personal ambitions are relinquished as one becomes more receptive to life and tunes into the understanding of what is right, what works, and what is the Truth. The person ceases to impose his or her desires on life and instead humbly accepts being a disciple of life, continually learning and practicing what is understood to be true. Accordingly, one engages to consciously purge negative Karma, foster Dharma, transcend duality, live in holism, neutralize evil, and foster enlightenment through Truth realization.

Progressing through the stages of the Spiritual level of consciousness, one aligns personal values and priorities with the higher Truth. Over time, the gap between what is subjectively desired and what is objectively right decreases. For example, service is put before pleasure, and yet as one evolves through this state, service becomes pleasure. Using another example, one may understand that it is beneficial to meditate at the crack of dawn when vibrations are in a purer state. Initially, the commitment to such a practice is perceived as important despite the sacrifice of sleep because spiritual development is prioritized over personal comfort. Yet over time, waking up in the early morning to meditate ceases to be a routine that requires discipline because it now provides one with tremendous fulfillment and pleasure; discipline is no longer required in order to be able to do the right thing. As the ego becomes better aligned with higher principles, less internal resistance is experienced and doing the right thing becomes less of an effort; this is the essence of spiritual development—consciousness shifts from personal wants to harmonizing with life.

Through the Individuated level of consciousness, one may have already absorbed a lot of spiritual knowledge and understanding. The difference in the Spiritual level is that the commitment to lead a spiritual lifestyle is all encompassing. Before, spiritual knowledge was used as a tool to understand the self and get in touch with one's inner creative and living potential. For example, the person may have used spiritual concepts to free him or herself from guilt or emotional blockages and to experience self-empowerment and healing. Through the Spiritual level, this orientation continues but the main focus is directed toward the betterment of life as a whole and personal attachments are more readily relinquished to serve this cause. Truth becomes more important than personal comfort because Truth is the ultimate comfort.

Through the Spiritual stages, freedom is better understood to result from living according to life's laws, for this is the only way to self mastery and collective well-being; freedom ceases to be about personal liberties and instead is experienced in the growing capacity to overcome negativity. Compassion and service replace the need for experimentation, decreasing unnecessary stimulation and grounding one's psyche. As this occurs, fear decreases because living in the Truth transforms what was detrimental into something beneficial through neutrality.

Neutrality does not mean that one is self-negating, egoless, and without any attachment or desires. Attachments are essential and important because without them one cannot self-invest and make choices in life. However, neutrality means that the moment an attachment obstructs the expansion of consciousness and comes between the person and the Truth, it is naturally severed. Non-attachment is in fact the ability to release an attachment when life requires it to be so.

The more aligned one is with the universal Truth, the more one harmonizes with existence and the greater the support from life. In the course of aligning the ego with higher meaning, new perceptions, faculties, and skills gradually develop. For example, a person may tap into finer vibrations and transcend the immediacy of time and space. This dynamic may be experienced through sudden awakenings and new realizations, as if literally downloading knowledge from cosmic pools. One may also develop healing capacities or be able to see the future. Speaking and living the Truth allows one to see and experience the Truth with more clarity.

It is important to realize that living a spiritual life does not shelter one from pain and failure. While a person may at first engage in a spiritual practice with expectations of being saved and having a smooth sail through existence, spiritual disillusionment is bound to happen. The learning process is never ending and thus pain still surfaces, requiring one to learn from mistakes. However, spirituality helps one diminish pain and cope with life more successfully. A consistent state of well-being cannot depend on having a life without challenges or turmoil but instead depends on knowing how to sail through the storm with better mastery.

Harmonizing and becoming one with existence naturally opens one's heart. In this developmental phase, oneness and unconditional love are not idealized concepts but actual realities the person naturally grows into. Seeing oneself in every living thing, including the ignorant and greedy, allows one to transcend negativity and inspire through love—a love that is not personal to anyone, but personal to everything.

It is important to realize that most people in the Spiritual evolutionary level are not necessarily accomplished saints! The process of alignment does not happen overnight and many internal struggles can be expected. While inspired to live according to spiritual values, finding the right balance between these values and egocentric creativity is not something that can be taken for granted. For example, at some point it is common for the person to develop a spiritual ego and become attached to messianic complexes. Experiencing divine inspiration can be intoxicating and blur one's sense and reason; it easily causes one to get carried away in naïve idealism and feelings of invincibility. Downfalls are part of the growth process and serve as a test of character.

There is an important distinction to make between conventional religion and spiritual consciousness. While conventional religion is certainly a part of a spiritual practice, it belongs more essentially to the Consensus level because it usually relies on blind conformity for the sake of maintaining order and discriminating vice from virtue, and necessarily so in that context. However, through conventional religion, the person is not encouraged to personally research life through his or her own experiences and access chaos so that spiritual realizations can be genuinely integrated. Religion relies on faith while spirituality relies on knowing. Moreover, conventional religion usually discourages the study of other religions and the full acknowledgment of their virtues; it is more protective and narrow because it main purpose is to avoid chaos. Notwithstanding, religiously oriented people can experience genuine spiritual awakenings and can accordingly evolve their consciousness to oneness and the Truth.

Through the Spiritual level of consciousness, one embraces a collective and universal approach that attempts to unify all fragments of life, distinguish the Truth from illusion, and inspire without discrimination—love is for life in all its diverse forms.

Spiritual level of consciousness keywords
Alignment of the self with the laws of life, neutral mind, flexible attachment, discrimination of sensory stimulation, oneness with all, service, impersonal love, illusion of salvation, messianic complexes, harmonizing with existence, freedom of peace, transcendence of negativity, heart-centered approach, sacrifice, egocentric purification, divine inspiration and guidance.

The Three Spiritual Stages of Consciousness

First Stage Spiritual
The first Spiritual stage of consciousness describes one's initial steps into a life fully committed to spiritual practice and values. The transition from the third Individuated stage to the first Spiritual one follows an inner realization that there is a higher intelligent mechanism operating behind life, and this realization now overcomes all personal ambitions and wants. One may have been involved in spiritual studies prior to this transition, but in this stage the importance of spiritual realization opens one's heart and mind in ways that radically transform one's attitude and life direction.

This spiritual awakening can generate a conquering sense of elation as the person feels more connected to life, nature, and the universe, and he or she may experience bouts of blissful joy. Abstract spiritual concepts become more tangible and life's complexity clearer because one feels closer to the intelligence of life.

Sometimes it is a deep inner void that stimulates this evolutionary transition. Despite having achieved important things in life, instigated progress, and stimulated the senses in all possible ways, one may feel a deep existential void and realize that happiness remains fleeting and whimsical. While enjoying a sense of internal freedom, true meaning may remain elusive and generate a sense of alienation from one's seemingly accomplished creative life.

Similar to previous transitional phases, it may also be that an emotional shock or a health crisis serves as a trigger to the awakening. The person realizes that intellectual competence, creativity, and control abilities do not always help when facing pain, prompting him or her to seek deeper answers. Overall, the transition only occurs when the person is consciously ripe for the evolutionary leap.

A holistic approach to life allows one to firmly realize that all seemingly separate life phenomena and occurrences are truly united—death, love, duality, pain, nature, science, flesh, and spirit are all interrelated and represent different forms of the same thing. This dynamic inspires a greater sense of harmony with existence, and the person is increasingly more focused on consciously becoming part of this oneness.

Often with a commitment to a spiritual path, a fundamental reassessment of one's values and behavior ensues. More aware of unhealthy habits—unnecessary attachments, reactive behavior, negative emotions, selfish motivations, illusive projections, or avoidance patterns—one goes through a purging process to strip down attitudes that hinder growth. The purging process may engender guilt and remorse for having done wrong in the past, sometimes excessively so, but this is part of the realignment process. Consequently, this phase of development commonly serves as a major karmic discharge because lifetimes of karmic debts are being released. The person *consciously engages* in ceasing to create negative Karma and fosters the Dharmic path of service to life (note that the person does not necessarily use these terms). Becoming more in tune with the Truth, one's approach becomes less personal because one better understands that the key to personal happiness is found in fostering collective well-being, from the small details to the bigger picture.

Through the realignment process, it is common for the person to follow a specific spiritual path and a teacher who offers guidance and support. Following one or more teachers over time also trains the person to surrender and cultivate humility. Yet regardless of the specific nature of one's spiritual path, the identification with universal unity eventually brings one closer to all beings and nature beyond prejudice or individual identities; there is a greater capacity to transcend seeming differences and thus to address living beings on a soul level beyond time and space attributes such as religion, origin, or gender. There is a greater feeling of compassion and openness, and one learns to respect each person for who he or she is within the greater whole of Creation. Similarly nature—including animals, vegetation, and rocks—is understood to be consciously intelligent and an integral part of oneness.

It is not uncommon for the person to be somewhat spiritually naïve in this evolutionary stage because the resonance with higher meanings may make him or her less discriminating and easily carried away with salvation expectations. Passion for life is revitalized when committing to a spiritual life; everything may seem open and accessible. The person may unconsciously perceive the chosen spiritual path as a final answer to all ills and entirely dedicate him or herself to a practice with the belief that it is the promised way to enlightenment and healing. This dynamic can manifest in giving too much power and becoming too attached to certain practices, philosophies, or spiritual teachers who may eventually lead to disappointment. When disillusionment occurs, it does not necessarily undermine the validity of one's spiritual path or teacher, but it does point to the need to adjust personal attitudes—letting go of personal projections and cultivating a more neutral mind is the first step. Attachments serve their purpose, but ultimately neutrality must prevail in order to maintain clarity and avoid letting the ego manipulate circumstances.

Usually the person in the first Spiritual stage focuses extensively on finding a balance between the ego and the divine laws of life. The tendency to revert to old patterns and sink again into negativity such as power struggles, jealousy, infatuation, or manipulation is recurrent; but as these themes resurface, one progressively exposes and resolves them because the dedication to spiritual values remains stronger and serves as a reference.

It is also important to realize that while devoted to spiritual values and practice, the person in this stage of consciousness may still have a profession that is not necessarily spiritually oriented; the need to make a living in daily life is part of the necessity to maintain a balance between matter and spirit. Questions about relinquishing a "regular job" are likely to arise because less meaning is found in a traditional vocation. Yet remaining involved in the everyday world can serve its purpose, especially for the sake of integrating spiritual values into the modern world and testing one's capacity to remain spiritually centered in the midst of daily struggles. At some point, the time may be right to transition to a spiritually oriented profession that is more in tune with one's values.

Second Stage Spiritual

Progressing into the second Spiritual stage of consciousness, stronger foundations are now established on the spiritual path. Coming from richer and more diverse experiences, the person possesses a deeper and more sober understanding of universal principles and life's mechanism; the abstract reality of what operates beyond the realm of matter is second nature and further integrated into everyday life. In the context of the modern world, it is more common in this stage of consciousness for the person to have a spiritually oriented profession and become an authority in spiritual matters because of a greater level of maturity in this field.

This higher level of integration manifests in various ways. The person may experience divine inspiration and thus become a conduit of higher knowledge or capacities, often becoming oneself a spiritual teacher. One may be well versed in different spiritual bodies of work, but the essence of one's wisdom and spiritual capacity is often the fruit of one's own *direct* spiritual experience. This depth of wisdom usually speaks for itself, filled with an inspiring and guiding quality. Beyond the depth of insight and vastness of spiritual understanding, there is an obvious devotion initially untainted by prejudice or pride that emanates from one's service. Thus a higher level of purity and heart-centeredness is more apparent.

Acquiring considerably deeper meditative and transcendental capacities, the person is likely to develop stronger spiritual faculties; the power to communicate with higher dimensions, to transform the negative into positive, to heal, dissolve resistance, or spiritually inspire others is now more readily accessible. During the first Spiritual stage, the transformation of values and alignment to divine principles is processed on a more personal level; it includes purging personal negative Karma and fostering one's Dharmic path. Through the second Spiritual stage, the individual is spiritually mature to become a vehicle through which negative Karma can be purged and Dharma enhanced on a larger scale. The inner foundation is solid enough to allow collective dynamics to be addressed.

As one gains more authority and addresses collective needs, the second stage Spiritual person requires the greatest egocentric alignment with the Truth; gaining influence and responsibility simultaneously intensifies the self-purifying process as the need emerges to measure up to higher standards. It is a time for the person to confront his or her deepest shadows and test his or her spiritual commitment and level of egocentric purity.

For example, as the person gains more insight and influence through this stage, it is common to think of him or herself as invariably protected by divine forces. As a result, one may develop a savior's complex and attempt to save everyone from pain, taking on much more than one is capable and entitled of handling. Disregarding personal limitations provides a sense of invincibility in the face of the salvation quest. Albeit the desire to save comes from positive intentions, it is usually not divinely inspired but rather a reflection of one's own existential pain and wishful thinking; consequently, it causes crisis. Typically, the crisis occurs as personal resources run out and the effort of salvation cannot be sustained when "the well dries up" so to speak.

This reality forces the person to face his or her limitations. For example, if the person is a healer, taking on everyone's burden may make the person sick as a result of overloading his or her system. Being a teacher and inspiring people is different than doing the work for them. Facing crisis, the person may interpret personal failure as a form of abandonment by the divine when he or she sacrifices so much for collective well-being and "selflessly" so. One may not immediately realize that the failure results from the personal attachment to salvation that engenders personal expectations and fears of pain.

In another way, the person enjoying influence and capacity may become intoxicated by the power he or she has over followers and become overly attached to the role of supreme teacher. The individual may lose the initial value of collective service, and personal motivations may become corrupt if teachings are manipulated for self-serving motives. The degree of corruption varies from case to case and accordingly the karmic debt. For example, after having acquired a certain level of prominence through spiritual service, the person commonly magnetizes tremendous projections from students and followers. These projections may be sexual in nature or else projections of divinity. Thus staying centered in the purity of one's intention and maintaining humility requires constant attention in order to avoid being seduced by these naïve projections.

In this context, each person faces different challenges relative to his or her personal evolutionary requirements. Shadows may be experienced through overzealous attitudes, the inability to "walk one's talk," and discrepancies in one's behavior showing, for example, in kindness on a public level and rudeness on a personal level, among others. If corrective measures are not implemented in a reasonable amount of time, the risk of evolutionary regression and downfall increases. The person may need to reprocess emotional dynamics and further cultivate his or her dedication to the Truth.

Third Stage Spiritual

The third Spiritual stage of consciousness reflects the highest level of spiritual mastery. In this stage, the person's egocentric alignment with divine principles is among the most sophisticated on the planet and manifests in extraordinary powers and unquestionned inherent humility. The degree of understanding of the principles of existence touches on the most subtle layers, providing one with an ability to affect the undercurrent of life's mechanism. As a result of the vastness of one's consciousness, personal efforts naturally influence larger life trends; consequently, the person is essentially focused on collective dynamics and primarily leads an impersonal life devoted entirely to service. Because the connection with higher dimensions is well integrated, the person needs less feedback and resources from this world as one feeds mainly from other dimensions—hence the capacity to be entirely devoted and oriented toward giving. This dynamic applies on all levels, but it can also literally manifest as the person needing little sleep and food and yet operating in a highly potent way.

Different paths may unfold in this dimension; the person may naturally mature into celibacy, marrying the divine rather than another person, while another may adopt the path of the householder master, embodying the essence of the divine in having a family and integrating into everyday life. Some people express their spiritual faculties and role in isolation, working toward refining the subtler levels of the collective vibrations in a rather anonymous fashion. Sometimes the person delivers his or her service to intimate groups of spiritually advanced disciples while in other circumstances the person is destined to lead an essentially public life through open teaching. Despite the various expressions, these souls have transcended their shadows and embody a high level of purity and mastery.

Because of the depth of their meditative capacities and high faculties of transcendence, people in this stage possess powers that may be considered supernatural by normative standards. These powers can include transcending limitations common to this realm of existence such as time and space or gravity. Some may get to the point where they can defy aging, levitate, relinquish their dependence on food, heal the sick, or see the future, but the importance of these faculties is not so much in their extraordinary quality but rather in the high level of mastery that reflects the person's success in harmonizing with the principles of life.

A common challenge in this stage of higher consciousness is learning how to remain grounded and deal with the denser vibration of existence on this plane. Having attained higher levels of realization, the need to be of service and contribute, whether publicly or anonymously, often requires constant adjustment and effort as it can be difficult for the person to integrate into the environment and remain accessible. Some of these souls may even come from higher dimensions and incarnate on Earth for the sake of service and fostering progress on this plane, making the integration process even more demanding. Sometimes even speaking or interacting can be disconcerting as it takes them away from their meditative space.

On another level, the need for adjustment may not necessarily be only physically, but also morally and culturally. Being connected to a purer channel of being, some of these souls may have difficulty understanding the development of the modern world such as managing computers or being exposed to the high stimulation of modern life. In other ways, a more modern approach to social issues, for example divorce or homosexuality, may require some cultural updating in order to prevent them from being removed from such issues. Some people may need to better understand modernity when operating outside the bounds of time and space, sometimes even learning from the development of modern life.

While people in this realm are considered enlightened, fully realized, or close to that, it is important to understand that imperfection remains. These souls are ready to depart and incarnate into other dimensions of existence, but they are part of the process of evolution; therefore, learning continues for them. Since they serve as guides and masters, expectations of flawlessness are projected onto them; as a result, mistakes are seldom tolerated. In this context, it is important to maintain a level of understanding and compassion realizing that the common collective desire to be free from pain engenders these idealistic expectations of perfection.

Important Facts about the Evolutionary Levels of Consciousness

- A person's evolutionary level of consciousness is assessed by the *value system* and the essence of his or her consciousness. One leads a lifestyle and makes life choices that reflect one's level of evolution. Some people may express enlightened ideas but manifest greed or bigotry through their actions; it is through values and choices instead of sophisticated discourse that one's evolutionary level is determined. Moreover, a person's true essence shows during a time of crisis for decisions made under stress can be the most revealing.

- A person may be born into a particular environment that reflects a lower level of consciousness than what he or she actually is; therefore, he or she may act according to that lower level of evolution during the early years of life. An awakening can occur at some point, and from then on this person is able to reconnect to his or her true essence and lead a new lifestyle that is aligned with higher values. For example, an Individuated soul may be born into a Consensus family environment and while not really fitting in, there would not be any explanation for this person's feeling of alienation. During childhood this person may act according to family standards, without a role model to know any differently, until a life event makes him or her aware of his or her true nature. The event triggering the awakening may be, for example, reading a life-revealing book or meeting a mentor. When this occurs, one can leap over many stages of consciousness, but in fact, one is simply going back to where one truly and always belonged on a soul level.

- Once a person is fully connected to his or her true self and authentic evolutionary level of consciousness, progress through the levels of evolution is relatively slow. While the pace of evolution is not a fixed pattern, usually the most one progresses in a single lifetime is to evolve from one (sub) stage to the next. The reason the pace is slow is because evolution occurs through the emotions and therefore processing and integrating new insights takes time. Experiences have to be repeated many times before they are emotionally integrated. In extraordinary cases, a person may progress through more than one (sub) stage, but it is not common. The latter usually occurs when uncommon circumstances in a person's life promote this significant leap forward. For example, this might happen if a person meets an enlightened teacher or goes through a trauma that tremendously shocks the system. This significant leap forward must not be confused with the situation where one's authentic level of consciousness is recaptured after having been misled by the environment.

- Sometimes, when a person seems to have evolved relatively quickly, necessary processing phases may have been skipped. Consequently, the person may create a more evolved environment that reflects apparent progress, yet if the transformation is not well integrated, a crisis occurs that reflects the discrepancy. Eventually, life circumstances bring one back to the steps that were skipped because more time is needed to assimilate them. For example, a person in the third stage Consensus level may feel inspired to individuate and leave a secure life behind to immerse him or herself into a passion for art, but over time miss the privileges of a secure life and revert back to previous attachments. This type of choice reflects the fact that values were not firmly integrated and that there is still a need to process past patterns. Change and evolution cannot be rushed; growth occurs when it is emotionally integrated.

- Intimate relationships usually have more meaning and a greater chance of survival if two people are more or less at the same evolutionary level of consciousness. When this is the case, a couple is better able to understand, support, and challenge each other.

Applying the Evolutionary Levels of Consciousness

The following examples illustrate how a particular chart configuration can express itself differently depending on the person's evolutionary level of consciousness: the same themes intrinsic to the configuration are taken to different dimensions. Explanations follow each example to clarify the described dynamics. The examples include the following astrological configurations: *the Aries Moon, the Gemini Sun, the Virgo Moon, the Scorpio Sun, the Aquarius Moon, and the Pisces Sun.*

Aries Moon Examples

Aries Moon: Second Stage Consensus—male in Western society

Having lived all of his life in a small Nebraskan town, Jim gained a reputation as a dedicated football player. He openly asserted that winning games is what drove him in life and that he could not tolerate anything short of that. His emotional attachment to victory, however, was encumbered by numerous difficult episodes—notably when he destroyed a local bar after his team lost a game.

Had he managed to dampen his temper, he might have been able to achieve a successful sports career; but the recurring act of quitting his team following any disagreement sabotaged his development. However, he managed to become a successful salesperson, travelling across the state to sell construction equipment. This job enabled him to have a changing routine and, truth be told, get away from his wife when things became too heated. Most often after a few days away from it all, he came back home again, realizing that he missed her.

Explanation

The Aries Moon is highly emotionally responsive, absorbing life experiences in a very direct way. The person establishes a connection with existence based on a capacity to independently take charge of his or her life and defend the needs or elements he or she associates with.

In the context of a second stage Consensus male in Western society, the competitive, defensive, and protective attitude of the Aries Moon can manifest in a strong emotional attachment to sports. However, as much as the person identifies with his favorite sports team, conflicts can erupt between personal needs and team needs. Because little emotional self-awareness exists, reactive behavior is bound to reoccur because the person is easily threatened by any form of disagreement.

The same issue applies to a personal relationship where the thing that holds it together is the ability for each person to have an external outlet; in this example, travelling for work provides relief and an exit from the emotional intensity. The flexible routine of a salesperson and selling something Jim emotionally associates with suits his independent nature and provides the opportunity to develop his personal ambition, fitting the second stage Consensus reality.

Aries Moon: Second Stage Individuated—*male in Western society*

Adrian moved from his hometown of Pittsburgh, Pennsylvania, to Amsterdam, Holland. After moving to Europe, he felt that his life had increased exponentially in meaning.

Growing up in Pittsburgh had been difficult as he always felt out of sync with his environment; as a child, all he cared about was painting and taking care of his pets, something his peers did not understand. His environment offered little creative inspiration. He was bullied at school and traumatized by his father who kept telling him how "girly" he was while continually fighting with his mother.

One day, on the spur of the moment, he was inspired to leave it all behind and travel to Europe—two weeks later, there he was! Deeply appreciating Europe's architectural refinement, he couldn't get enough of the Van Gogh Museum in Amsterdam where he emotionally immersed himself in each painting. Eventually he found a fellow painter to share a studio with, the studio also serving as his exhibition gallery.

Now still passionate about animal rights, he participates in a local campaign to promote vegetarianism and volunteers his artistic talent to design the organization's posters. On a personal level, his life is interesting but also somewhat unpredictable; he's easily infatuated with powerful women and falls hard when they do not reciprocate the intensity of his feelings, leaving him with a bleeding heart and yet more inspiration that manifests in more edge to his art.

His father still reserves a place for him in his insurance company, hoping that one day he will return to his senses and join the successful business instead of wasting away with "American haters." However, so far, none of that is in sight.

Explanation

The emotionally responsive nature of the Aries Moon manifests in a high level of sensitivity that requires an outlet of some sort. As Adrian feels isolated, typical to the second Individuated stage of consciousness and an Aries Moon, he finds an emotional outlet through art and activism.

Immersing himself in these activities, he separates from his family and environment to follow his emotional truth. He is emotionally empowered by taking action, physically leaving his hometown to live in a more liberal environment; the sudden decision and the act of leaving are both Aries Moon expressions while his choice of location fits the context of a second Individuated person. Feeling passionate and infatuated with women of strong character is another Aries Moon expression; expressing his emotional idealism and deception though activism and his art describes the second Individuated stage Aries Moon.

Aries Moon: Second Stage Spiritual—*male in Western society*

Ralph was raised in a middle-class environment in Germany, and even as a young boy, he was the one who gave morality lessons to his parents. At the age of seven he told his father, a businessman, that ambition and greed would eventually backfire on him and that he should donate a percentage of his income to charity.

Soon after graduating from school, Ralph bought a one way ticket to the East, telling his family that he would come back when he was ready; he travelled to China, Japan, and India and learned acupuncture, Tai Chi, and Falun Dafa, among other disciplines. Falun Dafa is a forbidden practice in China; consequently, many of its practitioners are persecuted and tortured by the government. Experiencing the depth of the practice, Ralph was deeply troubled by the inhumanity perpetrated by the Chinese government. He knew that to create a change he would have to go back to Germany and increase public awareness of this injustice.

Upon returning to Germany, he was completely focused and emotionally invested in this cause. Every day, he and fellow practitioners performed Falun Dafa in public places and raised awareness of the government's injustice through nonviolent means. Ralph knew this discipline had tremendous power and could potentially bring a person to spiritual enlightenment. Through the years, he became one of the most devoted activists and practitioners; the practice bore its fruits as he began to manifest natural healing capacities—he could cure ailments simply by touching people. Using donations, he eventually built a center for the study of this discipline. Spiritually, he felt ever more connected—he saw himself as a divine warrior, dedicating his life toward service, healing, and justice.

His commitment was obvious and unquestioned; however, when students and followers eventually left the path and abandoned their commitment to the cause, his reaction became increasingly more extreme—he became severely depressed and even used a magic practice to curse a "deserter."

This dynamic significantly affected his mental health and forced him to eventually face his shadows. Underlying his need for control and his high expectations of others was an unhealthy attachment that could be traced back to misplaced childhood emotions. He subsequently resigned his position as the leader of the Falun Dafa center and is now committed to a lifestyle of self-healing and more anonymity.

Explanation

In this example, the Aries Moon manifests in an independent spirit and an all encompassing emotional investment with a chosen cause. Ralph defends and fights for what he perceives to be a just cause. In the second stage Spiritual context, this cause is spiritual in nature and values of service inspire him to dedicate his time toward healing and inspiring others. He is courageous, defiant, and totally committed, as an Aries Moon would be.

He grows spiritually to the point of becoming a leader because his spiritual practice is sincere and without compromise. Yet the second Spiritual stage exposes him to spiritual powers that he ends up misusing, forcing him to discriminate between truth and egocentric manipulation.

Gemini Sun Examples

Gemini Sun: First Stage Consensus—*male in India*

Abhijat grew up in the slums of Calcutta, living in utter poverty. At age seven, he left his family, who could not provide for him anymore, and wandered the streets begging for his next meal. A man took pity on him and gave him a job distributing newspapers; in return he was allowed to sleep in a storehouse and given one or two meals a day.

Abhijat soon found out that he could make an extra income from the many tourists visiting the city; he learned a few words in English, German, and Hebrew, and used his pitiful eyes and smile to gain their sympathy, convincing them to hire him as a tour guide. He split the gains with his friend who owned a rickshaw, and together they drove people around the city. However, of the pair, Abhijat was the leader because he knew more foreign words and could quickly negotiate any circumstance.

He married at age fifteen and had seven children, four of whom did not survive infancy. At some point, his brother told him of better job opportunities in the big city of Mumbai where tourism was considerably more vibrant. Subsequently, he left Calcutta and joined his brother's rickshaw business in Mumbai, sending a monthly allowance to his family who remained in Calcutta.

Explanation

The Sun in Gemini reflects creative expression through merging different sources and using language or mobility to bring people of different backgrounds together. Living off the street from an early age, Abhijat is exposed to diverse people and currents, and learns how to create something out of these circumstances relatively quickly. In the first Consensus stage of consciousness, survival needs are what matter most and life is led in a rather impersonal fashion.

Relationships are functional and family is important, but closeness and emotional intimacy irrelevant. Relying on family ties is a survival need in this evolutionary stage; it is not about personal likes and dislikes but instead about making do with what is available without asking many questions: the primary focus is on establishing basic order and having food on the table. In this context, the Gemini Sun expresses its creativity by making use of the environment and promoting mental exchange through meeting tourists and developing foreign language skills.

Gemini Sun: First Stage Individuated—*male in India*

Sarasvat grew up in a traditional Hindu family in the capital city of New Delhi. His family expected him to go to the temple, prosper in his profession as an English teacher, and find the right wife. His mother kept bringing potential brides home hoping for his approval, but to no avail: none of them pleased him. Sarasvat just could not relate to the idea of marrying a girl because of her looks and the "credentials" of her family background. He needed someone who was equal to him, educated, and not submissive.

He enjoyed regularly meeting with his intellectual club and discussing foreign philosophers such as Nietzsche and Sartre, but he never brought the related books back home anticipating they would create more family drama. Frustrated by the constant complaints and pressure from his family, Sarasvat decided to leave India for a while and visit his cousin in London.

He loved London and ended up marrying a British woman who was an anthropologist, a decision that also granted him permanent residency in Britain. He worked as a translator and completed a master's degree in philosophy. Inspired by his wife's research in anthropology, he joined her to study the cultural heritage of the Mayan culture—an experience that opened a whole new world of insights and wisdom for him.

Explanation

The Sun in Gemini celebrates existence through mental stimulation and exchange—understanding more about different perspectives and ideas feeds passion and stimulates creativity. Sarasvat is an intellectual aware of the mentality limitations of his culture, particularly when it comes it gender inequality roles.

In the context of a Gemini Sun in the first Individuated stage of consciousness, he admires a partner who is intellectually developed and unafraid of challenging traditional ideas. His higher awareness prompts him to move to a more liberal environment where his needs and creativity can be better addressed. He eventually rebels against family and societal expectations, making choices without considering the fear of shame. He experiences a sense of liberation when making his move and deciding to be truly loyal to his nature.

Gemini Sun: First Stage Spiritual—*male in India*

As a child, Shailesh was the pride of his family. He was a bright and pious boy who showed promising signs of becoming a Hindu priest (a pundit). His eloquence was remarkable as he could recite and analyze scriptures with relative ease. But when it was time for him to become a Hindu priest, things did not go according to plan. Instead of rejoicing at the privilege and pride of such a prospect, he became depressed. To the shock and dismay of his parents and peers, he declined the position and embarked on a soulful journey across the country.

Shailesh needed real answers and had to stay loyal to what he perceived as truthful and authentic. On his journey, he met a wide variety of people, from the most profane to venerated spiritual teachers. One of the masters he met particularly touched him, instructing him to spend time meditating in the Himalayas because his "monkey mind" needed to focus and embrace the stillness of meditation. This made so much sense to Shailesh that off he travelled to Nepal.

While in Nepal, he was deeply impressed by the Buddhist tradition and learned a lot from that system of thought. He eventually realized why he could not become a traditional priest—the Truth is found in unifying diverse streams—he could not lead a lifestyle where one religion is considered superior to another. After immersing himself into Buddhism, he went on to study other religions and synthesized the diverse approaches. Now, he continues to work on calming the "monkey mind" and is increasingly more at peace with the flow of his life. He inhales every piece of wisdom gathered from the lectures of various spiritual leaders and hours spent in the huge spiritual bookstores. His natural wisdom has grown richer, and indeed, he was delighted to learn that for the first time he has been invited to speak at an interfaith institute in Kathmandu.

Explanation

Born in the first Spiritual stage of consciousness, Shailesh is a child who expresses wisdom from an early age. The only way his parents know to address this capacity is to associate him with conventional religion—something he naturally feels is limiting.

The Gemini Sun is aware of the need to synthesize different approaches. But the tendency to become overly mentally stimulated makes him restless, and he comes to realize that he does not really find peace. His sense of purpose is directed toward enriching his spiritual understanding while learning to better master the function of his mind through meditation.

Virgo Moon Examples

Virgo Moon: Third Stage Consensus—*female in Western society*

Jennifer was born into a very privileged family from Long Island, New York. Her father owned real estate across the country while her stay-at-home mother had a live-in hairdresser at her convenience. Jennifer and her two sisters were sent to privileged private schools, and her nannies were affectionate and giving.

Jennifer's parents noticed that from a young age she was the most beautiful of their three daughters, sincerely believing that she had the potential to become a top-notch supermodel. When she was six, her mother decided that Jennifer also needed to have her own private hairdresser because she would be auditioning for various commercials and could not afford to neglect her image.

Problems arose when it appeared that she would not be tall enough for the modeling profession; consequently, serious decisions needed to be made to "treat" her condition—her mother wanted her to take growth hormones. Initially, no doctor would agree to start Jennifer on such a treatment plan because by common standards her height was normal, but with persistence and financial incentives, a more "open-minded" doctor finally complied.

Jennifer spent hours on her training and grooming regime and became quite a popular child model. She sacrificed playtime with her friends for the cause, but as she put it, her friends were a bit "dense" anyway. The growth hormones worked well—Jennifer's height met industry standards. However, one night during a dinner together, a family friend noticed that something seemed wrong with Jennifer; she was full after ingesting only a small salad and a cube of protein and threw a hysterical tantrum when she found out that her mother forgot to buy her a new dose of laxatives.

Her parents agreed that Jennifer's behavior must be addressed, so they scheduled an appointment with a psychologist who immediately prescribed medication to curb her obsessive compulsive tendencies. The psychologist advised Jennifer and her parents to slow down her modeling career in order for her to be able to regain a sense of balance and health in her life. This advice made her feel very insecure and inflicted self-doubt, something that was further processed during her therapy.

Explanation

The Virgo Moon finds emotional security in high function, beauty, and predictability. In the context of the third Consensus stage of consciousness, the ambition for the "perfect" look can be particularly strong, especially for a female. Looking to supermodels as symbols of success and role models, Jennifer's sense of security and belonging becomes associated with the image of being perfect, and she is willing to work hard to establish that. However, external perfection comes at the cost of emotional dysfunction resulting from her parent's lack of awareness about the deeper meaning of health and proper function. A crisis blows the image of perfection and the sense of superiority that comes with it, forcing Jennifer to explore what health and high function is really about. Chaos shatters the sense of order in her personal world and generates further insecurity for her.

Virgo Moon: Third Stage Individuated—*female in Western society*

Alison knows about hard work! She grew up with her single mom who worked long hours to make ends meet in order to take care of her and her three brothers. Alison excelled in her studies but was distraught by the school's system which emphasized competition and ambition at the expense of support and academic quality. She was rather popular socially, but she did not date until much later than her peers because she did not relate to the sexist and overly sexual culture that was prominent at school. She was quite athletic and trained in the martial arts, eventually mastering a black belt in Aikido.

When Alison was in her twenties, her mother was diagnosed with cancer—doctors were pessimistic about the prognosis. Alison immediately knew that she had to intervene; she took some time off from her design career and did everything possible to help her mother. Moving back home, she and her mother both started a raw food diet and pursued a whole range of alternative treatments conducive to healing.

Alison knew that her mother had become sick because of the stress in her life, so she organized a trip to Brazil where her mother could relax and meet with a famous healer. In the course of spending time with the healer, and being surrounded by people struggling with various diseases, Alison realized that she identified with this kind of work more than anything else. Her mother overcame the cancer, and Alison went back to school to become a holistic practitioner with a primary focus on healing through nutrition. She is now highly successful in her practice and draws tremendous meaning from helping others through her work.

Explanation

The Virgo Moon person is usually unafraid of having to invest time and energy to make things work—whether this means working for an additional income or focusing on health. In the context of the third Individuated stage of consciousness, Alison is not conditioned by social norms when determining what to do in a time of crisis. There is no internal struggle or people to convince; her authority is established.

Her natural gravitation to alternative healing practices reflects her level of consciousness as does her instinctive decision to change careers and become an alternative nutritionist. Because her value system is established in a more holistic perspective, she naturally gains authority in her chosen path and finds tremendous satisfaction when she is able to be of service in this context.

Virgo Moon: Third Stage Spiritual—*female in Western society*

Elisabeth was a sickly child; she went through periods when she could not tolerate any kind of food, sometimes coming down with a high fever that confined her to bed for days—no doctor understood what was happening. At one point, she was so frail that doctors feared for her life. With her mother crying at her bedside, Elisabeth suddenly whispered, "Don't worry mother, this all has a purpose. I'm going to live and help many people get better." She was, in fact, purging the negative Karma of her ancestors and clearing the path for more healing to come.

At age fourteen, all her ailments disappeared and she returned to leading a normal life among her friends. Her parents rejoiced but did not understand why she spent so much time in the garden apparently talking to herself! They feared that the years of struggling with her physical condition had adversely affected her mental health and left her with post-traumatic stress syndrome. Nonetheless, she appeared happy and glowing.

As a young adult, she became a forest ranger in order to further cultivate her connection with the natural world. In spite of being very fond of her, her employer became frustrated when Elisabeth disappeared for hours alone in the forest. She asked him to trust her, telling him that one day she might be able to share with him what this was all about. In the meantime, she told him that he needed to take his wife to the doctor because she was likely in the preliminary stages of ovarian cancer; to his amazement, the doctor confirmed Elisabeth's premonition and consequently his wife was saved. Thereafter, he never questioned her disappearances.

In the hours of solitude she spent in nature, Elisabeth meditated and communicated with trees and spirits from other dimensions. Together, they purged the earth of energy carrying the trauma of massacres that had previously occurred there. Eventually, Elisabeth's spiritual duty required a full-time commitment; she could not go through the motions of having a regular job anymore.

The task of purifying and healing demanded everything from her. Despite keeping a relatively low profile, some people became aware of Elisabeth's healing and clairvoyant capacities; they decided to establish a fund to financially support her so that she could continue her mission. Her greater purpose of healing the natural environment and the earth provided collective healing well into the future.

One day out of curiosity, a dignified politician came to visit her. She pleaded with him to do more to protect the forests. Later that night, the politician noticed that his psoriasis had completely disappeared.

After living a life dedicated to the healing cause, Elisabeth passed away when she was forty-three; despite showing no sign of fading, the night before her time had come, she shared with her beloved sister her vision that in her next incarnation she would continue the healing work but do it through wider public exposure to increase global awareness of healing processes.

Explanation

A person with a Virgo Moon in the third Spiritual level of consciousness finds a connection to this world through restoring healthy function on both physical and energetic levels, and in ways that affect the greater collective. From a young age, Elisabeth accepts the task of purging collective Karma and healing dynamics that are beyond the immediacy of her personal existence. In this stage of evolution, she is capable of managing and handling the burden, first as a child and then as an adult.

Her sickness as a child can also be associated with her struggle to integrate into this earthly dimension. She has difficulty integrating into her body because in her personal universe this earthly dimension is very dense, toxic, and hard to adjust to: heavy Karma creates the dense vibration. But compassion and her sense of duty compels her to overcome these obstacles and purify the energy. She is naturally clairvoyant and masters time and space as she is able to control her death and know how her work must unfold.

Scorpio Sun Examples

Scorpio Sun: First Stage Consensus—*male in the Middle East*

Namir was born in a village in the Afghan countryside. When he was just a boy, his father died in an accident; henceforth, his life completely changed as his mother could no longer take care of him and his eight other siblings. All of the children were divided between the extended family, and Namir ended up living with an uncle who worked in the opium fields. He joined the workforce along with his male cousins.

As an adoptee he was not considered pure, so he was not included in the side-trade gains of the poppy harvest, and yet he was often used by the drug lords to deliver messages so they could assert their control over their share of the fields. This situation ended up working to his advantage because he gained a lot of proprietary information from the different groups holding power.

One day, he asked one of the most powerful lords to grant his daughter to him for marriage. He knew that this was his ticket to gaining more respect and being included in "the family"; given Namir's strategic role, the lord could not refuse him the favor—it was a matter of either complying or killing him. Namir knew of this risk and consequently informed the lord that if he were to return to his village unmarried, his uncle would have access to his personal belongings where compromising information could be found. And so, the marriage celebration took place the next evening; Namir's life was radically transformed. His new father-in-law made him responsible for all transactions, granting him power and respect among the clans.

Explanation

A Scorpio Sun creates life out of death and darkness. As everything is lost for Namir, he manages to quickly learn his survival lessons and use circumstances to extract himself from a pitiful state. From a position of utter powerlessness, he changes and gains power. In the context of the first Consensus stage of consciousness, life is impersonal, and he is judged by the perceived status of his clan and his orphaned status rather than what he himself is about.

Life and values are measured according to basic survival needs, and his identity is community based. There is no awareness of emotional needs or traumas; instead, those who are not innately strong simply perish mercilessly. Life circumstances bring Namir to a place of weakness, but he manages to gain strength and respect against the odds.

Scorpio Sun: First Stage Individuated—*male in the Middle East*

Bashir grew up in war-torn Lebanon; his mother was a Christian and his father a Muslim; the cultural mix was not always easy for him to handle when he was growing up, but he was proud of his unique identity and saw it as an important statement of unification. His family was relatively well-to-do socioeconomically, so Bashir benefited from a higher education in France. He opted to become a journalist because like his older brother he wanted to pursue a career in Europe where he would enjoy a more peaceful and progressive environment.

Life took a different turn, however, when his uncle back home was assassinated. Following the grieving period, he vowed to uncover the circumstances of his uncle's death as the authorities seemed pleased to cover up the event as an accident. Bashir never imagined that he would end up in an entangled story of racism and political corruption, and that his own life would be jeopardized because he kept pursuing the truth. He was not able to accept the game of deception because knowing truth had transformed him—he knew his life would not have any meaning if he were to avoid trying to expose what had really happened.

Threats escalated to the point where he feared for his life; he moved his entire family to France where enough support was available to carry on the investigation. The whole truth was finally revealed, first making headlines in France and Lebanon, and then eventually across the globe as major political figures were exposed in arms trades and corruption. This episode launched his career as a well-respected journalist, and he vowed to pursue his career for the sake of exposing conspiracies and bringing the truth to light.

Explanation

The creative purpose of the Scorpio Sun is to bring light where there is darkness. Bashir aimed to live a life away from trouble and intrigue, but once realizing the truth, he could no longer look the other way. The purpose of the Scorpio Sun is to challenge dynamics and confront shadows; in the context of the first Individuated stage of consciousness, Bashir confronted the traditional order and the power structure because he is aware that authenticity and truth are more important than safety and personal status. Making the choice to get out of his comfort zone, he experienced a sense of liberation because he knew that he was doing the right thing even though it was dangerous. Taking this further, he made a profession out of his controversial reporting.

Scorpio Sun: First Stage Spiritual—*male in the Middle East*

Ahmed had always been fascinated by death; he spent days next to his ailing grandmother before she passed away, and even though he was only a young boy, he knew that she was in altered states of consciousness during this time. The whole family dramatically grieved her death, but with her last breath, Ahmed saw that she was smiling. Though he did not know how to verbalize it, he also saw the angels who greeted her in another dimension.

His father kept telling him that he should get an education and a proper job, but all he was really interested in was reading philosophy and sacred texts; yet his uncle, who was an Imam at the local mosque, did not see his practices as religiously acceptable because Ahmed was asking too many inappropriate questions about death and sexuality—

Ahmed even dared calling an Imam evil as he had ordered the "rightful" punishment of throwing acid on a woman's face because she had had sex before marriage!

One day, he met a tourist from the United States who introduced Buddhist philosophy to him. This encounter had a tremendous impact on him; the tourist's description of the Bardo phases following death deeply resonated with him. He had a sexual experience with this foreigner and was glad to have had it because it offered him another layer of understanding about intimacy, vulnerability, and affection.

He did not have all his answers about life and death, but was passionate about researching all the different layers of expression and being. One person sincerely understood Ahmed and encouraged his soulful search; he was a friend of his father's and a Sufi practitioner. He told Ahmed: "Whatever you wear, whatever you speak, it is love and only love that ultimately matters—and this love is found in the presence of God in everything." These words of wisdom resonated with his soul; it comforted him to know that he was not alone in thinking this way.

Ahmed studied psychology and started working in a mental hospital, but in his spare time he joined international internet forums where he discussed reincarnation and the path of spirit. At some point, he had an existential crisis; disgusted by the way the system treated the patients, he felt he could no longer work at the mental clinic; yet he knew the patients needed him and benefited greatly from his compassionate approach. In the end, he did not have to quit; he was fired because the committee would not tolerate his unconventional, costly, and "irresponsible" approach whereby he encouraged the patients to hug each other and pray together, spend time freely roaming the garden, and paint their dirty walls bright colors.

Explanation

Exploring the meaning of life and death, and having the creative capacity to bring change where it is needed is a function of the Scorpio Sun. Ahmed is spiritually inspired but does not find immediate support for the truth he perceives and follows, making him a target for the traditional authority figures around him. This does not deter him from pursuing his quest and spiritually learning from life by exploring the taboos of his culture; sexuality is part of this life and death fascination and he is capable of putting fear and prejudice aside in order to have direct experience and adequate answers.

He is inspired by the truth and dedicates himself to that cause, even if suffering ensues. Eventually his truthful nature, courage, and sincere desire for the truth lands him in the hand of a Sufi practitioner who confirms his convictions and offers him support. He is still struggling to manifest his creativity because the environment constantly sabotages his initiatives and generates a sense of limitation. Ultimately he will need to find ways to overcome his sense of powerlessness and transform the way he approaches life so that he can successfully manifest his capacities and goals.

Aquarius Moon Examples

Aquarius Moon: Second Stage Consensus—*female in Western society*
Ashamed of her family since she was a young girl, Kathie never invited her friends over to play telling them that her mother was too sick to have visitors. After graduating from high school, she went on to study chemistry at a university and thrived in an environment of scientifically oriented people. She fell in love with a fellow student who later became a pharmacist. When he asked her to marry him, her dreams came true; together they had a great gene pool and she would lead the suburban lifestyle she had always aspired to.

However, as her wedding day approached, she worried about introducing her fiancé to her family. How would he react upon realizing that her parents were illiterate and her brother mentally challenged? She had to tell him the truth, and when she did, she promised her future husband that he would never have to deal with them—she would do everything possible to protect his reputation. He was disappointed by these circumstances (although he never admitted it to her), but trusted her promise.

They moved to another city, purchased a beautiful home, and sent an occasional check to help pay for her brother's treatments. The rare phone conversations with her family always culminated in extreme stress, often ending abruptly with her hanging up the phone. Her new life was perfect; she even had friends with PHDs and could not let her family drag her back into their more primitive world!

Explanation

The Aquarius Moon describes an emotional association with elements that promise progress and growth; it compels the person to reflect on his or her emotional associations and assess what is worth keeping. In the second Consensus stage of consciousness, the person is ambitious and wants to improve personal life conditions. Kathie's emotional disassociation from her less refined background reflects this need for more sophistication. She experiences an identity crisis because she wants to improve her life and let go of the past. Her insecurities cause her to be edgy, impatient with her family, and emotionally inaccessible, but what keeps her connected to life is her vision of a "better" future.

Aquarius Moon: Second Stage Individuated—*female in Western society*

Casey was born in the Midwestern United States. During her teenage years, she felt so alienated from the mainstream that she joined the punk subculture. To the dismay of her highly respected lawyer parents, she got a Mohawk and showed up at school wearing leather outfits. Her friends represented a freer way of thinking; however, soon enough she tired of that too, feeling that her friends were overly obsessed with the "freakiness of their look" instead of really understanding the point of it all. For her, the purpose was to make a social statement that expressed the dischantment of young people with the poverty of the educational system and the lack of support for creative political alternatives. She left her friends and her dramatic look, and ended up spending hours completely bored, surfing conspiracy theory websites.

Her father was aware of her intelligence and begged her not to waste her potential. She started studying political science and for a period of time she excelled, but then she eventually lost interest again feeling that no one really cared: everyone was in it for the grades and the "piece of paper!" She eventually joined a communist movement with radical Marxist views that advocated the death of religion, and claimed that Jesus Christ never really existed but was invented as a means to control the masses. She vowed never to have children "in this corrupt world" and lived in a platonic relationship with the leader of the movement.

Explanation

The Aquarius Moon reflects an emotional association with ideals of progress and betterment. The person's capacity to be emotionally objective can manifest in pronounced maturity and natural wisdom. In the second Individuated stage of consciousness, Casey has political and social perspective and wants to be an instrument of social change—she is inspired by a more radical approach. However, when she objectifies on the deeper motives of her peers, she realizes that they are not up to the challenge.

With an Aquarius Moon, she cannot fool herself, and the naked truth makes her jaded. She is extremely intelligent but does not initially find a platform that supports her vision until she finds a community that is truly radical and committed to their vision the same way she is. She gets carried away identifying with a rather radical ideology, but this is necessary in the Second Individuated stage where the person needs to test boundaries and explore taboos through actual experience.

Aquarius Moon: Second Stage Spiritual—*female in Western society*

Judith belonged to a spiritual group that completely revolved around the teachings of Rudolph Steiner. This spiritual movement possessed a staggering wealth of knowledge about diverse aspects of life from education, to agriculture, and so on. She stood out from the rest of the group—the purity of her practice, devotion, and loyalty to the teachings were remarkable. She eventually developed the capacity to channel divine entities and prophesize about the future of mankind. Followers had never encountered someone who had such a high caliber of knowledge and understanding of universal forces. From that point on, she was called Nanu, and within the community she was elevated to the status of prime teacher.

Nanu became very sensitive toward people who were not dedicated enough to the teachings and practices, feeling that they distracted from the serious course of study. Her level of discrimination increased as she proclaimed that the refinement and sophistication of the spiritual path must be protected. She presided over the ceremonies of the community, only initiating the few rare students who demonstrated that they had the exclusive potential of becoming enlightened. Chosen people were allowed to participate in and witness the initiation; obviously this was considered an exceptional privilege.

Nanu became more and more consumed by her position and lost her tolerance toward anyone outside of her immediate entourage, fearing that their "polluting energies" would taint her ethereal nature. She decided that she would no longer appear in public in order to preserve the purity of her auric field. Followers had an increasingly harder time keeping up with the high fees that were required for any type of participation; consequently, the community dwindled to very few.

Nanu became angry, claiming the world was not ready for her message. But over time, even her close entourage started to lose faith in her when her channeled messages decreased in substantial content and true inspiration. Nanu was eventually exposed for tax evasion and had to move back with her excommunicated ex-husband who took pity on her. Her demise had a traumatic effect on her mental health: irrational fears completely consumed her. Despite his meager means, her ex-husband diligently took care of her and provided a much needed support system as all her community friends cut ties with her upon realizing the level of her corruption. Nanu eventually realized that what she truly needed to learn was the purity of her ex-husband's love and dedication.

Explanation

The Aquarius Moon can reflect a dichotomy between mind and emotions. The initial purpose is to gain a greater understanding of emotions so that they can be better expressed and processed, but it is common to get lost along the way and end up having the mind override the emotions.

In the second Spiritual stage of consciousness, Judith developed unique spiritual capacities that drew many followers. Her level of refinement makes her a conduit of higher inspiration. But as she gains greater power, it is time to face her shadows and reevaluate the true intention of her work. She fails to walk her talk and loses credibility because when her heart closes the inspiration dries up. Yet she is saved by grace and love in uttermost simplicity and purity—she recognizes her ex-husband's devotion to be greater than her spiritual intellect.

Pisces Sun Examples

Pisces Sun: Third Stage Consensus—*male in Western society*

Henry moved from Toronto to Calgary where the oil industry was booming. His decision to move there happened almost "coincedentally" as he didn't really know what he wanted to do after graduating from business school. Dating over the internet, he met a girl from Calgary whom he decided to visit. During his stay with her, she showed him around the city. At a social event, he met a CEO of a local petroleum firm who told him all about the opportunities in the oil industry. The romance ended, but Calgary stayed!

Henry quickly amassed a small fortune, married his secretary, and had three children. After a few years, his wife started to complain that he was more enthusiastic about going to the field and checking the refineries than spending time at home with his family. He didn't understand why she complained—they had everything money could buy! Tired of her criticism, he further avoided spending time at home; instead, he focused on work or spent the weekends hunting with his colleagues. He loved the natural setting around Calgary and found satisfaction in accumulating hunting trophies.

One day his wife was waiting for him at the door, hysterical (he had turned off his cell phone so that he could not be reached). Their son had been hospitalized because of a massive cocaine overdose. Henry did not understand how this could have possibly happened. His son was a great hockey player and popular with the girls; he was not the type to use drugs. Henry was convinced his kid was framed! Yet when the police revealed that his son was actually the dealer and would get correction time after recovery, the truth finally sank in.

Explanation

The Pisces Sun finds its path in surprising ways. Unconsciously relying on the greater forces of life to manifest what needs to be, the person can passively follow the motions and enjoy the fruits that are handed down in all simplicity. Henry rides on that wave and refrains from asking too many questions. In the third Consensus stage of consciousness, he manages to manifest financial success and then takes that success completely for granted. He shies away from his wife, who wants to "complicate" everything and ruins his smooth sail, until he is made to realize that his level of denial is so profound that he did not even notice his son's degeneration. He is made to realize that life cannot be addressed so simplistically without consequences for neglect.

Pisces Sun: Third Stage Individuated—*male in Western society*

Manuel grew up in Barcelona, Spain. From the time he was a young child, he demonstrated amazing creativity. He organized stage plays with his friends and wrote the scripts and soundtracks for the performances. He was only a teenager when he was approached to produce a video clip for a local band whose popularity had grown strong.

He eventually left Barcelona for New York City where he enrolled in theater studies. The atmosphere was creatively liberating but extremely competitive, something he clearly did not relate to. His play, about a transvestite who communicated with Jesus Christ through his dreams, granted him critical acclaim. He converted to cinematography, planning to direct a full motion picture film about a romance between two Basque Separatist activists who decide to sacrifice their love for the revolution. His script drew the interest of Hollywood producers, making him ecstatically happy! However, disillusionment ensued when the producers completely rewrote the story and changed the setting from the Basque countryside to the California beaches. Although having only minimal means, he eventually produced the film independently, which allowed him to preserve the story's authenticity. The film was not a huge commercial success but won significant critical acclaim at various film festivals for its powerful emotional content. His second film was a greater international success in the independent market and distinguished him in the field for his very unique and controversial style.

Manuel and his partner, a yoga teacher, decided to adopt two Chinese girls rather than have children of their own. She was aware that Manuel's habit of going days without properly sleeping or eating would eventually take its toll. At least he made a point of practicing yoga regularly—something that kept him grounded and in touch with his body.

Explanation

Natural talent and inspiration make the Pisces Sun rich with content; opportunities knock on the door when one stays creatively authentic. Yet without caution, passivity and flow can lead to a loss of self; Manuel catches himself at the last moment before the Hollywood studios completely hijack his project and take over. The themes of spirituality and sacrifice captured in his creations are part of the Pisces influence.

In the third Individuated stage of consciousness, authenticity and truthfulness are more important than popularity, so his values save him from temptation. He knows that his talent lies in the quality of his script and the depth of his message—he trusts that he should not compromise the content to attain the desired creative result. Typical to the Pisces Sun, he neglects his personal life and needs when immersed in his creative inspiration, but in the indiviudated stage, exposure to a spiritual practice such as yoga helps balance the issue.

Pisces Sun: Third Stage Spiritual—male in Western society

Joseph's parents knew their son was special; signs were there from the moment his mother became pregnant with him. Deer, foxes, and other wildlife creatures regularly rested on their backyard doorsteps. An easy child to raise, he mostly befriended children from underprivileged neighborhoods because they embodied simplicity and liked to climb trees like he did.

Before he was even ten years old, he developed a fascination for ancient languages and effortlessly learned Latin and ancient Greek, followed by Hebrew and Sanskrit. He wrote poetry in Latin but at the same time still enjoyed mundane activities with his friends.

One evening he did not come home for dinner. Perceiving him as naïve and "too good hearted," his parents feared for his safety. Eventually, they received a call from the center of Kabalistic studies where apparently he had been frequently visiting and was known for his insightful interpretations of sacred texts. Joseph matured to become a beloved spiritual teacher of the highest order.

He led a life of service, tirelessly sharing his universal wisdom. He occasionally went into trans-states through which he apparently completely exited his body. He did not share much about these experiences with others, but soon after people who spent time with him experienced a feeling of immense love and bliss—practicing what he preached, he always said he was here to teach through the experience of love, not only through words. His simplicity and accessibility were well documented.

Explanation

A third Spiritual stage soul commonly exhibits pronounced spiritual tendencies from infancy. The connection and response from the animal world reflects a level of inner purity that is authentic and speaks for itself. As a child, Joseph already manifests unconditional love with his friends at school and recognizes the purity of those who maintain a connection with their simplicity—those who enjoy climbing trees.

The Pisces Sun recognizes the power of life through natural elements and people who are stripped of artifices and fancy costumes. Joseph's transcendental capacities and expression of love is the result of lifetimes of work and alignment; in the course of this life, he naturally shares his wisdom through words and experience; he is where he is needed and does not discriminate who, where, or what to teach. He is open, accessible, and serves as a pure spiritual channel, offering his service without pretense.

Glossary of Astrology Terms

Angles: The cusps of the first, fourth, seventh, and tenth houses. In most house systems, the angles are determined by the intersecting points between the Earth and the ecliptic namely the Ascendant, the IC, the Descendant, and the MC. The angles are highly important points in the chart, representing new cycles of becoming.

Archetype: Each of the twelve astrological archetypes consists of a sign, a planet, and a house. The three components embody the same themes but play a different role in the chart dynamics. For example, the Cancer archetype consists of the sign of Cancer, the Moon, and the fourth house.

Ascendant: The sign that rises on the eastern horizon at any given moment. It is one of the four chart angles in most house systems.

Aspect: A relationship between two or more factors in a chart defined by a particular geometrical distance between them.

Asteroids: A multitude of small bodies orbiting around the Sun between Mars and Jupiter. The biggest asteroids are Vesta, Pallas, and Juno. Ceres was once considered an asteroid but is now a Dwarf planet.

Centaurs: Bodies of the solar system located between Jupiter and Neptune that have an unstable orbit. The most commonly used centaur in modern astrology is Chiron, which was discovered in 1977.

Constellations: Subdivisions of the heavens named after major stars in the area. The twelve constellations of the ecliptic are the ones that are used in astrology (from the constellation of Aries to the constellation of Pisces)—they represent the zodiac.

Cusp: The beginning of a house defined by a degree of a sign.

Descendant: The sign that rises on the western horizon at any given moment. It is one of the four chart angles.

Dwarf planets: A term defined in 2006 that represents a subcategory of planets possessing some of the attributes of planets, but not all of them. Currently, Dwarf planets include Ceres, Pluto, Haumea, Eris, and MakeMake. Of the Dwarf planets, only Pluto rules a sign—the sign of Scorpio.

Ecliptic: The path of the Sun as viewed from our perspective on Earth.

Equal house system: A house system dividing all houses equally by 30 degrees beginning at the Ascendant degree.

IC: The initials for *Imum Coeli*, the lowest heaven. The exact opposite of the MC. It is one of the chart angles in most house systems.

Inner houses: The houses situated between the chart angles, namely the second, third, fifth, and sixth houses and their exact opposites the eighth, ninth, eleventh, and twelfth houses.

Koch house system: A relatively new house system that quickly became popular among astrologers. Some consider it to be the house system that is the most related to the location of birth.

Kuiper Belt objects: A region extending beyond the orbit of Neptune which includes a multitude of special objects including three Dwarf planets (Pluto, Haumea, and MakeMake—Eris is beyond the belt).

Luminaries: The Sun and the Moon.

MC: The initials for *Medium Coeli*, also called the Midheaven. It is the intersection between the local meridian of the birth place and the ecliptic. It is the Sun's highest point of passage in a particular location. It is one of the chart angles in most house systems.

Meridian: An imaginary circle that passes from the North point of the horizon to the South point of the horizon. It corresponds with geographical longitude.

Outer planets: Planets located beyond Saturn and not visible to the naked eye including Uranus, Neptune, and Pluto. The outer planets describe objective development.

Personal planets: Planets ruling the lower hemisphere signs of the zodiac including Mercury, Venus, and Mars. This term may or may not include the Luminaries depending on the source. The personal planets describe personal development and survival issues.

Placidus house system: The most commonly used system in Western astrology notably because tables for this system were the ones most available during the nineteenth and twentieth centuries.

Porphyry house system: A house system developed by Porphyry that divides the chart angles into three equal parts to determine the inner houses.

Retrograde planets: Planets are considered retrograde when their motion appears to move backward from our perspective on Earth. It is an optical illusion, but the phenomenon carries important meaning in astrological interpretations.

Social planets: Jupiter and Saturn. The social planets describe personal development in the larger framework of society.

Transpersonal planets: See Outer planets.

Zodiac: A band or a ring that extends eight to nine degrees on each side of the ecliptic defining the path of the Sun, the Moon, and the planets. The constellations that are part of the zodiac, from Aries to Pisces, are the signs that are used in astrology.

Glossary of Spiritual Terms

Consciousness: One's current level of understanding of the Truth.

Dharma: The fulfillment of one's destiny by living in the Truth resulting in one's contribution to existence; as a result, Dharma enhances the essence of love.

Ego: The operating arm of the soul in the current life through which one forms attachments necessary for the evolutionary process. These attachments come to define one's separate sense of self and identity; through the ego all of life's experiences are emotionally processed.

Evil: A parasitic force that serves the role of tempting a soul away from the Truth into illusions and delusions so that the Truth is realized through effort.

Evolution of consciousness: Increasing the understanding of the Truth.

Evolutionary levels of consciousness: The levels of consciousness a soul acquires and progresses through in the course of incarnations. The maturity level of the soul.

Fate: Choices or circumstances that are predestined and sometimes cannot be changed in the course of evolution.

Free will: Decisions and choices made by a person on an ego or soul level that are not predestined and influence the course of evolution on a personal and sometimes collective level.

Karma: The subordination of personal action to divine order. Corrective measures and possibly negative consequences that occur when a person's actions are misaligned to divine order. Conversely, positive circumstances that result from aligned actions. The law of cause and effect that is in force through one's incarnations.

Reincarnation: The phenomenon of a soul incarnating repeatedly into a physical body in order to pursue its evolutionary process throughout time and space.

Soul: One's consciousness incarnated and evolving throughout lifetimes.

Spirituality: The study and practice of aligning the ego with the soul and the soul with the Truth.

Truth: The sum of all principles and laws governing life within and beyond the realm of human understanding: what works. Divine intelligence and order.

Vessel of consciousness: An abstract container of one's consciousness.

CPSIA information can be obtained at www.ICGtesting.com
Printed in the USA
LVOW080054040512

280267LV00006B/63/P